More Praise for *Secondhand*

"With grace, a keen eye for detail, an interesting cast of characters who spend their life reselling used things, and the perennially curious mind of a great journalist, Minter takes readers from the backs of thrift stores all across the United States to small apartments and vintage shops in Tokyo, and from a truck in Mexico to an office in Mumbai, to show the inner workings of one of the world's largest markets . . . a gripping narrative. Minter is a superb storyteller who knows empathy is easier to connect with than numbers. In this book, there are plenty of both, but the people he interviews and the stories he tells are what make it an enthralling read . . . It's a book I'd recommend buying now instead of waiting for it to show up at your local thrift store." —NPR.org

"A sprawling, insightful travelogue through the world of repair, reuse, and waste . . . Adam Minter . . . delivers a book as crammed with oddities and gems as the secondhand shops he loves to haunt." —*Nature*

"An anthem to decluttering, recycling, making better quality goods, and living a simpler life with less stuff. The book is a compelling argument for tempering acquisitions, especially now that global warming compels people to rethink how they live." —Associated Press

"Minter tells stories and offers insight suffused with legitimacy, pragmatism, and optimism." —*Science*

"Minter's approach manages to be both detail-orientated and a page-turner." —*Foreign Policy*'s *China Brief*

"*Secondhand* tells an important story about consumerism gone wild, the complex industry that has grown around its detritus, and how we can push back on an entrenched culture of disposability." —*New York Journal of Books*

"If you are curious, downsizing, or trying to be a conscientious consumer, you'll want this book. Having it on your shelf is perhaps the ultimate irony, but that's exactly where you'll want it because *Secondhand* is not something to toss aside lightly." —Terri Schlichenmeyer, The Bookworm Sez

"An epic journey across continents to untangle the used-goods market . . . Minter's greatest contribution is his balanced look at the economies of India, Ghana, and other countries that have figured out that most things can have a second consumer life, if only we let them." —*Providence Journal*

"[Minter's] new book moves up a step in the classic environmental hierarchy of 'reduce, reuse, recycle,' to see what becomes of our stuff once we let go of it." —*Sierra*, the national magazine of the Sierra Club

"A fascinating, eye-opening look at a dynamic, largely unseen world that only starts when one drops off something at a thrift store." —*Publishers Weekly*

"Well written and packed with intriguing details, this is a great look at a global industry to which virtually all of us contribute." —*Library Journal*

"A character-driven, detailed, eye-opening report." —*Kirkus Reviews*

"In Minter's capable hands, [this] topic comes alive . . . Minter designs a workable path forward to combat the glut of stuff." —*Booklist*

"Accessible and engaging . . . An unparalleled look at the lifespan of everyday things and the unexpected ways our society's abundance of discarded items are, refreshingly, being repurposed for a second life." —*Shelf Awareness*

SECONDHAND

SECONDHAND

TRAVELS IN THE NEW GLOBAL GARAGE SALE

ADAM MINTER

BLOOMSBURY PUBLISHING

NEW YORK · LONDON · OXFORD · NEW DELHI · SYDNEY

For Christine

BLOOMSBURY PUBLISHING
Bloomsbury Publishing Inc.
1385 Broadway, New York, NY 10018, USA

BLOOMSBURY, BLOOMSBURY PUBLISHING, and the Diana logo are trademarks
of Bloomsbury Publishing Plc

First published in the United States 2019
This edition published 2020

Portions of the preface, chapter 2, and chapter 5 were originally published in
different form in *Bloomberg Businessweek* as "Japan's Lonely Death Industry."

Portions of chapters 2, 5, and 8 were originally published in different form in
Bloomberg Opinion as "What's in Marie Kondo's Closet?," "Used Goods Could Be
the New Thing in Asia," and "No One Wants Your Used Clothes Anymore."

Portions of chapter 12 were originally published in different form in *Scrap* as
"Continental Drift" and the *Shanghai Scrap* blog as "Anatomy of a Myth:
The World's Biggest E-Waste Dump Isn't."

Bloomsbury Publishing Plc does not have any control over, or responsibility for,
any third-party websites referred to or in this book. All internet addresses given
in this book were correct at the time of going to press. The author and publisher
regret any inconvenience caused if addresses have changed or sites have
ceased to exist, but can accept no responsibility for any such changes.

ISBN: HB: 978-1-63557-010-6; PB: 978-1-63557-011-3; eBook: 978-1-63557-012-0

LIBRARY OF CONGRESS CATALOGING-IN-PUBLICATION DATA IS AVAILABLE

2 4 6 8 10 9 7 5 3 1

Typeset by Westchester Publishing Services
Printed and bound in the U.S.A. by Berryville Graphics Inc., Berryville, Virginia

To find out more about our authors and books visit www.bloomsbury.com and
sign up for our newsletters.

Bloomsbury books may be purchased for business or promotional use.
For information on bulk purchases please contact Macmillan Corporate and
Premium Sales Department at specialmarkets@macmillan.com.

Took my diamond to the pawn shop
But that don't make it junk.

—LEONARD COHEN

CONTENTS

PREFACE: THE DONATION DOOR

A blue Mazda CX-7 is next in line at the Goodwill donation door at South Houghton and East Golf Links Roads. A fortyish brunette in black yoga pants and a baggy yellow T-shirt emerges slowly, iPhone to her ear. Three cars and two pickups are lined up behind her, but she's in no rush. "Put the frozen dinner in the microwave for two minutes," she says as she saunters from the driver's seat to the rear passenger door on the opposite side. "Yes, two minutes," she repeats as she slowly opens the door.

Standing nearby is Mike Mellors, a fifty-seven-year-old attendant. He stoops over the back seat, pulls out a white garbage bag bursting with what appears to be clothing, and places it on the top shelf of a two-level gray cart. He stoops farther and pulls out an ironing board and a pair of plastic deer antlers. "Thank you for your donation," he says.

The woman lowers her phone and voice. "There's a community yard sale at Sierra Morado," she says with a knowing smile, as if providing a hot tip. "It's getting hot, and people are saying, 'Screw it—I'm done.' So that's why people are coming." With that, she gets into her car and drives away.

It's eleven A.M., Saturday, and the Tucson heat is drenching Mellors's six-foot frame. But there's no time to retreat into the air-conditioned warehouse on the other side of the donation door. The donors are lining up. A Kia Sorento is next, its back seat piled with garbage bags. The youthful woman in the driver's seat lowers the windows and unlocks the doors, but she doesn't get out.

"Yard sale?" Mike asks as he opens the door and starts tossing the bags on a cart.

"Over at Sierra Morado."

"Nice." He hauls out six bags of clothes, an Ogio golf club bag holding two putters, a stack of 2014 World Cup commemorative cups, a ceramic drinking horn roughly the size of a trumpet, a beat-up Braun coffeemaker, four frying pans, and at least ten bags of party favors priced at twenty-five cents each, according to the bright pink tags. Mike pauses at the drinking horn, turning it in his hands. "Thanks for your donation!" he says and closes the door.

Three hours ago, just before the store opened, he told me that Goodwill is where Tucson's garage salers unload the things they can't sell and don't want to keep. It's a weekly phenomenon, boosted by the comings and goings of Tucson's military families and retirees. When they arrive, they need things; later, they realize they can't take it all with them.

The Sorento pulls away, and a large black Ford pickup carrying a ratty sofa takes its place. I walk through the donation door and into the wide warehouse. It's busy with employees who've arrived to process the rush of donations. Four women sort through boxes of clothes at the far end, and two young men sort through stacks of electronics not far from the donation door. A supervisor strides over from the clothing area to encourage Mellors to work faster.

Between 1967 and 2017, the money that Americans spent annually on stuff—from sofas to cell phones—increased almost twentyfold. Some of that stuff will become treasured heirlooms worthy of future generations. Some will be buried in landfills, turned to ash by incinerators, or—in rare cases—recycled into new goods and heirlooms. And some will persist, packed in basements, closets, attics, garages, and storage units. The precise breakdown is unknown, but there are hints. For example, one 2006 study of Los Angeles middle-class homes found that 90 percent of garage space is now used to store stuff, not automobiles.[1]

Americans aren't alone in their love of stuff. But they are unique in having so much space to store it. That's a luxury other people would love to have. For example, the Japanese are just as shopping-mad as any CX-7-driving Tucsonan. But their homes are much smaller. So, to make room for new, many Japanese purge. There's nothing particularly unique in their approach, but millions of Americans—keen to bring order to their homes—have embraced what Marie Kondo, the entrepreneurial Japanese organizing consultant with bestsellers and a hit television series, calls the KonMari Method. It's an enticing system: keep only what sparks joy; toss everything else. It also leaves open an essential and pressing question: What happens to all that stuff after it's been KonMari'd?

I pondered the question for the first time in 2014, shortly after I published my first book, *Junkyard Planet: Travels in the Billion-Dollar Trash Trade*. In it, I followed U.S. recyclables like cardboard, shredded automobiles, and Christmas lights around the world, primarily to China, and argued that "if what you toss into your recycling bin can be used in some way, the international scrap recycling business will manage to deliver it to the person or company who can do so most profitably."

Readers soon contacted me to share how they recycle. Some wrote with descriptions and pictures of art projects that incorporate junked electronics like circuit boards and overhead-projector lenses; others offered detailed accounts of furniture and home restorations; I received notes from folks informing me that they were writing on computers and phones they'd repaired at home; and I was the lucky recipient of many, many invitations to visit flea markets, thrift shops, and antique stores.

As the descriptions and invitations accumulated, I felt torn. It's good to have one's work appreciated. But my readers weren't writing to tell me about the sorts of things I described in *Junkyard Planet*—like giant, multistory automobile shredders. They weren't even writing to tell me about small-time junkyard dealers like my immigrant great-grandfather—dealers who made a living by collecting and purchasing the waste of their neighbors and selling it to bigger industrial recyclers. Despite my best efforts, the most enthusiastic readers of my book (judging from the notes they send to me) understand "recycle" as short-hand for "reuse."

That's understandable. For most people in affluent countries, the process of recycling ends at the point they sort their trash into a recycle bin. The highly industrialized processes that follow belong to faceless others. In contrast, the buying and selling of used stuff is intensely personal. Anyone can hold a garage sale, purge their closets on eBay, or visit a flea market. Reuse and resale give consumers a rare, tangible connection to the afterlife of their stuff.

Two weeks after *Junkyard Planet* was published, my mother passed away unexpectedly. Like so many Americans with parents who accumulated stuff over a lifetime, my sister and I were left with an uneasy question: What do we do with her stuff? From a sentimental standpoint, it was hard to let go of anything for fear it meant something to her. From a practical perspective, neither of us had the space to keep much. My sister and her family live in a two-bedroom New York City co-op; at the time, my wife and I rented a one-bedroom Shanghai apartment.

Our problem wasn't unique. Around the world, questions about what to do with the material leftovers of a life are becoming as much a part of the mourning process as the funeral. There's so much, and the children all live somewhere else. Who's to clean it out?

Much of my mother's modest estate wound up at Goodwill. I concede I have no idea what happened to her china after I handed it to a donation door attendant. But I had faith that—like the recycled metal that I wrote about in *Junkyard Planet*—my mother's secondhand items would be *used* in some way—not landfilled, incinerated, or recycled. In part, I started this book to reassure myself that my instincts were correct.

That turned out to be harder than I expected. As a business journalist, I am accustomed to confirming my suspicions and assumptions by double-checking them with the data collected by governments, businesses, and trade associations. Want to know the weight of all Christmas-tree lights exported from China to Luxembourg over the last decade? That number exists. Similarly, thanks to a growing and professionalized environmental movement, volumes of data are available on what's trashed and recycled in wealthy countries. Want a graph showing how much furniture Americans heaved between 2003 and 2013? It can be plotted.

I looked into whether similar data exists for secondhand goods. Data on used cars is plentiful and accurate—so long as you aren't looking for how many move between international borders in the developing world (at which point many seem to disappear). But beyond cars, the numbers become fuzzy. For example, nobody keeps data on how much clothing moves from closets to rummage sales, there's no metric on the number of pieces of furniture that flip from college apartments to Goodwills, and no government agency tabulates or even estimates the number of garage sales held annually in the United States and how much revenue they generate. It's not just a U.S. issue, either. Trade data related to the booming global business of secondhand is even worse. For example, there's almost no data on the vast trade in secondhand between the world's developing economies, especially in Africa, where consumers embrace imported secondhand as the ubiquitous material of daily life.

Fortunately, a lack of data doesn't mean the trade in used goods is untraceable. But instead of finding it through data, a reporter must travel to the places where secondhand goods are collected, bought, repurposed, repaired, and sold. That might entail watching someone take a picture of a shirt and post it to Facebook, eBay, or Poshmark. Or it might entail following a Ghanaian buyer of old laptops from the United States to the city in northern Ghana where he sells them.

Both are small acts that underline an often overlooked truth. Secondhand goods clothe, educate, and entertain billions of people around the world. And all this is accomplished using less energy and far fewer raw materials than what's required for new goods. However, because governments tend to focus on the value of things made and sold new, the value of used things exchanged between people and businesses is generally invisible except to the people who are involved in buying, selling, and moving them.

This book seeks to uncover that value and restore it to a central place in the daily life of the planet. That's not easy. Just as no single book can cover the new-goods trade in all its geographic and economic immensity, no single book can hope to cover all secondhand goods, either. Though I'll touch on a wide range of items, especially in the early chapters, I will eventually focus most intently on clothing and the electronics that accumulate around us. Both are among the most valuable and traded secondhand goods in the world today, and they are the ones with the most interesting—and potentially troubling—futures.

Thanks to innovations in mass production and marketing dating back to the industrial revolution, the world is filled with more things than at any time in history. That's often a blessing. But not always. As I traveled in the world of secondhand, I was repeatedly overwhelmed by the scale of unwanted stuff. In Tucson, only one third of the donations to Goodwill sell in the charity's stores. Who buys used plastic antlers (who buys the new ones)? A tattered sofa? A pilled T-shirt?

The flood is rising. Just twenty years ago China was a major importer of secondhand clothes; now it's a major exporter, with a huge supply that's driving down the price of used clothes—and the economics of the used-clothing business—globally. It's not just China that's shifting to new, either. Growing affluence across the developing world means that more and more consumers are opting for new stuff. Sustainably minded consumers in wealthy countries with the best of intentions simply aren't numerous enough to make up for the global erosion in secondhand demand.

That imbalance manifests itself in growing piles of unwanted stuff.

According to a 2018 study by the World Bank, humans are on track to generate waste at a pace more than double that of population growth through the year 2050.[2] Most of that growth will occur in developing regions of Asia and Africa striving to achieve American-style consumption-based economies.

Let's not pretend: that growth will have negative consequences for the environment. But those consumption-based economies will also bring tangible benefits to billions of human beings, including better health and education. Nothing that an affluent American minimalist can say about consumerism and stuff is likely to change the mind of a developing-world teenager whose only experience of minimalism has been involuntary.

The good news is that this doesn't need to be the end of the discussion. Social problems have social solutions. One of those social solutions is the already existing secondhand industry, which supplies billions of people with goods around the world. In the latter chapters of this book, I'll argue that this crucial industry isn't suffering from a crisis of stuff so much as it is from a crisis of quality. Simple, voluntary steps by manufacturers and consumers to encourage the production of more durable and repairable goods could go a long way toward ensuring that secondhand thrives and grows for decades to come. It doesn't need to be a revolution, either. Already, manufacturers big and small are building better for growing numbers of consumers who demand it. I'll highlight a few of them and show how their approach creates a secondhand future.

Quality isn't the only barrier to a secondhand future. Opposition to globalization also inhibits reuse. But the most serious trade barriers involved in secondhand aren't tariffs and bans. Rather, the most intractable barriers are prejudices that inhibit people in wealthy countries from selling and shipping their unwanted stuff to people in developing countries. Throughout this book, I'll explore the origins and impacts of those prejudices, including how they're promoted, and how and why they should be overcome. There is no secondhand economy that excludes the developing world, and consumers in the wealthy, developed world need to embrace that reality.

If this book succeeds, readers should come away with a much better understanding of how the afterlives of their purchases impact the global economy, the environment, and, ultimately, their closets and basements. With any luck, you'll have a better idea of what happened (or didn't happen) to those bags of clothes and that beat-up sofa Mike conveyed through the donation door. And just maybe you'll change how and why you purchase stuff, if only to make sure you don't leave a mess for others to clean up later.

Like most Americans, I have done my own share of accumulating over the years. Researching this book helped me let go of some—but not all—of it. I can't promise readers of this book that they'll have a similar experience. But they will find a surprising world where what's old becomes new again, over and over, and the desire to profit from castoffs creates innovation and livelihoods—all over the world at all hours of the day. Finding it is a treasure hunt, one that anyone can join.

CHAPTER 1

Empty the Nest

Highway 169 runs north-south through the affluent western suburbs of Minneapolis. High brown walls that serve as sound barriers block views of most of the neighborhoods, but here and there a mini-storage business appears along the way. Beige seems to be the preferred color, and during the dry Minnesota fall, when the highway scrub turns tan, they're all but camouflaged.

Everyone knows they're available and the purpose for which they're erected. To meet the ever-growing demand from Americans for space to store their stuff, hundreds, sometimes thousands, are erected across the United States every year. As of 2017, there were at least fifty-four thousand mini-storage sites in the United States, with enough rentable space to cover all of Palm Springs, California, golf courses included. In recent years, the industry's annual profits are triple those of Hollywood.

Those profits won't be threatened for many years. At a time when personal identity is wrapped up in brands, Americans are prone to keep things longer, and sometimes value them more than they value themselves. At Ace Mini Storage,* located along Highway 169 in Plymouth, the cost for a square foot of unheated storage space exceeds the cost per square foot of many studio apartments in the surrounding area.

On a brisk fall day I stop into the Ace Mini Storage office to ask about price and availability. The balding clerk picks up a piece of paper with a grid printed across it and squints. Outside, a pickup pulls into the parking lot with furniture piled into the bed; a lamp hangs off the side. "We might have something available later in the week," the clerk declares and pushes a business card across the desk. "A ten-by-forty unit."

It turns out that particular unit is the reason Sharon Kadet is now pulling up in her car. She's the account manager of Empty the Nest, an eight-year-old local business that empties homes of their property.

The reasons for these cleanouts vary, but they typically revolve around downsizing and death. Business is booming: by 2030 senior citizens will account for one fifth of the U.S. population. Some of those seniors want to remain in their large single-family homes packed with stuff. But many others downsize, either by their own or someone else's choice. And some will pass on, leaving the heavy responsibility of cleaning out a life's accumulations to somebody else.

Plenty of companies and individuals will clean out homes and drive the stuff to the dump after skimming the easily marketable objects. But Empty the Nest is unique in its commitment to finding reuse and resale markets before giving up on an object. Empty the Nest has a thrift store, and what can't be sold there is donated to organizations that might have better luck.

As Sharon steps out of her car, a cold breeze whips past, ruffling her black windbreaker and shoulder-length hair. "The deal is that we're

---

* The facility was recently rebranded as a Storage Mart.

There are 753 individual units for storing excess stuff at the former Ace Mini Storage in Plymouth, Minnesota.

cleaning out two units for this man whose mother filled it up with all kinds of collectibles," she tells me as we walk toward a large truck parked at one end of the facility. "It's pretty incredible how much she left. I think she might've had a store."

A truck is parked in the driveway beside two storage units with their doors raised. Three crew members are passing boxes from the units into the truck, where they're stacked neatly. Standing in silent witness is the woman's son, a retired auto mechanic happy to chat, so long as I don't ask for his name. "These were my mother's units. She had a knickknack store. Not antiques, but collectibles."

One unit holds dozens of boxes marked "Beanie Babies" in black marker. I pull back the top flap of one and see it's packed with colorful stuffed animals. "I looked on Craigslist," the mechanic tells me. "They're going for three dollars. But nobody wants them."

Sharon peers into the truck—it's about one third full. Then she looks at the larger unit and wonders if there'll be enough room. The crew assures her that they can manage.

I have my doubts. At the front of the larger unit are display cases. The remainder of the space is filled with unopened boxes from collectible companies. The mechanic's mother seemed to have a particular affinity for small porcelain Christmas villages made by Department 56, a manufacturer of holiday baubles. There could be a hundred of those alone. And as the movers work deeper into the storage unit, it's revealed that she was also passionate about limited-edition porcelain dolls marketed by something called the Consummate Collection. "I don't know what she was thinking, buying all this stuff," the mechanic says. "Was it for us? When she had her store, I don't think she had dolls." He picks up an unopened box. "Made in China," he mutters.

I step gingerly into the larger unit. On the floor is an unopened six-pack of Coca-Cola with a Santa Claus design and CHRISTMAS 1996 printed across the cans. I look back at the mechanic. "How long did she have this unit?"

"Rented it in 2006 or 2007," he answers. "We've been paying over five hundred dollars per month for both."

"That Coke is twenty-one years old."

He shakes his head. "Mother's house was full of stuff, so she put it here. You kind of wonder if she had a problem with stuff. They sell it to you on credit." We both step back and watch as Empty the Nest's crew methodically stacks boxes of dolls in the truck. "Tell you what," he tells me. "I won't leave my kids this kind of mess. My wife and I already decided that."

Most American homes contain very little of value beyond the sentiments of the person who purchased them. The contents of a bathroom—from toothbrushes to soap—can't be reused. Kitchen utensils are typically too beat up to serve anything but the scrap-metal industry. Old CDs, DVDs, books, and media players are generally worthless unless they're scarce, in good condition, or of interest to collectors. Furniture, unless it's an antique of value, has a diminishing market, especially if it's made by Ikea. Used clothing, unless it's made by a well-known and expensive brand, is often barely competitive with the flood of new garments made in low-cost factories around the developing world. And electronics, from desktop computers to phones, rapidly depreciate into a state of worthlessness—at least to consumers in places where the next upgrade is just a season away.

Few Americans know it better than Sharon Kadet. In the six years she's worked for Empty the Nest, she's taken thousands of photos of potential and actual client homes before they've been cleaned out. It's an impromptu, inadvertent, and largely unprecedented archive of American consumption, discreetly contained in Dropbox folders accessed through an iPad she carries everywhere. When she sits down with me at a Caribou Coffee along Highway 169, she places it on the table to her left. As she checks a message, I notice her inbox contains 25,322 emails.

"Okay, let's find a good one." She opens a folder that holds hundreds of additional folders, each labeled by address. Most store between twenty-five and thirty-five photographs of the things filling up the homes of potential and actual clients. For Sharon, the photos fulfill two purposes. First, they allow her to quote a price for a cleanout. Labor and dumpsters are costs; the potential resale value of the stuff in those photos is value that can be deducted from those costs. Second, the photos allow a crew to plan a cleanout, some of which can last for days.

"This is a good one," she decides, opening up a folder devoted to a home located north of the Twin Cities. "Split-level house," she adds and leans in. "From the outside, you know nothing." She scrolls quickly through images of a bedroom dominated by stacked books and a kitchen table piled with binders, and she stops on an image of hundreds of VHS cassettes stacked on shelves, on tables, and stashed in open boxes. She zooms in. "They're all homemade," she notes, pointing at the handwritten labels on the spines. Then she zooms out and points to rows of three-ring binders. "I think he cataloged the tapes. This is a very passionate townhouse. A very passionate guy."

"Is any of that worth anything?"

She leans back and crosses her arms over her black EMPTY THE NEST T-shirt. "Homemade VHS tapes, no." Sharon pauses for just a beat. Reuse is what makes Empty the Nest unique in an increasingly competitive cleanout industry. "The idea that your stuff isn't going to be wasted is more important than packing your own vases," she explains.

Why that's so important is a complicated question. Sharon, with hundreds of cleanouts in her background, has watched the difficulty that clients have in letting go. "Yesterday we cleaned out a place, and later the sister called and said he [the client] died at four A.M." She throws up her hands. "I don't know . . . but coincidence?"

Historically, personal identity revolved around religion, civic participation, and pride of (oftentimes small) place. But as those traditional bonds disintegrate in the face of industrialization, urbanization, and secularization, brands and objects become a means to curate and project who we are. Users of iPhones "think different" than users of Android-enabled phones do. A Volvo station wagon, a brand and model favored by liberal residents of academic communities, isn't likely to be found in the drive-through at Chick-fil-A, a fast-food chain favored by conservatives.[1] Small acts of consumption add up to a picture of who we are—just ask Google or Facebook, companies that keenly track consumer identities online. And for many Americans, objects packed into a home present the complete curated package.

Like most people in a very new industry, Sharon Kadet didn't aspire to her current position in home cleanout. She grew up in a middle-class Minneapolis family, attended college, and spent much of her career working for large philanthropic foundations like the United Way. Then, in the late 2000s, her father passed away, and the family hired a company to help her mother transition to a smaller home. The manager of that move eventually founded Empty the Nest in 2011. Not long after, Sharon ran into that "move manager" at the gym and later looked up what she was doing. "It made sense to me from a human stand-point," she says, recalling her first online encounter with Empty the Next. In 2013, Sharon joined the company as a packer. Then she started visiting senior housing communities to market Empty the Nest's services.

In addition to generating profits, Empty the Nest also generates knowledge. Sharon opens another folder and clicks on a photo. It shows a cluttered basement with a treadmill in the center. "Exercise equipment has no value," she says, then clicks through to an image of bookshelves stacked with magazines, many with yellow spines. "Basements full of *National Geographic*s on the shelves." She sighs. "People thinking they're valuable." A moment later we're on a particular peeve: hide-a-beds. "Nobody wants used ones, and they're dangerous to move. Can't sell them."

Sharon is aware that talking about the difficulties of her job can make it feel like every cleanout is an episode of *Hoarders*, the wildly successful American television series about people who compulsively acquire objects and never unload any of them. "But not every home or transition from a home is extreme," she reminds me. "Most aren't." Even so, each Empty the Nest client finds themselves in the same position: they have more stuff than they can handle.

Before we go, I ask Sharon if the job has impacted her personally. "Materially, no. I have a house full of stuff. But personally, yes. Life is short."

The idea that a person may reach the end of life with more stuff than he or she can manage is new. For much of human history, senior citizens were among society's most destitute and left little material evidence of themselves. That changed, like so much else, in the mid-twentieth century. Thanks to large houses (the average U.S. house has more than doubled in size since the 1950s), a robust social safety net, and longer lifespans, Americans have had the opportunity to acquire more stuff over a longer period of time than any nation in history.

That's mostly a good thing. Living standards have never been higher. But eventually, people—and their stuff—wear out.

In 1987, Mercedes Gunderson of suburban Edina, Minnesota, moved her mother—and her stuff—from her lifelong home in small-town Wisconsin to the Twin Cities. It was one of four moves that the elder Ms. Gunderson would make during the final seven years of her life. The stress of those relocations made an impression on the younger Ms. Gunderson, and in 1990 she founded what's believed to be the first U.S. company devoted to moving senior citizens and their stuff: Gentle Transitions.

The business case is simple. Families are geographically scattered and increasingly busy, so someone other than the kids will have to pack Mom and Dad for the move to senior living. It's a sensitive task. Seniors with three-bedroom houses have more stuff than they can take to their new, much smaller homes in assisted living. So a new job category—"senior move manager"—was created to help them end to end, from the packing to the unpacking.

Gentle Transitions is a lucrative and influential business. In 2018, it coordinated more than 1,200 moves in the Twin Cities, for fees that average $1,500 to $3,500 (not including the cost of the moving truck). Gunderson's son, who owns and operates a California branch of the company, was one of the cofounders of the National Association of Senior Move Managers, a trade association with more than six hundred members in forty U.S. states.

As the industry grows, new job categories proliferate. "Sorter" is the most interesting. In addition to helping pack up for the move, the sorter works with a property owner to choose what stuff makes the move to a new home—and, more important, what doesn't.

Jill Freeman, a marketing associate at Gentle Transitions as well as a professional sorter, is one of the best. I meet her at another Caribou Coffee on Highway 169. "Hoarding is a spectrum disorder," she tells me. "It's just a question of where you land on that spectrum. And we all do."

Freeman has a blonde bob, blue eyes, and endless charisma; I'm not at all surprised when she tells me she's a former actor, or that she's scheduled to lead a decluttering seminar in ninety minutes. "When I first arrive at a house, the first thing I do is have a discussion," she explains. "I want to be a friend, not an adversary. Because that's how they see me, as someone who throws away stuff."

That's just the starter. Inevitably, the job is about convincing people to let go and assuring them that the things they love aren't lost. "There's a grieving process," she says. "When you got that wedding china, you were going to keep it forever. I have clients break down." As possessions are set aside, a more profound grieving takes place. It's not just the loss of a sentiment; it's the loss of an identity.

The process is made even more difficult by changing tastes. The fine china and antiques appreciated by Americans born in the middle of the twentieth century aren't in much demand from the younger generations. "People just don't want it. But seniors want people to want it," Freeman says. " 'Oh, my kids will take it.' No, they *won't*." It's not their identity.

In the course of sorting someone's stuff, Freeman's best tactic is to persuade the clients that stuff won't be wasted. "Men won't get rid of tools. Women, Tupperware. So we tell them the Tupperware can be recycled. The tools can be used by someone else." Then it's left to the senior move manager to figure out what to do with what's left behind, and quickly. Freeman and other sorters have an hourly rate. Efficiency, not sustainability, must be their first priority.

That can be painful. Tammy Wilcox, a Gentle Transitions move manager, recalls sorting a photographer's belongings. "His whole life in pics," she tells me over coffee at the south Minneapolis home of another Gentle Transition sorter. "I went through pics of safaris, animals, his whole life. I told family they should take them. They said no. 1-800-JUNK came, and it broke my heart. They cleaned out three storage units." Tammy doesn't know where it all went, and it's not in her job description to worry about it. "They're paying us fifty-two dollars per hour, and the family's goal is to get rid of the stuff."

The Empty the Nest thrift store is located in a long beige office strip just off Highway 169, behind a Culver's restaurant. Out front, a handful of rakes and garden tools in metal buckets set it apart from the office tenants. But open the front door and the bland and beige give way to a riot of the very best stuff: a midcentury white leather sofa, side tables, metal buckets of vintage photos, farm equipment, shelves of glassware and plates, vintage magazines. The cash registers are perched on a desk made from hundreds of books; random objects hang from the ceiling. And all of it, every last object, was extracted from someone's home in the last month or so, with the promise of being reused.

For someone like me, the son of a junkyard owner, this is the best sort of playground. If my grandmother, the daughter of a junkyard owner, were still alive, it's where I'd take her for an outing—and then, after an hour, wonder if we'd ever leave.

But on this particular Wednesday, I don't get to linger. Sharon Fischman, the owner and founder, has agreed to sit down for an interview. But if we do it at the store, she'll be distracted. So, looking for a reason to get away, she suggests we go across the street to a Perkins restaurant. She's barely five feet tall, her wide eyes are constantly moving, and she walks at a single pace: straight-ahead fast. I practically chase her across the street.

At Perkins, Sharon leads me to a table and orders breakfast. It's the middle of the afternoon. "So," she says, "what do you want to know?"

A native of the western suburbs of Minneapolis, Sharon spent her early career working in television and, later, doing sales for a ground-beef processor. "Traveling around the U.S., calling on McDonald's and Perkins," she recounts with a fond smile. She married, had kids, and took time off to raise them. But after a health scare in her forties, she looked to reenter the workforce. There was no plan or direction. Reflecting on what she liked to do, she circled back to a childhood passion for organizing. One night, while surfing the internet, she googled "organizing" and Gentle Transitions turned up.

She started as a packer and progressed to move manager. The part of her job that required finding somewhere for all the stuff to go, post-move, made an impression. "I would end up calling the mover who moved them and saying, 'I have a bunch of stuff here. You want it?' And they'd be like, 'Yeah! We'll come get it.'" Sharon wondered if there wasn't an easier, more efficient, and more sustainable way. "I hate—*hate*—throwing away stuff." She pauses. "But I'm not a hoarder. My staff thinks I'm a hoarder because of the store. They should see my house. Not a hoarder."

As Sharon saw it then, the price of an Empty the Nest cleanout could be offset by the money recouped from the resale of the stuff—and marketed accordingly. Eight years later Empty the Nest has around thirty employees and a thrift store that's become a bit of a Twin Cities landmark. But Sharon insists this wasn't the plan at all. "It was just kind of like—it was more kind of like—there is all this stuff. And there are so many people who could use this stuff. How can we get it together with them instead of having it be so difficult." She pauses to cut into the omelet that was just delivered to the table. "And then when it hit me on that personal level, when we had to empty my parents' house, and we had an estate sale, and then there was this amazing stuff left in the house."

"Do you remember anything specifically?"

"The dining room table. It's gorgeous. Nobody wants this? Yeah."

At nine A.M. on a Tuesday, Sharon Kadet is standing outside a modest split-level home on leafy Vincent Avenue in North Minneapolis. A crew of four is already inside, cleaning out the contents. She's on her phone, checking on the delivery of a dumpster to take away what can't be reused. I gaze through the windows and see a relatively empty living room with a few spare pieces of furniture. "Doesn't look too bad," I tell her.

Sharon slips the phone into her jacket pocket. "Wait till you see the basement. You can't be fooled."

Inside, Denise Dixon, a willowy, middle-aged woman, is seated on one of the three chairs remaining in the living room. Each has a piece of blue tape affixed to it, indicating that it's going with the family—not Empty the Nest. The dining room table at the far end of the room, blue tape affixed, has an assortment of glassware and what appear to be antiques, most of which lack blue tape.

As packers descend the stairs with cardboard boxes, Denise crosses one leg over the other. "I could've gone down to the corner and hired a couple of guys for a few hundred bucks to do this job," she says in a businesslike manner. "But I wanted the stuff reused in the community. That makes me feel good."

A crew member walks in through the back door. "There's a grill in the—"

"My dad's smoker and charcoal," she interrupts. "It's promised to a gentleman who's coming this morning." Then she turns to me. "I'm unsentimental because I have to be." The house belongs to her parents, who bought it in 1973. Mom was a covenant minister ("We were the first African Americans to integrate a Covenant church in Minnesota"); Dad was a surgical tech for the Veterans Administration. They raised Denise and her two siblings here and wanted for nothing. "We had an awesome life," she says, her voice suddenly breaking. "We had everything." In 1982, she tells me, they were named City of Minneapolis Family of the Year.

Both parents are now eighty-two, and they'd managed to remain in the house until nine months ago. Then Denise's father, already suffering from dementia, "got sick," was hospitalized for a month, and spent an additional month in an aftercare center. "And it became clear to me they couldn't stay here anymore. So I bought them a condo in a co-op for seniors where there's a pull cord if you need anything."

That solved much of the problem. But there was still the question of what to do with the stuff. Denise, an entrepreneur, took the initiative and cleaned out what she could with family members. Most of what they kept has value to nobody but the family: photos and books. Then she hired Empty the Nest to handle the rest. "It was so clear to me that my mom was okay with this." Other family members feel otherwise. "You don't see my sister PJ because she's probably crying somewhere," Denise says with a sisterly roll of the eyes. "Well, PJ, if you feel that way, we should buy the house. At some point, stuff is stuff. We've had generations of stuff. We've had grandparents' stuff."

There's a diesel rumble from the back of the house, and Sharon excuses herself to check on the dumpster delivery. Denise stands and invites me to look around. I follow her into the narrow kitchen, where two packers are carefully boxing sets of dishes stacked on shelves and on cabinets. "Hard to say how we got so many," she says. "But hopefully somebody else can use them."

From there she descends down creaky stairs into a basement lit by just a few bulbs and held up by exposed beams. There are boxes and garbage bags bursting with stuff; tools and vacuum cleaners; appliances. Three packers are arrayed at strategic points within the room, sorting and depositing stuff into boxes and bags bound for Empty the Nest, the Salvation Army (for what Empty the Nest can't justify selling), and the trash. At the far end, behind the stairs, stuff is so dense that there's no room for a packer, yet. "This is stuff my dad did over the years," she says, pointing at a box. "Who knows?" I lean over it, but it's covered in newspapers. Denise takes a long gaze around the room and then excuses herself. "I have an appointment at ten."

As she walks up the stairs, I wade gingerly into the stilled tide of her parents' material life. Tracy Luke, a sinewy sorter with a strong jaw and an air of unsentimental efficiency, is kneeling beside boxes of clothes. "This requires making some judgment calls," she tells me. Unless the garments are vintage and collectible, the margins are too small to interest Empty the Nest. So they pack them for the Salvation Army.

Generally, packers sort into five different categories: new, vintage, collectible, and resalable stuff goes to Empty the Nest's thrift store; reusable stuff too cheap or common for the thrift store is bound for the Salvation Army or a similar charity organization; old electronics are bound for a specialized electronics recycler; recyclable paper and metal goes to a general recycler; and trash is bound for wherever the hauler takes it that day.

"When I first started working at Empty the Nest, I didn't think I had much stuff," Tracy tells me as she pauses to examine a carefully folded blouse before tossing it into a bag for the Salvation Army. "Then I started downsizing."

Tracy's experience with the hoarding spectrum preceded her work at Empty the Nest. She's a retired police officer who worked for more than two decades in an affluent Twin Cities suburb and called on many hoarder homes. "Older generations—things get away from them," she says. But her sympathies have limits. "How many gifts do we need? Over there is a cook set, all new in the box. Probably a book in there too." It's just one hint of the new and unused things that are stashed in American homes. And it's not just an American problem. A 2016 study sponsored by the British retailer Marks & Spencer and Oxfam, a British confederation of twenty charities, revealed that British closets contain 3.6 billion unworn garments.[2]

Across the basement, Ally Enz, another packer, stands up amid the boxes. "There are four vacuum cleaners down here."

Tracy nods. "That's super common in hoarder houses."

"I think older people are recalling back when you'd repair the things."

I wander up the stairs and into a first-floor bedroom off the living room. Inside, Kristy Dueffert, a four-year packing veteran, is sorting through clothes. Three vacuum cleaners are perched in a corner.

"People hold on to a lot of stuff. If they have one piece of paper," she tells me, "they have a thousand." She's younger—and breezier—than her colleagues. "I have two kids, and I used to keep a lot more stuff," she explains. "Then they grew up, and I realized it didn't mean as much to them." She folds undershirts into a bag for the Salvation Army. "You should take a look in the attic."

It's reached via a set of stairs that ends at a tight landing further constrained by the angle of the roof. The overly warm space is cramped, and made more so by the wild assortment of stuff that's spread across the floor, a bed, tables, and a dresser. I open a large black garbage bag and find a sparkly paper Santa Claus staring back; beneath him, ornaments. I close the bag and scan the piles. There's another vacuum cleaner in a corner.

Downstairs, I mention the Christmas stuff to Kristy. "It's still summer, nobody wants it," she tells me. "If you try to donate it to the Salvation Army, they'll say no. Nowhere to store it." She shrugs. "Things accumulate. Working with Empty the Nest, you learn 'you bring something in, you take something out.'"

Prior to World War II, little that Kristy just said would've made sense. The United States, like the rest of the world, was still an agrarian society, families were large and localized, and property of any kind was scarce, oftentimes homemade, and valuable. Nineteenth- and early twentieth-century practical housekeeping manuals (a genre that's largely disappeared) were, in many respects, repair manuals.[3] Some included basic cement recipes to aid in the repair of broken dishes. Others offered advice on basic strategies to prolong the usable lifespan of pottery, ironware, and glass. What little a parent or grandparent owned and left behind was bequeathed to the next generation for uninterrupted use.

As the industrial revolution drew families into cities and mass-production jobs, society's relationship to stuff began to change, and modern notions of "waste" emerged. For example, in traditional farming communities, food scraps are fertilizer. But the nineteenth-century urban tenements into which rural families relocated provided little space or opportunity to "recycle" food. In the absence of waste collection, food scraps often literally went out of the window, into the streets. In 1842 the *New York Daily News* estimated that ten thousand pigs were roaming the streets of New York, consuming mostly organic garbage. Modern trash collection and disposal had yet to be invented.

Likewise, before mass production rendered clothing cheap and large wardrobes a middle-class entitlement, garments were homemade and expensive. A shirt could require days of labor; bed linens and blankets were heirlooms. When they wore out or tore, they were mended, reused in other garments, or—ultimately—reduced to rags for cleaning.

Industrialization and urbanization changed everything. Busy days spent in a sweatshop provided little time to mend a shirt, repurpose it into a new garment, or reduce it to rags. As a result, store-bought alternatives emerged, and families used the money earned from hourly or daily wages to buy them. They were still expensive—it would be decades before middle-class Americans could afford multiple changes of store-bought clothes. But the idea that a garment or other object was a resource that should be renewed at home was eroding. In the process, the sentimental value associated with clothing declined as quickly as the material value. After all, it's easier to discard a store-bought shirt than one made at home by a mother, a wife, or a sister.

Of course, a preindustrial agrarian lifestyle is more environmentally sustainable than a modern one. But so too is the brutish nomadic life that preceded the development of agriculture. Nobody is clamoring for either, and it bears repeating that neither is worth romanticizing: sanitation and nutrition were poorer, and the average lifespan was considerably shorter and less interesting. No doubt, there are downsides to an economy built on mass production and consumption. Factory production, in particular, can take a significant toll on air and water quality. But even in places where that toll is most tangible, such as contemporary China, consumers understandably embrace mass production and urbanization over the alternatives.

That's worth celebrating. But spend a few hours at an average American home cleanout, and there will be moments when you doubt that you're celebrating the upward arrow of human progress.

I meet Sharon Kadet in the garage of an upscale multilevel townhouse in the trendy Uptown neighborhood of Minneapolis. Empty the Nest crewmembers—Sharon says there are "eight or nine"—are maneuvering chairs and boxes between the hills of other furniture and boxes cluttering the garage and into an Empty the Nest truck partly filled with stuff acquired during another cleanout earlier that morning. Sharon says she typically organizes seven to thirteen cleanouts per week. But thanks to several complicated multiday jobs—including this one— there's just seven scheduled this week.

"I've seen everything," she reminds me. "But the family really built this one up." The townhome belonged to an elderly woman who'd recently passed away. According to her relatives, none of them— including the sister who lived nearby—had been allowed into the house in years. "She was embarrassed," Sharon says. "But this actually isn't close to the worst I've seen."

She leads me into the house and up a stairway covered in carpet with years' worth of grime ground into it. At one end of the landing is a room that was used as an office. Three crew members are inside, opening drawers and rapidly emptying them into trash bags. "They're not looking for anything," Sharon explains. "But they're going through everything." Personal papers go into recycling bags; broken staplers, used pens with ink leaking out, a stray plastic paper clip—that all goes into a trash bag. Unopened reams of paper, of which there are several, land in boxes for the thrift store. "A job like this, there's probably not much Empty the Nest stuff. So we become more of a service."

A tall and muscular older man walks into the room and kneels beside a desk and bookshelves covered in white vinyl. "Particleboard," he mutters as he presses a hand against them, testing their weight and build. Sharon introduces him as Carl, and he is excited to reveal his knowledge of moving to a journalist. "I've been doing moves for thirty years," he tells me as he stands up. "And I'd never buy something from Ikea. We'll shrink-wrap them, but it's only fifty-fifty they make it."

Sharon leads me out of the office and up the stairs. As she does, she reminds me she's not as optimistic as her movers. "That desk and those shelves aren't the sort of thing we can salvage in most cases. Particleboard can survive one move, maybe. Then it's done. Nobody wants to buy it—it's so cheap already."

This upper floor is what must have horrified the owner's relatives. It's a bright, high-ceilinged space, and the main living area is a forest of banker's boxes, books, and loose paper. The tan carpet is stained brown; two vintage exercise machines—the HealthRider and the SoftWalk Plus—are in the center of the room; bottles of nutritional supplements are scattered randomly until they concentrate and overtake the kitchen. Every spare filthy counter is covered in stacks of bottles and containers of something allegedly healthy: slippery elm, tiger balm, organic barley sprout powder, reishi extract, organic wheat juice. Perhaps hundreds more are stashed in boxes.

A smashing occurs downstairs, and I jump. "The white particleboard shelves will not make it," Sharon announces with a shrug. "The boys are breaking them up. Not worth the trouble."

Ally Enz is here, seated on a box, going through banker's boxes of paper and binders. "This would all go faster if we could just toss all of the paper into the recycling," she says as she shakes out a binder, seeing what falls from it. "But you never know what's in these binders, or books that we might be able to reuse." Three books are on an end table next to Ally: *Office 2008 for Mac*, *Webster's New Collegiate Dictionary*, and *Clutter Free* by Kathi Lipp. "Folks usually know they have a problem," she tells me.

She reaches the bottom of a box and pulls out a handful of small porcelain cats. They land in the trash. "We're not doing anybody any favors saving these kinds of tchotchkes," she says dismissively. "I've seen stuff like this in really nice houses, with Goodwill tags still on them. How many more times are we going to send them through the reuse cycle?"

Spend time around cleanouts, and a few patterns emerge. Seniors born during the Depression tend to hoard more. Ally mentions finding plastic bags containing plastic bags among those clients. Baby boomers, by contrast, tend to have more electronics and less stuff in general. "The real interesting cleanouts are the ones where people have lived in the same house for forty, fifty, sixty years. Interesting and emotionally hard. They even kept the kids' artwork. Even baby books." She pauses and gives me a sad smile. Nobody cares about your old baby books but your family. And sometimes they don't care, either. "If they're vintage, the baby books can go to the thrift store."

After a lunch of Domino's pizza, Empty the Nest's movers and packers continue. I descend to the first level and the office, which has been largely emptied of furniture and is now a shell containing loose papers. Around the corner is a bedroom not much bigger than the queen-size bed and two end tables that fill it. The perimeter is jammed with boxes that must be sorted.

Amy Rimington, the lead packer on this cleanout, is seated on the edge of the bed, sorting through a box of envelopes and documents. "I'm a bit of an environmentalist," she tells me. "One reason I joined Empty the Nest was to reduce, recycle." She takes a large envelope from the box and reaches inside. It's filled with old color photos that she sorts through like they're playing cards before tossing them into the garbage. "If they're vintage or postcards we'll send them to the store. People like to collect them." Next, she pulls out a stack of personal letters still in their envelopes, shakes them out to make sure there's no money or other valuables inside, and then tosses the remainders into the recycling.

I step farther into the room and see that there are several similar boxes at the bottom of a closet still heavy with winter clothes and coats. They remind me, at least, that whoever lived here was something more than a consumer of supplements. She, too, had things that she valued more than a thrift store ever would. And now much of it is on the way to a paper mill and the massive garbage incinerator on the edge of downtown Minneapolis.

Amy dispels whatever sentimentality that my face has betrayed. "When you're running a business, you can't take the time to examine every piece of paper. I do four or five homes per week, and I throw away a lot more than I used to. Still, this is a particularly bad one."

At the bottom of the first box of letters and photos is a blue leather purse. The color is faded, and the stitching is frayed. She drops it into the trash and pulls out a smaller handbag with a needlepoint cover. "I'd like to recycle this, but nobody's going to want it. So I make up for it myself, and reduce, reduce, reduce."

She reaches into the closet and pulls out several additional cardboard boxes. To her surprise, dozens of pairs of new shoes are stored behind them. "Hey, Carl," she calls out. "New shoes! Can you box them up for our store?" The stout mover strides into the room, gazes into the closet, and says he'll be right back. "This house had hundreds of shoes and inserts," she adds. "Lady had OCD, dementia. Her new and vintage shoes will go to our store. The rest we'll give to charities that sell them for funds."

"What percent of the stuff in this room is reusable?"

"Fifteen to twenty percent. Shoes mostly." Amy leans over to pick up a handwritten letter that must've fallen out of an envelope earlier. Uncharacteristically, she pauses to read a few words—and then tosses it into the recycling. "I sometimes get mad at people. They buy things for no other reason than it's cheap. And they hold on to things that people gave to them. 'Oh, it meant so much,'" she says sarcastically. "Well, what're you going to do with it?" She shakes her head and opens up another box of photos and letters.

Multifamily homes emptied of stuff are assets. And they are becoming more common. People over age sixty-five will account for one quarter of the U.S. population by 2030, and senior housing demand is expected to grow with their population. That's why Sharon Kadet is seated at a small coffee table in the corner of a windowless conference room at a Coldwell Banker real estate office in Minneapolis at nine thirty A.M. on a weekday. She's been invited to pitch Empty the Nest to the agency's roughly forty agents. Also invited: a move manager, an odor-elimination company, and a woman who creates hand-lettered real estate closing gifts.

But first there's coffee. As Sharon sets out Empty the Nest brochures, a handsome realtor in a very expensive-looking blue suit approaches.

He's heard of Empty the Nest and wants to know more. But it's not for a client. "My dad is aging. He's not a hoarder, and we're talking about an estate sale. But the problem is that nothing sells at estate sales anymore."

Sharon has heard this before. "With an estate sale, you don't know what you're going to make. And you'll still have a project, stuff left behind when you're done." They exchange business cards, and as he walks away, Sharon whispers to me, "This is so common. You're here to talk to realtors about a solution, but it quickly becomes about their family. It's just how we live. We don't just keep what we need. I'm the same way."

As we're talking, a short, late-middle-aged realtor in a bright red coat approaches us. She introduces herself as Lesley Novich and tells me she's sold homes for twenty years. She also knows Sharon and uses Empty the Nest. "As a realtor, you can tell people to declutter. But to do it yourself . . ." She shakes her head.

Sharon tells Linda that I'm writing about Empty the Nest and the secondhand-goods industry. Linda puts her hand over her heart. "Love it! When I moved out for college, my mother held a secondhand party for me. All that old heavy wooden furniture, we wanted it."

Sharon lets out a big laugh almost too loud for the room. "Now nobody wants it."

Linda leans toward Sharon as if she's getting ready to confide. "My nephew, moving into a new apartment, wants all new. He's happy with Target."

Sharon, the blunt marketer, takes it in and pushes it right back out. "Target is purposeful. Secondhand is the experience."

CHAPTER 2

Decluttering

The United States wasn't the only country to boom after World War II. And it's not the only place struggling to find a home for excess stuff left behind by an aging population. In Japan, the population isn't just aging—it's declining. Often, there aren't any family or friends left behind to claim the property, much less hire a cleanout service. Meanwhile, homes packed with belongings and garbage—hoarder houses, in the American parlance—are discovered daily.

That's a state of affairs very much at odds with the image projected by Marie Kondo and other representatives of Japan's minimalist and decluttering movements. But it's worth noting that part of the reason those movements have achieved popularity in Japan is that the Japanese want decluttered homes as much as Americans do.

Jeongja Han rushes up the stairs at the Ebisu subway stop in Tokyo and greets me with a polite smile and a bow. She has a round, youthful face framed by a short bob of hair, and she wears a tan apron with two large pockets filled with pens, markers, and tape. She is the director of the

Tail Project, a six-year-old company based near Tokyo that specializes in cleaning out and disposing of the property accumulated by Japan's shrinking population. At age fifty, she is ten years retired from her first career as a flight attendant. But there's a hurried efficiency in her words and manner that echoes her former life.

I am joined by Toubi Cho, who translates Japanese language and, often, culture for me during my visits to Japan. Except in cases where I explicitly note that a Japanese person speaks English to me, Toubi is the intermediary.

Han's business card lists three professional accreditations: a government license to sell secondhand goods; a certification from Japan's National Association of Cleanout Professionals, an organization representing eight thousand of Japan's cleanout companies; and, from the same organization, an accreditation as a *shukatsu* counselor.

The last is unique to Japan. During the country's post–World War II reconstruction and economic boom, *shukatsu* described the process of finding a job. But in recent years, older Japanese have changed the first Japanese character in *shukatsu* so that it takes on a new, grimly ironic meaning: the process of preparing for the end.

The need is acute. In 2018, Japan celebrated 921,000 births—and mourned 1.369 million deaths. That was the lowest number of births since records were first kept in 1899, and the eighth consecutive year of population decline. Despite decades of government efforts to encourage couples to have more children, Japan's population could shrink by one third over the next fifty years. As a result, the business of preparing for death is growing rapidly. *Shukatsu* "fairs," where Japanese familiarize themselves with vendors for everything from grave clothes to estate planning, are common. Workbooks for putting one's end-of-life affairs in order are widely available, and entrepreneurs like Han are also available to consult on what to do with your stuff after you're gone—or to send it off on behalf of your paying relatives after you've departed.

Today Han is cleaning out the apartment of a woman whose husband was recently killed in an auto accident. The couple had no children who'd want to salvage heirlooms, memories, or simply help with the process. So this one, like most, is total. "Some families say, 'Keep something,'" she says as she hails a taxi for us. "But most say, 'Get rid of it.'"

It's a process that wouldn't have made sense sixty years ago. Japanese families were big, mostly rural, nearby, and willing to do the duties surrounding death. But that changed quickly. During Japan's post–World War II boom years, young Japanese could look forward to benefits-rich, lifelong "regular employment" in big cities far from their rural roots and families. It was a prosperous arrangement that fueled unprecedented levels of consumption for a historically conservative country. By the 1960s, affluent Japanese joked that Japan's mythological three "sacred treasures"—the sword, the mirror, and the jewel—had been supplanted by three new sacred treasures: the television, the washing machine, and the refrigerator.

Eventually, Japan was so rich and its homes so full of stuff that televisions and washing machines were no longer sacred or worthy of self-effacing jokes. The jokes became even less funny after Japan's asset bubble burst in the early 1990s, sinking the economy into a recession and a decades-long stagnation. Since then, regular employment has progressively given way to low-paying, benefits-poor, irregular jobs, especially for younger Japanese. Economic insecurity has forced those young Japanese to put off marriage and children—or skip them altogether.

What's left behind is one of the world's most aged societies, millions of homes filled with property accumulated during Japan's boom years, and a dearth of heirs. Japan is already home to eight million unoccupied homes, colloquially known as "ghost homes." By 2040, the total amount of vacated residential real estate in Japan could equal the total area of Austria, according to a recent government study.

The situation isn't unique to Japan. Across affluent developed East Asia, populations are aging just as fast, leaving behind a similar legacy of stuff. Western Europe, too, is facing similar demographic challenges. What will eventually happen to those 3.8 million unused fondue sets that one U.K. insurance company estimated were stashed away in British homes in 2003? Even assuming that most of them still work, it's hard to believe there will be enough population growth (even via immigration) to create a secondhand market.

Fortunately, there are many clean and environmentally secure options for recycling or trashing unwanted objects. If a fondue pot doesn't make its way to a metal scrapyard—and it probably won't—it will be safely turned to ash in a technologically advanced, environmentally secure trash incinerator (especially in Japan, home to the world's finest trash incinerators). It's just a matter of delivering it to the flames and paying the disposal fees, which can be considerable. A twelve-gallon garbage bag filled with stuff will incur a fee of around fifty dollars at the incinerator; a futon, twice that. Some of the to-be-burned stuff might have resale value, but the trouble of sorting it is worth less than the value of having more time to charge for another cleanout.

At least, that's what Jeongja Han thought. But recently she's found that her clients have different ideas. "They want to know that somebody is using their things," she says. "It makes them feel good." As a businesswoman, she's obliged to provide the service.

*   *   *

On the second floor of a Doutor coffee shop not far from Ebisu, I meet Rina Hamada, the editor of Japan's *Reuse Business Journal* and Japan's foremost expert on everything related to the country's secondhand-goods industry.

It's a big job.

In 2016, secondhand was a $16 billion industry in Japan. That's roughly 4 percent of Japan's overall retail market. But the actual impact on Japan is much greater. For example, according to Hamada's data, Japan had twenty million used-clothing consumers in 2016—or roughly one sixth of the population. And even though used clothing sells for substantially less than new, it still accounted for 10.5 percent of the total retail apparel market. Among younger Japanese, secondhand is a taken-for-granted method of assembling an identity.

Hamada is physically tiny—generously five feet tall. On her left shoulder is a massive handbag into which she's stashed several copies of the *Reuse Business Journal* for my use. It looks like the *Wall Street Journal*, and its contents are just as thorough and serious. There are articles on auction houses, online secondhand start-ups, and market prognostications; they are bordered by hundreds of advertisements for auctions, pricing data, and newly opened resale shops.

"*Mottainai*," she says to me, invoking a difficult-to-translate Japanese word that expresses a sense of regret over waste, as well as a desire to conserve. "Before the 1960s, Japanese had this feeling," she explains. "Even during the Edo period [1603–1868], a kimono would be reused." But everything changed in the 1960s as the country entered its proud era of hypergrowth. "Japanese forgot who they were and just bought, bought, bought."

In her view, that ethos faded over the last two decades, thanks to Japan's slowing economic growth and changing demographics. Hamada also cites another factor: the March 2011 Tohoku earthquake and tsunami that caused the Fukushima Daiichi nuclear disaster. "After that, we remember who we are," she explains. "People start to send their things to Tohoku because the people in Tohoku have nothing. People think, 'Maybe we should reuse things.'"

The Japanese home-cleanout industry predated the earthquake, and—initially, at least—had little relationship to the secondhand industry. Instead, it was about getting rid of stuff quickly and efficiently. In that sense, it was the perfect offshoot of Japan's go-go economy of the mid-twentieth century. But that changed in the early 2010s, too. Several cleanout companies in Hokkaido, the northern Japanese island renowned for its beauty and tourist economy, were caught dumping objects culled from cleanouts into natural areas (rather than paying the high disposal fees). The resulting press coverage produced an uproar—and a noticeable uptick in the public's awareness of the cleanout industry's services. The Association of Cleanout Professionals was formed in response to both. It's worked hard to change the industry's image, in part by offering in-depth training on how to profit from recycling and reuse markets.

These days, even Buddhist monks are getting into the business. As Hamada explains it, Japanese Shinto and Buddhism posit that spirits come to inhabit objects that have been used for years. "Families go to the monks and temples after the death for prayers," Hamada says. "And then the monks go to the home and clean it out." It's such an attractive business model that some cleanout companies are working directly with the temples, offering to tie up the deceased's spiritual and material needs in one simple package.

But despite Japan's re-embrace of its traditional values, its more contemporary values retain their power. "Of course in Japan we have the *mottainai* spirit," Hamada acknowledges. "But the living standard is high." She raps her knuckles on the wooden table separating us. "This table is a good one, but if it's dirty, Japanese won't use it."

"So who will?"

"Developing countries."

Jeongja Han steps out of our taxi on a quiet, affluent street lined on one side by expensive apartments and the other by a park filled with cherry trees shedding their blossoms in a late-spring breeze.

I follow her into the lobby of an apartment building, up four flights of stairs, and into a two-room apartment in an advanced state of disassembly. Two Tail Project crew members are lifting a wardrobe, preparing to transport it down the stairs. A third crew member is kneeling on the floor, pulling up cables carefully secured to the floor years ago. To the right is the kitchenette, with several boxes filled with kitchen utensils and glass, two boxes jammed with half-drunk bottles of scotch and sake, and a stack of new boxes still flat and tied together. On the near wall is a poster of Bob Marley smoking a joint and another advertising the Rolling Stones' Voodoo Lounge tour.

In the middle of the room a woman sits on a stool, right leg crossed over her left. She's in her midfifties, wears skinny jeans and a short black coat, and her hair falls past her shoulders. She is the widow, and there are dark circles below her eyes. As a condition of my presence, she asked that I not use her name.

Han settles back into what she was doing before she fetched me from the subway station: packing the widow's glassware in newsprint. "I pack things we can resell at the recycling markets," she explains. "The crew packs the furniture."

I lean in closer to look at two cloudy beer glasses that she's wrapping carefully. "You can sell these?"

"It's very difficult to sell in Japan. They prefer things that have only been used a year, including electronics. So we export, if they want it."

She works through the widow's kitchen as if she's collecting meal trays in a packed wide-body jet well into its descent for landing, dumping what must be dumped so that she can move on to the next item. "Our first choice is the Philippines. But recently Africans are buying more things. But not everything. Sometimes we leave things in front of the office, just so people will take it."

"I want the things to go to people who will use them," the widow pipes up. She's fidgeting with a finger-size toy bicycle that she pulled from the disorder. It strikes me that the desire to see one's things take on a second life is as much a matter of vanity as it is a concern for the planet or dismay at waste. It's as if she's saying that her stuff is worthy.

One of the crew walks over with a box of vinyl records, and the widow kneels down and flips through them. I see Elton John's *Don't Shoot Me, I'm Only the Piano Player* and *The Best of Cream*. In Japan, collectors of old vinyl are passionate, and the objects of their desire are highly sought. Old beer pints may not have much value, but these records surely do.

Han's eyes flash in the direction of the records but she doesn't say a thing.

The widow smiles. "My husband used to make tapes and bring them to bars for them to play. I remember neighbors yelling, 'Turn it down!' when he made them. We used to have parties here all the time."

Han seals a box of glasses with tape and, without looking up, asks, "Can I take the records?"

"Take them."

It's a good score. Despite the emphasis on resale and reuse, most of her cleanout revenues come from the fees that the clients pay her, which range from $2,200 to $3,200 for a one-day job (multiday jobs scale up in price). But that revenue shrinks as she pays salaries and steep disposal fees that sometimes reach $1,000.

Jeongja Han of Tail Project during a Tokyo-area cleanout.

Han isn't struggling, though. The Tail Project, like most Japanese cleanout companies, is busy. On average she does ten to twelve jobs per month. "I could do more," she acknowledges. "But I like to do a good job on the ones I've accepted." The day before, she cleaned out a home in Fukushima Prefecture, 180 miles to the north, and after this job she's bound for Yokohama, 20 miles away, to meet another client. "When I started out, it wasn't so easy to find business." She opens a junk drawer. Unopened boxes of staples go in the resale carton, while pens get tossed into the nearby garbage bag. She picks up a small brown cylinder. It's a personal seal that's used like a signature in Japan. She turns to the widow. "Do you want this?"

During the course of the morning, the widow has swung from quietly contemplative to chatty, even humorous. But with that question, she settles into what appears to be her ground state: exhausted. "No, thank you," she says with a shake of the head.

It lands in the trash bag.

*   *   *

Jeongja Han's decluttering methods are practical, not spiritual. Everything has a place or—better yet—a market. It's a way of thinking with relatively shallow roots in contemporary Japan. In the 1910s, Japan's modernizing bureaucrats and industrialists embraced the "scientific management" theories of Frederick Winslow Taylor, an American mechanical engineer who became one of the world's first management consultants.[1] Taylorism, as his approach has come to be known, sought to measure and maximize the efficiency of the workplace and to reduce waste, whether of time or materials.

Toyota adapted the Taylorite idea to create its famous "lean production" system that's become synonymous with Japan's manufacturing prowess. But Taylorism isn't just about factories. In a Taylor'd office, executives should be seated close to the door because they leave the office most often, and shared items should be placed in designated areas so time isn't wasted looking for them.[2]

Some of Taylor's Japanese acolytes decided that such advice is also applicable to the home, and in the late 1940s advice literature emerged that focused on reducing waste and improving the efficiency of home life. For example, in 1949, Omoto Moichiro published *The Scientification of Home Life*, a guide that sought to create the optimal division of labor in the home, with the housewife as manager. Taylorite advice such as "things should have a designated place in the home, and containers such as boxes or cans should be clearly labeled with a description of their contents,"[3] would become decluttering gospel in the 2010s.

None of this advice was geared to minimalists and other people who sought to reduce their reliance on stuff. Instead, it was explicitly aimed at helping Japanese manage the growing volumes of stuff—and waste— that they acquired. It's advice for people who like to shop, and few countries like to shop as much as Japan does (the size of their economy is in part the proof). Fashion turns over quickly; gadgets are adopted, upgraded, and tossed.

But even during Japan's midcentury boom, there were doubters. In the 1970s, a nascent environmental movement began voicing concerns about Japanese materialism. Those environmental concerns soon merged with social concerns. In 1979, respondents to Japan's annual national survey on lifestyles indicated for the first time that "affluence of the heart" and *yutori*—a word that roughly translates as "a search for time and space to enjoy life"—was more important to them than material affluence. As the roaring 1980s wore on, dissatisfaction with materialism deepened.

Eiko Maruko Siniawer, the foremost historian of Japanese waste and wastefulness, writes that seekers of *yutori* considered "not just whether a purchase was necessary or not but whether . . . it would bring pleasure and joy to their heart."[4] It's not a very big leap from acquiring things that bring pleasure to the heart to Marie Kondo's famous commandment that consumers should keep only those things that spark joy.

In late 2018, I called Professor Siniawer at her office at Williams College, in Massachusetts, and asked what had caused these multiple threads to converge and create the internationally popular Japanese decluttering movement in the late 2000s. Like Rina Hamada, she cited the influence of Japan's long economic slide. But she was careful to note that despite the economic slide and growing environmental consciousness, Japanese decluttering remains a movement aimed at organizing stuff to achieve immediate, individual happiness. It's about saving space, not money or the environment:

I think Marie Kondo has been popular in Japan for the same reasons she's popular in the U.S. and other relatively affluent, mass-consumer societies. Which is that she is addressing the problem of an abundance or excess of stuff, which is a problem only if you're of a certain class and can afford to have an abundance and excess of stuff. And she doesn't actually address the consumption side of things. Some people say it's implied that you should make do with less stuff. But she doesn't actually address how and why stuff ends up in your home in the first place.

That last problem—one that's metastasizing around aging, affluent Japan—is typically addressed only during the final declutter, when the consumer is no longer around to feel joy, and the person picking through the stuff might be a hired hand.

Jeongja Han doesn't have time to mourn for what her clients give up. It's a lesson she learned personally after her own mother died years earlier. Family members weren't available to help, and Han recalls thinking that she would have liked to hire a stand-in or two. Instead, she did it herself. "It was so hard," she recalls, showing a brief flash of vulnerability. " 'These are my mother's things!' " she says, quoting her younger self. "But I have to do it."

A few years later, Active-Techno, a manufacturer of sheet-metal painting equipment in part owned by Toyota, was reeling from the recession that followed the March 2011 Tohoku earthquake. The owner is a friend of Han's, and he mentioned that he was in search of new business lines and had recently read an article about the cleanout industry. "He said, 'Maybe I should do this business,' " Han recalls. "And I said, 'No, no, no. I'll do it.' " The Tail Project opened as a division of Active-Techno in 2012.

The barriers to entry are few. Han acquired a secondhand-goods dealer's license. For jobs that require she also do some cleaning, she acquired safety training similar to what a mortician might receive. Thanks to the thousands of Japanese who die alone every week, that work accounts for around 30 percent of the business.

Han steps away from the kitchen, takes out her iPhone, and scrolls through photos of cleanouts. "See," she says as she stops on a photo of a bed. The mattress is stained with a dark shadow in the shape of a body. "I don't remove the body," she says. "But I had to receive the training to clean what's left." She keeps scrolling, through images of hair still stuck to tatami mats, a pile of garbage upon which a body was found, and an entire decomposing body on a bed. She captures the images when she's visiting a potential client to bid on a job. If she lands it, those images prepare her and the crew for what they'll encounter.

Some cleanouts are "happy," Han says—occasions where the family gathers to tell stories about the deceased. And then there are the sad ones. "The family comes just for the things of value. Leave everything else behind." She pauses. "What about the United States?"

At this, the widow suddenly interjects that she'd been to Los Angeles with her husband, and while there she'd seen garage sales. "Americans hold them so they can have room to buy more stuff," she tells me and looks away to smile to herself and, perhaps, to the memory of the husband with whom she once might have shared this observation. "I think it's funny."

It's late afternoon and traffic is starting to choke Yokohama's wide thoroughfares. Takaharu Kominato, a public relations officer at Bookoff Corporation, Japan's second-biggest retailer of secondhand goods, is driving his BMW. Over the course of a quarter mile, we pass Tackleberry, a used-fishing-gear retailer with outlets across Japan, and Golf Effort, a used-golf-clubs retailer with outlets around the Tokyo and Yokohama areas. "Do they get much of their used stuff from . . . *shukatsu*?" As I say the word, it feels awkward, a pose.

Kominato smiles politely. "Much is from young people. They want to get rid of stuff and have room for new. Stores like these make it easy." It's a business that Bookoff pioneered in the 1990s, back when "second-hand" was synonymous with "down-market" in Japan. Today, Bookoff has more than seven hundred outlets across Japan buying and selling everything from books to camping equipment. The company's stock is listed on the Nikkei—along with the offerings of more than a dozen secondhand competitors.

Kominato turns into a parking lot set between two massive ware-houses identified with Bookoff's playful orange logo. He gets out of the car and pats the wrinkles out of his dark suit and tieless gray shirt, wipes off the tight oval lenses of his black-rimmed glasses. He's thin and bony, but there's a warmth to him. In part, I think it's because there's a magical quality to the operations of secondhand businesses. Visiting their backstage areas is a bit like lifting the curtain on an audi-tion. In this case, the performance is about how little our stuff matters once we've let it go.

We stride into a well-lit storage space that's divided by hundreds of red and blue carts holding roughly forty beat-up banker's boxes each. According to Kominato, the individual boxes contain at least twenty used books, DVDs, and CDs that their owners are selling to Bookoff Online, Bookoff's rapidly expanding e-commerce unit. Rather than go through the trouble of taking them to a used bookshop, they take advantage of a process Bookoff has designed to simplify the process of unloading stuff: simply pack a box, print a shipping label, and call for a pickup. Kominato says that Bookoff receives around 3,000 boxes per day containing around 150,000 items, the vast majority of which are books. This is no cleanout; it's a black hole that sucks in volumes the moment a book owner loosens her grip.

We walk up a set of stairs to the second floor. As we emerge on the landing, I step back to let a worker push past with a cart the size of a hot tub filled waist-high with hundreds of books. "Those are being recycled," Kominato says. Bookoff is Japan's largest used-book buyer and seller. But not every used book has a buyer and, as a result, Bookoff is likely Japan's largest book recycler, too. According to Kominato, the company sends thirty-five thousand tons of books to paper recyclers every year. That's three and a half times the weight of the Eiffel Tower, measured out in individual, unwanted volumes: romances, histories, dictionaries, classics, cookbooks.

It's a heartbreaking number—especially if you're an author. And it's a merciless cull that happens all day long in the long, thin second floor of this Bookoff Online warehouse. Running down the middle of the space are carts piled with books. And on each side are perhaps thirty workstations where workers spend their hours opening customers' boxes and evaluating what's inside.

Kominato introduces me to Mrs. Naya, a cheerful graying woman who's worked here for a decade. There's not much to her workstation. To her left is a hot tub cage full of recycler-bound books and, behind it, six unopened cardboard boxes sent by customers. In front of her is a computer screen, a bar code reader, and a printer. To her right are blue and red bins roughly the size of backpacks. That's where the books judged to be worth something will be placed.

The process is straightforward. Mrs. Naya slices open a box and grabs a book. If there's a blemish—a turned corner, a torn page, a sun-bleached cover—the book is immediately dumped in the recycling bin. Kominato concedes that this is a tough standard. "It's actually tougher than the quality standard used in our physical bookstores," he says. "The problem is that online customers don't get to inspect a used book before buying it. So it must be good as new. We don't want any returns because of condition."

Books that survive the physical evaluation are then slid beneath the bar code scanner and subjected to the judgment of Bookoff's vast and constantly updating database and purchasing algorithms. Bookoff won't reveal everything that goes into those, much less the people who control them. But Kominato says that the decision to buy a book and what to pay are based on a range of factors, including what's sold in the past, what the company's pricing staff expects to sell in the future (if a title is being made into a movie, the company might hold on to a book that's not selling now), and what's already jamming up the shelves.

Most don't make it. According to Kominato, roughly 60 percent of the books that people send to Bookoff have no value. "Most are manga, which is disposable," he says, referring to the uniquely Japanese comic books and graphic novels that are printed by the millions. "On the other hand, there are books that are super popular but we don't want them taking too much space on the shelf." He drops the comic book. "So they get recycled, too."

Each scan of a book produces a beep and—on the screen—directions as to whether it should be sent to the recycling bin or one of the blue or red bins for purchase. While speaking to me, Mrs. Naya scans and distributes books to bins as if she's dealing cards. *Beep.* "I always see all kinds of interesting things here." *Beep.* "Especially in the recycling bins." *Beep.* "But we're not allowed to take anything, which breaks my heart." *Beep.* "So that just encourages me to go out and buy new things." *Beep.*

"I do the same," Kominato says as he reaches into the recycling bin for a book that catches his eye. It's a thirty-year-old hardback novel, and he pages through it carefully. The condition is perfect, and the edition is rare. If it were at a traditional used bookstore, it'd command a premium price. But Bookoff is about volume, and there's a problem: not only does it lack a bar code, but it lacks an ISBN—the unique ten- or thirteen-digit identifying number assigned to individual books and editions. "So there's no way to price it in Bookoff's system," Kominato says. With a grimace, he gently places it on the top of the books filling the recycling cage and steps away.

It's a cold-blooded but necessary assessment. In the five minutes it might take to look up the price of one book without an ISBN, Mrs. Naya can scan and sort twenty books that have bar codes. If Bookoff received only a few books per day, that might not matter, while the spark of joy felt by Kominato might have. But Bookoff receives tens of thousands. If it's going to remain in business as the place where people can easily get rid of their excess, guilt-free, there's no time for joy.

Meanwhile, a cart full of blue and red bins like those at Mrs. Naya's workstation gets shuttled to an elevator, where they'll be sent upstairs for storage. Each contains one customer's inventory and an invoice detailing the value. A copy of that invoice is emailed to the customer, who needs only to accept it to receive payment. Kominato says 80 percent do. The remaining 20 percent agree to pay the costs of shipping their books home. Few will find a better appraisal than the one Bookoff offers, especially when the shipping costs are added into the total. And that appraisal typically amounts to pennies per volume. "But it's not really about the money for our customers," he says. "Whether they accept the offer or not."

For Bookoff, it's about the money. Once a seller agrees to a price, the books are sent to one of two destinations. A small percentage move upstairs, where they're packed for shipment to Bookoff stores around Japan in need of books to sell. Title, author, and subject don't matter. What the stores want are books—books of any kind—and this Yokohama warehouse has them.

But most move next door to a four-story structure that Kominato claims is the largest used-goods warehouse in Japan—and possibly the world. "I keep meaning to call the Guinness Book," he says. It contains five million items, mostly books, stored on shelves on dimly lit corridors just wide enough for an attendant with a cart and a handheld navigator to move between. This is no library. There's no cataloging by title, author, or subject. Instead, Toyota designed a system that catalogs by shelf number only. If there's room on a shelf, a book goes there. When somebody orders that book, the navigator sends the attendant to pull it for shipment, a nameless commodity bound for a buyer.

A small two-story home sits on the edge of a hillside on a winding road in Kamakura, a coastal tourist town roughly thirty-five miles south of Tokyo. It's behind a stone fence and a metal gate, and metal sunshades protect the inside from bleaching light and prying eyes. There aren't too many of the latter. During the late morning, at least, this neighborhood seems to belong to only a handful of elderly people on park benches. Jeongja Han will be here soon. She's spent the last two days cleaning out this house. This morning, though, she's away making a bid on another job.

It's a common house in a common neighborhood. The neighborhood and yard are impeccably clean, void of garbage and waste. Three years ago, the house was occupied by a family of three: a woman, now ninety-five, her daughter, and her son-in-law. The son-in-law died three years ago. A few months later, Saya (she prefers that I use only her personal name), his daughter, moved her mother and grandmother to live with her family in Yokohama, twenty miles away. Then late last year, Saya's mother died, too.

Saya meets me at the door wearing an apron over a checked shirt and jeans. She has a wide smile and thin glasses that give her a bookish look. She works as a part-time English teacher for children, and she's happy to chat with me. "Come, come," she says, beckoning me into the house. Despite the sunshades, the room is bright and yellow, and largely intact. There's a dining table and chairs, a full china cabinet, and a television on a stand. On the table, however, is a familiar sight: dishes wrapped in newspaper, along with a can of Premium Boss iced coffee, available to keep someone—probably Saya—alert. There are also several beautiful pieces of red lacquerware. "They were made by my grandmother," she tells me. "We will keep them."

One of Han's employees, a newly hired woman who is too shy to talk to a journalist, much less share her name, is also there, packing up dishes in the kitchen. Saya introduces her and leads me back into the sitting room. "This was my childhood home," she tells me with a grimace and a glance up the stairs. "I know I have to put away everything. But I have a job, a husband, and two children. I can't do it myself."

She took bids from three cleanout companies and settled on the Tail Project because of Han's personality, competitive pricing, and interest in seeking out reuse markets. "I didn't want to throw away everything. Someone can still use these things." She turns toward the table and several things that spark joy in her, still. "It's very hard. Once you start, you can't go back."

She leads me up a stairway to the second floor, where the roof slants over the rooms. We stop first in her grandmother's room. Rectangular tatami mats cover the floor. The walls are olive green, and the space is void of objects except for a small Shinto altar perched high in a corner against the ceiling. A length of twisted rope, known as a *shimenawa*, believed to ward off evil spirits, is hung in front of it. "Ms. Han will contact the local religious authorities to take the shrine," Saya tells me. "They will burn it. If there are emotions connected to other things, they can be burnt, too." According to the Association of Cleanout Professionals, the fee for burning an altar is similar to what would be paid for a Buddhist shrine (one-meter diameter) or a futon: around one hundred dollars.

Saya leads me into an adjoining walk-in closet that's dominated on one side by a wall-length wooden chest of drawers. The rest of the room is filled with boxes and storage bins. "Japanese religion is very interesting. This chest has its own spirit," she says, "because it's been used a long time." A piece of string ties down a drawer-length piece of rice paper that Saya lifts gently to reveal a heavy blue hemp garment and, below it, wool woven into a floral pattern. "These are kimonos made by my grandmother," she says, lifting one and then another. "She sewed them." Six kimonos are in this drawer, and at least as many are in each of the three drawers below it. She walks into the bedroom and reaches into a box that I didn't notice earlier. It contains at least ten more.

"You're keeping these, right?"

She kneels down and unties the rice paper covering two more kimonos. "A kimono. A mother wears it, a daughter wears it . . . not so easy to give it up." One is brown with intricately woven swirling patterns; the other is covered in a green and orange tangle of art deco angles. "But some of these I can't keep. I don't have room. But maybe someone can reuse them." She stands and wipes a tear. "It hurts my heart, but I cannot take everything. Already some are gone and sold."

We walk from her grandmother's room into her mother's—a journey, it turns out, from an older Japan to a modern one. The room is filled with boxes piled high, a full-size bed on which more boxes are piled, a vanity, a dresser, and a chair. Framed family photos are spread on empty surfaces. Saya touches the sleeve of her black-and-white-checked shirt and says, "These clothes are Mother's clothes, so I wear them." She turns me toward a closet where plastic storage bins are stacked six high, opens one, and pulls out a hand-knit sweater. "Grandmother made these, too," she says, and starts to weep again. "I cannot keep everything."

As we descend the stairs, I tell her about a used-kimono market that runs on the weekends in the bustling Harajuku neighborhood. "The customers are mostly foreign tourists," I say carefully, figuring that she'd want her grandmother's work to go to someone who can appreciate it.

She gives me a hard, affirmative nod. "Good. Let the foreigners enjoy them. It's good someone values them." Then she turns away, eyes again wet with tears. I'm not sure what to say. But thankfully, the door swings open. Jeongja Han has arrived, ready to get to work.

CHAPTER 3

The Flood

It's the rare object that's passed from generation to generation. And it's an even rarer object that increases in value over time. As the volume of stuff surges, it's only natural that consumers entrust the care of things to others. An independently owned antique store or collectible mall should be able to obtain value from the handful of truly valuable objects in a home. Anyone can sell a diamond necklace. But twenty-five used wool sweaters per week? That requires somebody with money, patience, and plenty of other products to sell while the sweaters don't move.

For decades, that role has been fulfilled by thrift stores. And no set of thrift stores has been more successful in squeezing the value out of the everyday objects in an American home than Goodwill Industries International. In 2017, it generated $5.87 billion in retail sales, making it the king of an American thrift trade that generated at least $17.5 billion in revenue. Its business model is widely imitated, both in the United States and abroad. For Americans, it's the brand that represents an entire industry, the Kleenex of charitable giving. It's the past, and the future, of what's left behind.

*   *   *

By mid-afternoon, the donations are coming without interruption at the Goodwill on South Houghton and East Golf Links Roads in Tucson. Inside the donation door, gray pushcarts overflow with jigsaw puzzles, sofa cushions, picture frames, pillowcases filled with clothing and shoes, two high chairs, and at least one vacuum cleaner. I also spot a bag of garbage—actual garbage—that someone dropped off; three uneaten Hershey's Kisses, tinfoil still intact, spill out. Outside, a headboard with a coffee table propped against it blocks half the entrance, and two carts, one covered with fake house plants, blocks the other half. Scattered around the perimeter are an awkward ancient rowing machine and several large, taped-up boxes. I've been here all day, and I can't remember seeing most of these items unloaded from vehicles.

The flood isn't likely to let up. Four cars are in line awaiting the chance to donate, and—according to Michelle Janse, an unflappable forty-three-year-old with a social critic's eye for what passes through the donation door—the rush is only beginning. She's just punched in to help.

Next in line, an elderly gentleman slowly steps from a Nissan Frontier pickup carrying a pair of fur-lined hunting boots. "Gave a pair to my ex-wife, she loved them," he announces. "Cost a hundred and fifty bucks. Gave this pair to my current wife, she hates them. Says I gave a pair to my ex-wife." Janse takes them with a look of distaste and, as she turns, calls out, "Thanks for your donation! It supports twenty-two employees at our store!" She turns to me and says, "That's our mission statement this month."

Next in line is a white Impala with New Mexico plates. I recognize the driver—a teenage girl in a striped, sleeveless top who dropped off at least a dozen garbage bags full of clothes and linens not more than thirty minutes ago. This time she opens the trunk to reveal boxes of dishes. "This is all from my grammy. She's kind of a hoarder. We had a garage sale . . ." She shrugs.

Janse pauses to gaze at the haul.

"This isn't too much stuff, is it?" the girl asks with a hint of panic.

"Nope! We can't refuse donations—only certain categories like mattresses and hazardous chemicals."

"Oh good. We were worried you wouldn't take it all."

Janse unloads the boxes onto a cart. As she pushes the haul through the donation door, she shakes her head. "Garage sales aren't where it's at anymore. Half the stuff doesn't sell because the prices are too high. Everyone thinks they're on *Antiques Roadshow*." She reaches for a green glass vase that's resting atop a pile of garbage bags stuffed with clothes. It has a pink, handwritten two-dollar garage-sale price tag on it. "People see that and they know they can get it cheaper at a thrift store."

"They do?"

Boom.

Behind me, Frank Kaphan, a stout fifty-year-old former construction worker, slams a garbage bag full of clothes onto a large, overflowing washing-machine-size carton of clothes. His face is drenched in sweat, and his shoulders tighten as he lifts the garbage bag over his head again. *Boom.*

Michelle rolls her eyes. "That's how we fit more when we're running out of boxes," she explains. "We're not supposed to get on top and jump." It's a safety violation. *Boom.* "Donations arriving," she says, and heads back out the door.

During its 2018–2019 fiscal year, Goodwill Industries of Southern Arizona, comprising around forty stores and donation centers in the Tucson area, received 504,519 individual donations. They included everything from sofas to baseball card collections, with each donation averaging 60 pounds. Conservatively estimated, that's around thirty million pounds of stuff, out of the more than fifty million pounds of stuff that the half million people in this modest-sized American city sold or donated that year.

That's nothing.

In 2015, Americans tossed out 24.1 *billion* pounds of furniture and furnishings, according to the most recent data from the U.S. Environmental Protection Agency. Along with all those old sofas went 32 billion pounds of textiles—including clothes, bedsheets, towels, and wiping rags—and 45.3 billion pounds of what the Environmental Protection Agency calls "miscellaneous durables." This catch-all comprises products that aren't generally destroyed in the course of use, including everything from rakes to forks and spoons, jigsaw puzzles to jigsaws, rotary telephones to smartphones. It's a flood that's yet to crest.

Goodwill Industries of Southern Arizona is a midsize Goodwill organization among the 162 regional, autonomous Goodwills in the United States and Canada. Collectively, they operate more than three thousand stores and donation centers and divert more than three *billion* pounds of stuff from the trash heap annually. In other words, Goodwill

After Tucson's garage sales close on Saturday mornings, the Goodwill at South Houghton and East Golf Links Roads receives the flood of what didn't sell.

International collected just 3 percent of the clothes, furniture, and miscellaneous durables tossed out by Americans in the middle years of an affluent decade.

And it collected more than anybody.

In February 1932, *Scientific American* published "Jobs from Junk— Wages from Waste," a brief feature introducing Goodwill to its readers. The organization was three decades old at that point, but most Americans were just starting to hear about it and other charities that accepted old goods as donations. According to the author, the benefits of giving weren't just spiritual. The average American home had fifteen dollars' worth of unused goods in the attic, and to most Americans those unused items were a "burden, contributing nothing to their welfare or happiness." Goodwill not only took that burden off their hands, but it employed the poor in repairing and refurbishing those unwanted goods—especially clothing—and sold them for many times the value they had in the attic.

It was a model of charity that could exist only in an era of mass production and consumption. Before the industrial revolution, churches often collected clothes for the poor. But as cheap store-bought clothes eroded the need to make clothes at home, hand-sewing skills declined, and the financial incentive to repair and remake garments began to evaporate. Changing fashions, and the perpetual need to upgrade and evolve one's wardrobe, accelerated the trend. As more and more Americans could afford new clothes, the distance between the poor and the rich became one defined by taste; the poor could dress just as elegantly as the rich, as long as they were open to being a season or two out-of-date. Closets and attics grew, as did the belief that one could be burdened with too much stuff.[1]

Charities seized the opportunity. In 1865, the Salvation Army was founded to evangelize to the urban poor of London. To make it work, the organization employed the city's indigent to collect, repair, and sell unwanted goods. It expanded to New York in 1897, where it built so-called industrial homes to house the collectors, repair operations, and evangelization operations. The homes were multistory and included retail stores (where poor consumers could be recruited for work) and shipping areas, which evolved into donation centers.

Around the same time, the Reverend Edgar James Helms took over Boston's Methodist Morgan Chapel and began a program to collect and repair clothes in local neighborhoods. As part of the collection program, the Morgan Chapel distributed burlap coffee bags to middle-class homes. These "opportunity bags" (soon to be renamed "Goodwill bags") were then returned with unwanted but repairable stuff. It was a successful model that expanded to Brooklyn, where the name Goodwill Industries was adopted in 1915. By 1920, independent Goodwill branches were operating in six major American cities. The Methodist affiliation was eventually dropped, and Goodwill expanded rapidly, in part because of its interdenominational nature and appeal to a mass American audience.

Early on a Friday morning, I sit down with Lisa Allen and Liz Gulick, the co-presidents of Goodwill Industries of Southern Arizona at the organization's headquarters in a sparse office park on the south side of Tucson. Collectively, they oversee a roughly thirty-million-dollar enterprise that spans sixteen retail stores, two outlet stores, a boutique for higher-end secondhand merchandise (mostly clothes), several warehouses, a vast social services network, and more than five hundred full-time employees. Allen oversees the retail and operations side of the charity, and she speaks in the fast, efficient sentences of someone deeply immersed in the American culture of selling stuff. "Goodwill has forty-seven percent of the thrift market in Southern Arizona. Ten years ago, it was twenty to twenty-three." Allen, with a traditional retailing background, isn't shy about letting me know that boost happened under her leadership. "It was an intentional development. We thought we were underserving the market."

"How do you know you're underserving a secondhand market?"

"You do an assessment," she says. "You see the unemployment rate and see that the community needs more training." It's not an answer to the question that I was asking. Instead, it's the answer to a more important question: What motivates Goodwill? It's not profit for profit's sake. Rather, the first motivation is social distress—youth unemployment, for example. Then Goodwill figures out how to pay for the solutions. "Stores are our economic engine, helping us connect people with jobs."

It's the identical mission that Goodwill had in the 1890s, but with one significant difference. Rather than employ the urban poor in repair shops or Goodwill stores, Goodwill now uses its professionally managed stores to fund social services focused on helping people become economically self-sufficient through work. Liz Gulick seems reluctant to speak over her co-president, even though she manages the half of Goodwill that uses the money earned in the stores. But when there's some space, I prompt her. "The mission is what we're all about," she reminds me. "It's why we do what we do, and everybody is a part of it. We have five-hundred-plus employees here, and forty, fifty of them are just devoted to career development in the community."

The individuals taken on by Goodwill are often the hardest, most expensive cases, the ones that government won't, or can't, handle on its own; and they—not secondhand stuff—inspire the greatest passion among Goodwill employees (regardless of whether those employees are involved in social services). For example, Pima County, home to Tucson, has a large population of youths who haven't completed high school, many of whom end up in the juvenile justice system. So, under Gulick, the organization has refocused its efforts on helping them in ways ranging from paying for GED test-taking fees to subsidizing salaries so that skeptical employers will take on at-risk youth. "We had thirteen hundred job placements last year," Gulick says. "So that tells you we're using that economic engine in the right way."

Allen nods in agreement. "The stores are the means by which we do what we do," she says. "If they aren't doing well, we have to look at ways to cut. If they are doing well, our options increase. So we are very focused on improving our store performance. But we are all invested in the work beyond retail that we do."

"Do you hire people out of your programs for the stores?"

Allen shakes her head. "Rarely. The stores can be a tool. If somebody needs work clothes, we can make that happen. But the stores are separate. It'd be a conflict of interest, in a way. We want to place people in the community."

Of course, not everybody loves Goodwill's economic engine. As far back as the 1920s, for-profit junk dealers and thrift stores resented having to compete with charities that acquire inventory via donations. Yet despite these bumps, Goodwill is consistently given top ratings by organizations that rate philanthropic management. And in Southern Arizona, where Goodwill uses 90 percent of its donations for mission-oriented work, the organization is widely lauded for what it gives back to the community. It's a crucial civic institution.

Inside the donation door at South Houghton and East Golf Links Roads, a Goodwill-donation tax-receipt book sits atop a neat desk, fluttering in a breeze cast by a fan. Across from it are eight bins, each six feet tall, called "cages." The two closest to the desk are devoted to clothing. Next to them is a cage designated for linens and another holding a hodgepodge category of large durable goods that includes everything from a large planter to a tricycle—Goodwill calls them "large wares." Next to them is a cage for "large electrical," like hotplates, stereo receivers, and PCs. On it goes, to "small wares," like silverware and children's toys, CDs and DVDs, and shoes. Everything has a place.

Mike Mellors has returned from a break and starts work on the piles of donations, ripping into garbage bags and boxes. Clothes are tossed into their cage, piles of neatly folded bedsheets into theirs. At the bottom of one bag, he finds a tangle of rhinestone jewelry and Mardi Gras beads, plastic pendants, bangles, and knots of what look like silver and gold chains ("fake for sure," he assures me). He drops the mass into a Tupperware pitcher on the standing desk nearly full with other gold and silver tangles. The next bag contains bedsheets, a paper party horn, a paper party hat, wire-rim sunglasses missing a lens, a Safeway card, and a nickel, which he tosses into a glass jar half full of coins that's next to the one nearly full with cheap jewels. It looks random, but it's not: Goodwill has strict guidelines for what can and cannot be on the desk, and bonuses are impacted by how well employees abide. In this way, Goodwill resists the junk.

I walk farther into the warehouse, past an area where furniture is laid out three sofas deep, and see two employees sorting through newly arrived wares beyond the dining room tables. Those are both important sources of revenue. But they can't compare with clothing, which is both the organization's most donated and most sold item.

Today, toward the far end of the warehouse, four women are busy with what Goodwill calls clothing "production." The idea is a simple one: the process of sorting through cages of clothes, pricing them, and hanging them is a kind of manufacturing. But unlike in a traditional factory, where raw materials and parts are made into something new,

Goodwill uses the cages of donated stuff to produce racks of clothes sorted by quality and price. As in a traditional factory, Goodwill has production targets. For example, yesterday this Goodwill had a production goal of $4,787 worth of sorted, priced clothes. It beat that goal by producing 1,115 garments worth $5,657.

Most of that production won't sell here. At this store, roughly 45 percent of the product on the sales floor sells (up from 33 percent a few years ago). That's high for an American thrift store, but maintaining that sales percentage is incredibly difficult. During a walk-through, Kevin Cunningham, director of retail operations for Goodwill Industries of Southern Arizona, summarized the challenge for me:

> Think of it as Walmart headquarters calling a Walmart store manager and saying, "You've got a truck of product coming." The manager is like, "Okay, yeah, I know." And the manager in HQ is like, "And oh, by the way, we don't know what's in that truck— no one thing in the truck is the same as any other one thing. And oh, by the way, you need to price all of it. And oh, by the way, you definitely need to make a profit selling it."

Smart, market-sensitive pricing is the difference between selling the stuff rolling through the donation door, making less money at an outlet store or via an export market, or losing money down at the landfill. Experience, taste, and a sense of what's happening at Walmart and other mass retailers figure into an ever-changing formulation. "If you price even with a Walmart, [Goodwill customers] won't buy it," Lisa Allen told me. "I have the numbers! People know the value of the stuff."

"What if the quality is better at Goodwill?"

Allen smiled and shook her head.

Making matters more difficult, each of the sixteen Southern Arizona Goodwills serves a slightly different market. What sells for $6.99 in one part of town is likely too pricey for another. To manage these market differences and ensure the optimal pricing, Goodwill relies on hourly employees that it compensates with good benefits, above-average wages, and—above all—bonuses based on how well sales and production targets are met. Hopefully, they stay long enough to really know their markets. If they don't, nobody does.

It's time-consuming and expensive work that requires lots of workers, knowledge of the local market, and sound judgment. As much as possible, Goodwill tries to systematize it. For example, on the wall beside the sorting area is a sheet labeled $2.99 BRANDS that lists in-house labels from mass retailers like Target and Kohl's. If a sorter picks up a top or a jacket from Old Navy, for example, or jeans from the in-house Target brand Mossimo (the brand relationship was dissolved in 2017), it's $2.99, no exceptions, and the garment is tossed into a large cardboard box labeled $2.99. Later, it'll be tagged accordingly, hung, and rolled out to the sales floor.

Upmarket brands are subjected to similar treatment. There's a sheet labeled BOUTIQUE BRANDS TO PULL AND SEND. It includes a list of eighty-six labels—from Brooks Brothers to Zara—to be set aside for sale at Goodwill's three-year-old high(er)-end boutique in an upscale neighborhood. "A pair of Miss Me jeans retails for $249 new," Cunningham explained. "But we can't get $6.99 for them here. People will look at the tag and say, 'This is Goodwill?' But at the boutique, they can go for $30 to $40." It's a savvy business move to compete with resellers who scavenge Goodwills for bargains that they mark up on eBay and other online platforms. Over the course of two weeks that I spent in and around Tucson-area Goodwills, several resellers complained to me that there aren't as many bargains on Goodwill's racks and shelves anymore. For the most part, that delights Goodwill. "We want that revenue," Cunningham said. "The boutique helps us get it."

Between the boutique and $2.99 is room for judgment, and large boxes for the $3.99, $4.99, and $6.99 price points. Mackenzie Williams is a sorter in her early twenties, with a long ponytail and a talkative manner. Like the others, she wears gloves to protect her hands from pins and other hazards in boxes two feet deep with donated clothing. "Talbots is a six," she explains as she tosses a Talbots blouse into the $6.99 box. "A four is a not-so-great brand, and tank tops are a two." She drops a blue halter into the $2.99 box. Next, she picks a green wool Dockers sweater from a cage and pulls it, searching for holes. "So this should be a six, because of the brand. But because it's hot in Arizona, it'll go as a four." A plaid, short-sleeve men's shirt is next. "Is David Taylor good?" she asks the other three sorters.

"Lemme see," says Julie Sanchez, an assistant manager. She takes the shirt, removes a glove, and rubs the fabric between thumb and index finger. "Four."

"How'd you know that?" I ask.

"Feel," she answers as she flips the collar up. "Never mind. There's holes in the collar. As is." She hands it back to Kelsey, who tosses it into a box labeled AS IS bound for a Goodwill outlet store that will sell it and other garments by the pound.

Sanchez has sorted clothes far longer than Mackenzie, and she talks right past her younger co-worker. "The brands you see on that chart," she says, referring to the $2.99 sheet. "You have to be careful. Quality has been declining for a couple years now. The clothes aren't as good. I used to buy Mossimo at Target, but now I don't. It falls apart after a single wash. We see it in the donations, stuff is so worn these days."

"Are people just wearing their clothes harder?" I ask.

"People are making clothes cheaper."

On the other side of the boxes, Kathie Greco, a quiet, older presence, pulls clothes from the $6.99 box, examines them, and, if the price is right in her experienced eyes, attaches a tag and hangs them on a rack. "People don't seem to keep clothes as long anymore," she pipes up. "And the people who make them know that and don't bother to make good ones." The data backs her up. Between 2000 and 2015, global clothing production doubled, while the average number of times that a garment was worn before disposal declined by 36 percent.[2]

Several factors account for those shifts, including the emergence of hundreds of millions of new consumers in China and greater Asia over the last three decades. To enable consumption, manufacturers in Asia, primarily, have become expert at making products that can be sold at an affordable price point. But for them to do so, the quality often suffers, and the lifespan of a garment is shortened. Key to the process is utilizing the low-cost labor and manufacturing processes located in emerging markets like Cambodia and Myanmar. By the 1990s, these practices made possible "fast fashion" and brands like Forever 21 and H&M.

These days, you no longer have to be wealthy or living in Paris or New York to have the latest catwalk look. You just need access to a mall or an internet connection. That's a great thing for young, fashion-minded middle-class consumers, many of whom won't wear a garment enough times to notice it falling apart in the wash. According to a 2018 survey by the online fashion reseller thredUP, millennials are the demographic most likely to discard a garment after one to five wears.[3] If those garments were as well made as the high-end brands they're meant to emulate, that'd be a wonderful thing for Goodwill. But, as Sanchez noted, they're often no better than disposable, and—at best—bound for the "As Is" bin.

"Customers are all about price, not quality," Cunningham told me when I asked him about the challenges of pricing at Goodwill. "They won't buy a $6.99 shirt that'll last. If that's the option, they'll buy a $2.99 shirt from Walmart. It's all price." It's this combination of factors—whether applied to a tank top or a cheap sofa—that makes pricing so difficult and product quality a crucial concern to the donation-based thrift industry.

At six thirty A.M. on a Saturday, Cathy Zach, manager of the Goodwill at South Houghton and East Golf Links, is standing ten feet inside the donation door, inspecting inventory. "My warehouse is too clean," she says. "Not enough stuff. Only five hundred dollars' worth of wares produced yesterday." She stops and looks at a cart holding two stereo receivers, a flat-screen television, a scanner, and three power bars. "But I'm really proud of electrical. For the first time in months, we're above the production goal."

Cathy is sixty-six, but she moves with the urgency of someone much younger. Today she has good reason. It's Goodwill's monthly 50 percent off sale, and the store will be swarmed with customers. At the front, she'll be challenged to get everyone's purchases checked out in a timely manner. Here in the back, she worries that there's not enough stuff to meet all the demand—and the $14,087 sales goal for the day.

She wears an orange BOO CREW T-shirt promoting Goodwill's Halloween products, a pair of loose-fitting jeans, and black Nike running shoes. Prior to Goodwill, she spent thirty-two years in traditional retail, including decades at Sears. Goodwill, she insists, is more challenging. "You have to have variety like no other retail environment," she says. "People come here every day, and if they see the same stuff over and over and never notice something new, they'll stop coming."

To ensure that doesn't happen, Goodwill changes the color of its price tags every week, enabling employees to track how long something has been on the sales floor with just a glance. Every six weeks, the cycle of colors is renewed, and six-week-old tags (and products) are pulled and placed in "As Is" bins. It's a ruthless system that keeps customers interested, keeps revenues up, and—most crucially—ensures there's always room on the shelves for the flood of stuff coming through the donation doors.

It's also not unique to Goodwill. Around the world, thrift stores— keen to switch up inventory—do something similar.

For example, the nearly eight hundred stores that belong to Bookoff, the Yokohama-based used-goods chain, have four different color-coded price tags timed to the seasons. As a cycle ends, goods are taken off shelves and racks. Bookoff refers to the process as *tokoroten*, named after a Japanese noodle that's made by pushing a seafood jelly through a press. "Customers doesn't care how old something is. They care about how long it's been on the shelf," is how Takaharu Kominato, the Bookoff spokesperson, explained it to me. "Like food, old stuff goes bad. We call it a 'poison apple.'"

Bookoff's *tokoroten* is widely imitated across Japan's secondhand industry, just as Goodwill's six-week cycle is copied by thrift businesses across North America. Cathy picks up a clipboard detailing recent production and frets that there just isn't enough that's new to interest her regulars. "That'll kill you in this business, if you don't have variety. Gotta have everything out there every day. And we need more wares."

Cathy gazes at the roughly 60 people gathering outside the front doors. "Some of them are stashers," she tells me. "They come in the night before and stash items in hiding places so they get fifty percent off today." In the clothing section, she reaches into a trench coat and pulls out two oil paintings. "Julie, can you take these?"

Julie Sanchez rushes over, grabs them, and looks at the prices listed on the backs as she walks off. "They're only $2.99!"

Cathy points to racks of shirts sorted by color, as orderly as in a department store. "This is the way it should look. Neat. Nothing fallen on the floor. Just as nice as the Walmart across the street." She speaks literally: there's a Walmart across the street, and it's the competition. There are $2.99 shirts there, too.

Goodwill Industries of Southern Arizona isn't alone in the quest to compete with Walmart. Across North America, Goodwills are using bright lighting, brighter color schemes, and professional product placement, as the organization works to upgrade the public's expectation of what a thrift store should be. As they do, Goodwill is attracting a more economically diverse clientele. "Things started changing for Goodwill around 2000," Lisa Allen told me. "You started seeing the higher-end cars in the parking lots."

As it happens, that was the point that things started changing for Bookoff in Japan, too.

The business of buying and selling used in Japan dates back centuries. Organized pawnshop guilds, protected by the government and police, emerged in the seventeenth century. As a protected industry, the pawnshops were profitable. But they had few incentives to invest in customer service, and their reputations suffered. "Back in the day, people didn't want to sell their things to used-goods dealers," says Mayumi Hashimoto, the former president and chair of Bookoff's board and now a senior adviser and director of the company. "People felt ashamed to sell their stuff to used-goods dealers."

Hashimoto, who's seventy-eight, is a corporate legend in Japan. She joined the company at age forty-one as a part-time employee. At the time, Bookoff was just a year old, had a single store, and was devoted exclusively to books. For years, she'd been a stay-at-home mom, but her kids were growing up and needing her less. So Hashimoto had a new ambition: "I wanted to make my own money." As Bookoff expanded into a national chain, Hashimoto rode it to the top, becoming one of the very few women to run a publicly held company in Japan, a country in which women have struggled to advance in the workplace. Hashimoto has stepped back in recent years, but only modestly: she maintains an office in a nearby Bookoff store because, she says, "I like to see what's going on."

"What'd you think of used bookstores in 1991, at the time you applied to work at Bookoff?"

"Dirty!" she says definitively, and then laughs. "I'd never go into one." Hashimoto has a matronly presence, but there's a steely directness in her manner that reminds anyone of her authority and how she earned it.

"Anything else?"

"Shame. We used to have lots of pawnshops in Japan. Very snobbish outfits. People would go there to get money, and the pawnshops treated you like you needed it. So if you were seen going there, it meant you didn't have money."

Over the next twenty-five years, Hashimoto played a key role in expanding Bookoff into the full range of consumer goods. Along the way, Bookoff transformed how Japanese consumers view secondhand. It wasn't easy. First, Bookoff had to destigmatize the act of selling used stuff. The solution was a slogan that Hashimoto devised: "Please sell to us." To English-speaking ears, it sounds like a platitude, not a slogan. But in Japan, it turned the table on the "snobbish" pawnshops and launched a revolution in secondhand dignity and politeness. Today, the phrase is posted outside secondhand businesses around Japan, including many of Bookoff's fiercest competitors.

Second, the company brightened things up. "Used bookstores are typically dark and frequented by men. We needed to change that," Hashimoto explains. So they turned on the lights, painted the stores in yellows and oranges, and streamlined pricing to a simple formula so that anyone—not just a snobbish bibliophile—could work behind the counter. "We wanted mothers to feel comfortable bringing their children to the shops. We encouraged them to read in them. And we hoped they'd work at them, too."

The third and perhaps most important revolution was a training program—directed at customers. Used books, Hashimoto explains, were often viewed as dirty. So Bookoff devised a machine that shaved away the stained and bent pages. The result was a good-as-new book that sold for a fraction of the price charged at a new bookstore. As selling to Bookoff became more acceptable, consumers changed their behaviors. "They realized that their things are worth money if they take care of them," Hashimoto explains. "Eventually we didn't need the machine anymore. The books they were bringing us were good enough to put on the shelves."

Stop by any of the three Bookoff shops within walking distance of the corporate headquarters, and the shift is obvious. The shelves are neat and lined with books that could be mistaken as new: paperback spines are uncreased, pages are white, corners unturned. It's not just books, either. In clothing, there's no musty "thrift store" smell, and the clothes are displayed by brand, in arrangements reminiscent of what might be found in a Uniqlo or Gap. In sporting goods, the tents and camping equipment look unused, and the displays wouldn't be out of place in a Dick's Sporting Goods.

"Before us, people viewed used as waste," Hashimoto explains. "Bookoff turns it into a product."

"So Bookoff is a kind of manufacturer. It produces a product."

Hashimoto nods vigorously. "Yes."

*   *   *

So far, no American organization has managed to emulate Bookoff and upgrade the manner in which Americans treat their used things. And there's good reason for that. In the United States (and in Europe), most secondhand goods are donated rather than sold. As a result, most people lack a financial incentive to take care of their things. So instead of seeing the end of an object's life as an opportunity to extract some last value from it (as people do with their cars), Americans view that object in philanthropic terms. It'll help the poor; it'll benefit the environment. For better or worse, both those reasons have proved to be little incentive to take care of stuff. In my experience, the quality of what's sold at a Bookoff is far superior to that of the stuff donated at an American thrift store. There's no comparison, really.

That's unlikely to change soon. The belief that used things should benefit the poor is deeply engrained in the cultures of North America and Europe. Indeed, when it raises prices or opens boutiques, Goodwill often faces backlash from communities, which expect thrift stores to serve as a resource for the local poor.

Meanwhile, for-profit thrift stores like Savers and online market-places like OfferUp, Poshmark, and eBay move far less stuff than Goodwill does, and that's unlikely to change, either. The $0.50 mixing bowls and $2.99 blouses that fill Cathy Zach's Goodwill store don't make economic sense to sell online (shipping would exceed the cost of most items) or in a for-profit store. If the donation system didn't exist, much more would be trashed.

At eight A.M., Cathy pauses in the middle of her Goodwill sales floor. She's standing next to an endcap filled with new kitchen utensils, like wooden spoons and plastic spatulas. Around the corner are stacks of secondhand pots and pans.

"What's with all the new stuff?" I ask.

She glances at the line of people outside her store. This really isn't the time for an in-depth discussion of retailing strategy. But Cathy, famously patient, offers an answer: "They'd buy it at Walmart if we didn't sell it. Since we can't sell used shower caps, we sell new, and people can do most of their shopping here."

"Do you sell much?"

"New is eight or nine percent of our sales."

The proliferation of new goods at Goodwill isn't just about convenience and immediate sales. It also upgrades the image of the store in the eyes of consumers. Displays are more orderly, and the dinge associated with some products is evened out by the presence of sanitized packaging. Cathy, with her years of retail experience, obviously appreciates the opportunity to exercise her skills.

Just before opening, she takes one last gaze at her store and walks toward the front doors. It's not quite a Bookoff, or a Walmart, but it's a long way from the garage sales, dingy thrift stores, and church basements that still inform so many American imaginations when it comes to secondhand. She unlocks the doors with a buoyant "Good morning. Welcome. Good morning. How are you? Good morning. Good morning. Fifty percent off today. Good morning."

The first customers dash past her for the items they've stashed. I watch to see if somebody heads for the trench coat that hid those two oil paintings, but nobody makes the run. Two minutes later, the first customers arrive at the register: a middle-aged, Spanish-speaking couple whose two carts hold a small dog kennel, a table lamp, a red silk scarf, a new Jiffy-Foil baking pan, several plastic utensils, two children's backpacks (Spider-Man, Teenage Mutant Ninja Turtles), a new box of cotton balls, and three new shower caps.

As cashiers ring up carts, clothes hangers pile up at the end of the counters. Cathy, in between taking handbags and other collectibles from the display cabinets, gathers them up and hangs them from nearby clothing racks placed just for that purpose. "At the end of the day, we'll have four or five thousand hangers," she says.

I think I misheard. "*How* many?"

"Four or five thousand. We'll wrap them in sets of tens and put them out for sale. Typically sell around three hundred." She grabs another bundle from a register. "The world does not need to make any more hangers."

At nine, one hour after opening, Cathy invites me to follow her into the back office. "Let's see how we're doing," she says. On her computer are the first-hour results: $1,407.11 in total sales spread over seventy paying customers. Of that, $380 was textiles, and $376 was furniture. "Not too shabby," she says. "Better than I thought." But even better, from Cathy's perspective, are the sales numbers starting to be reported from other Goodwill stores in Tucson. At nine A.M., her store is tops, followed by the shop in tony Bear Canyon, with $1,323 in sales. Casa Grande, the most distant outlet, and one that serves a low-income community, was at the bottom of the list, with $73 in sales.

Energized, Cathy returns to the floor. Lots of stuff will move today. Her numbers will look good, the sell-through will be boosted. "The line starts here," she says to people snaking through the store, directing them to an aisle perpendicular to the busy cash registers. For now, the flood out the front doors equals the flood coming through the donation door.

CHAPTER 4

The Good Stuff

In the two decades that I've written about waste and recycling, it's rare that I've gone through a week without somebody saying to me that "one man's trash is another man's treasure." It happens at American garage sales; it happens at the flea market beneath my home in Malaysia. It happened in Cotonou, the commercial capital of the West African nation of Benin. One afternoon I asked a used-shoe trader in the city's Dantokpa Market how he sources his nearly new plus-size Nikes. He replied with a toothy smile. "Trash is treasure."

Like many aphorisms, there's some truth there. But in my experience, not much. Generally, one man's trash is another man's trash. And as the world of stuff expands, the trash is becoming more common. Yet treasure continues to receive attention well beyond its representation in the world's used stuff. Walk into any bookstore and there's bound to be several guides to the price of collectibles sitting on the shelves (good luck finding a book on how to sell and price your old forks and ten-year-old acrylic sweaters). Flip through American television channels most any night of the week and you're bound to land on a show in which a casual junk picker happens upon an autographed baseball worth many times the sum paid for it.

That small percentage matters, though. In some cases, that little bit of treasure is what makes it possible for a secondhand business or charity to take all the stuff that doesn't have much value. Knowing the difference helps us understand how and why we come to value stuff, and how so much turns to garbage.

My grandparents lived in a split-level home in St. Louis Park, Minnesota, roughly a half mile from Highway 169. During my first five years, I lived around the corner on Quebec Avenue South, and I recall running between houses to reach their front door, where, without fail, I'd be greeted by my grandmother Betty. She'd usually bring me upstairs to the living room and kitchen. But if I had my choice, we'd slip down the creaking wooden steps to the basement.

It was filled with stuff, most of it "good stuff," as my grandmother called it. There were two large, heavy wooden china cabinets in the far corners (one had belonged to her mother, I believe), a wooden drop-front desk on the near wall ("I'm saving that for you," she'd say), antique lamp stands, a pharmacist cabinet ("that's also yours one day"), and tables covered in knickknacks, including U.S. presidential campaign buttons (IF I WERE 21, I'D VOTE FOR KENNEDY), vases, candlestick holders, postcards, bits of art glass, and random photos. A photo of Abraham Lincoln hung on one wall, a reproduced Napoleon portrait on another, and a framed coin collection near the stairs, with a random assortment of other images—mostly landscapes—scattered throughout.

If you were lucky enough to be invited into the basement—and not everybody was—she'd likely dig into the assortment of objects with the same curiosity as you, the first-time visitor. And if you picked up something—say, an antique iron—and asked where she'd found it, the answer was almost always the same: "That was so long ago. Probably a sale."

My grandmother's passion for collecting had immigrant roots. Her father, Abe Leder, arrived in the United States from Russia with nothing—no education, English, or transferable skills. So he did what millions of other Russian Jews did: he became a ragpicker, roaming Galveston, Texas, for discarded objects that could be sold. At first, he searched for discarded clothes, bedsheets, and other garments. But in time, he had enough capital to acquire metals, paper, and—eventually— "antiques" and collectibles. The underlying principle was always the same, no matter whether he was buying a pile of scrapped brass plumbing fixtures or an oak cabinet: the person selling didn't know the true value of an object, and Abe Leder either did . . . or thought he did.

The five Leder children—my grandmother was the middle one—all worked in the family recycling business at some point during their lives. And they all, to some degree, became collectors, holding on to objects in part because they acquired them for much less than what they believed they were worth. For people and families with living memories of immigration, of the Great Depression, bargains create a sense of security and identity.

As I described in my first book, *Junkyard Planet*, some of my earliest memories entail walking through the family scrap-metal warehouse, perusing inventory with my father. It was filled with value buys: metal cuttings from area manufacturers, scrap car radiators from repair shops, bundles of wire sold by electricians. If I returned a day or two later, all that inventory would be gone, sold onward to someone who paid more.

I have an additional set of early-childhood memories.

It's before dawn and I'm riding in the passenger seat of my grand-mother's long, powder-blue sedan. We stop in front of a single-story suburban house, shut off the headlights, and wait. The talk-radio station is playing softly, and the newspaper classified pages whisper as my grandmother peruses them for nearby garage sales. When the garage door opens, she closes the paper, and we walk up the driveway, tailed by other early arrivers hoping to get first crack at the sale. I remember plates covered in brooches filled with rubylike stones, and my grand-mother negotiating as the others leaned in to see what they might be missing. We always left with some "good stuff."

That was the mid-1970s, and the American garage sale was a preschooler, too. According to the historian Susan Strasser, author of *Waste and Want*, a landmark history of American waste, the term "garage sale" fully emerged in 1967, "when people made a verbal distinction between rummage sales for charity and garage or yard sales for profit." The charity sale emerged in the early part of the twentieth century, as affluent Americans found that mass production had blessed them with more stuff than they needed. They donated that excess to churches and other charitable organizations, which, in turn, sold them to fund charitable works. My grandmother spent years running a thrift shop that benefited the National Council of Jewish Women, all the while attending garage sales for her own enjoyment and profit. There were plenty to attend: according to Strasser, by 1981 Americans were holding six million per year.

The reasons for attending a garage sale in the 1960s and '70s varied. The American counterculture that emerged in the 1950s inspired a wave of anti-materialist environmentalism among young Americans, and some viewed the garage sale as a way to bypass the consumer economy altogether. Others saw vintage goods as a means of connecting with a simpler, less-materialistic past. And many others viewed the garage sale as a more interesting and diverse shopping experience than the uniform retailing found in America's booming midcentury shopping malls and department stores. For individuals whose self-image is located outside what they perceive to be mainstream American culture, garage sales are a toolbox for assembling a countercultural identity—albeit one that also must be purchased from mass-market stuff.

As young rebels grew into affluent baby boomers, garage-saling and thrifting went upmarket. In 1997, the American public broadcaster PBS began airing *Antiques Roadshow*, a weekly broadcast based on a BBC show. In it, collectors bring their antiques for experts to appraise, in hope of finding out they possess a treasure. The show has been a wild success, and it's inspired imitators in the form of second- and third-generation treasure-hunt series like *American Pickers*.

My grandmother enjoyed those television shows. When *Antiques Roadshow* visited Minneapolis, she was eager to attend and even brought along a vase for appraisal. But when offered the chance to appear on camera, she declined, saying she "didn't need the attention." By the late 1990s, she was mostly out of the garage-saling game, anyway. She had better sources for stuff, including my father's scrapyard, which she plumbed for brass vases and other metal objects that struck her as having value beyond the metal. But she also decided that the "good stuff" we used to buy as dawn broke was no longer around or cheap. Too many antique dealers were chasing it, she said, and there was far less to be had. "It's not like it used to be."

Main Street in Stillwater, Minnesota, runs parallel to the St. Croix River and between a handsome collection of two- and three-story brick buildings erected between 1860 and the early twentieth century. Many were built by the lumber businesses that once thrived in the area, supplying wood to communities around the Midwest, including Minneapolis, thirty-five miles away. Others housed a once-thriving manufacturing base that took advantage of the St. Croix's nearby connection to the Mississippi.

Nothing lasts forever, especially economies dependent on limited natural resources. Sure enough, the trees ran out, and the manufacturing was priced out. In their place, antique shops moved into the elegant old brick buildings, taking advantage of (then) low rents and property prices, and a vast inventory of antiques that could be found in the small towns of Minnesota and western Wisconsin. This new business grew. By the early 1990s, Stillwater was home to around thirty antique shops, many of which sold items likely made in or around Stillwater during its heyday. For residents of the nearby Twin Cities, the town's antique stores became a favorite daytrip.

But antique stores, too, seem to have had their day: just six antique businesses remain in Stillwater. The decline isn't confined to the banks of the St. Croix. The population of Minnesota antique shops overall has declined by roughly 20 percent over the past twenty years. And that reflects a global trend. *Antiques Roadshow* now runs reappraisals of antiques featured on earlier episodes, and they're typically in a downward direction. David Lackey, an appraiser made famous by *Antiques Roadshow*, claims that the prices of traditional American and British furniture—once antique-store mainstays—have fallen by 50 to 75 percent in recent years.[1] Christie's, the global auction house that sells collectibles at the very highest end of the market—and, in essence, that's what a million-dollar chair is—has seen the prices of some traditional European furniture decline by as much as 70 percent in less than a generation.

On the south end of Main Street, not far from where the tourist traffic enters town, is a husky three-story building that originally housed a furniture store and, later, a funeral home. In 1991, an antique business located across the street acquired the structure and transformed it into the Midtown Antique Mall, allegedly the largest antique emporium for hundreds of miles in all directions.

The brick exterior is unremarkable for Stillwater, but walk through the glass doors and you'll find a towering two-story room with a balcony hung with dated landscape paintings, old advertisements, a set of Japanese silk prints, and several clocks. Below is a tangle of cabinets and tables displaying the full range of things that somebody found valuable enough to extract from the jumble of worthless items filling up a home, a business, a church. There is china; there is art glass; there are advertising signs; there is jewelry.

Most days, Dick Richter, a wispy antique dealer in his seventies, presides. He has an expressive face framed by a wild head of white hair and an equally scraggly beard. "We have one and a half million items in here," he tells me as he leads me past the cash register and into the mall,

In the 1990s, small, independent antique shops began to fold and dealers relocated into large antique malls. Midtown Antiques in Stillwater, Minnesota, is likely the largest in the Upper Midwest.

where he's sold since the early 1990s. "And I challenge *any*one to say otherwise." Dick isn't the owner—that's Julie, who's presiding over the cash register. But his possessiveness is palpable. It reminds me of the affection you find in priests when they show visitors around their parish churches.

As Dick lopes up a stairway, he explains that the concept behind an antique mall isn't much different from the one behind a housing co-op. At Midtown, dealers pay rent, plus 2 percent of every transaction, and are required to spend a certain amount of time each month working the floor and cash register. In return, Midtown pays for the lights, heat, security, and marketing; collects the sales tax; and pays the credit card fees. It's a model that emerged in the 1990s as small, independent antique shops started closing in the face of a growing excess of "antiques" and dealers to sell them. Competition and shrinking margins forced those who had stuff to move into common quarters.

It's not easy to manage an antique mall. Politics between dealers, especially those with similar collecting interests, can be fierce. "I'll tell you about it—off-record," Dick says, shaking his head as he leads me quickly past a wash of children's books, vintage dresses, racks of old *Life* magazines, china, and glass. He turns into a booth lined on both sides by *Star Wars* action figures, *Austin Powers* action figures, and *Star Trek* action figures. "Twenty years ago, we wouldn't have allowed this," he says. "Now? People want what reminds them of what they grew up with. It's out of production, so we allow it. Not my thing, but gotta move with the times." He moves along, past cabinets of antique glass and jewelry, racks of vintage clothing, and stops at a cabinet full of antique cups and saucers.

"So what's your thing?" I ask.

"These days, stained glass. But my wife and I, we used to do a lot of furniture and dolls."

I gaze at the cups and saucers. "My grandmother collected cups," I say to him, lingering on the memory of the display rack she arranged just outside her kitchen.

"Nobody wants them, anymore. Sorry. Twenty years ago, we could get twenty to forty bucks for a cup. Now?" He points at a small sign: 50% OFF. He walks to the balcony and points downstairs at the front window. "See down there? That's Pyrex," he says, referring to a table covered in patterned casserole dishes, mixing bowls, and other pieces of durable glassware. Pieces manufactured for sale in the 1950s and 1960s have become highly collectible, especially by younger Americans, and can sell for thousands of dollars. "A year ago, that was Victorian glass in the window."

I almost interject that my grandmother loved Victorian glass. But he knows that. "The people who bought the Victorian just aren't around anymore. Tastes change. People want what they grew up with."

"I grew up with Pyrex," I tell him, remembering my mother's brown mixing bowls. "And I don't want it, especially for that price."

"Maybe not," he says. "But, believe me, we get people who do."

For decades, the collectibles market made sense. Demand for unique, precious things outpaced the supply, and so the price went up. What's changed is that notions of what's unique and precious have gone down-market. The ancient Greek statuary sought out by nostalgic and admiring ancient Roman aristocrats was definitely rare. Thus, the price was and is high. But a mint-condition *Star Wars* figure in original packaging? They sometimes sell for tens of thousands of dollars (a Boba Fett in the original package went for $27,000 in 2015), even though there are millions in existence (unpackaged). Will that packaged-price premium still hold fifty, one hundred, or two hundred years from now? I doubt it.

Though nobody could have foreseen it at the dawn of the industrial revolution, mass production democratized collecting and connoisseurship.

By the mid-twentieth century, everyone could own something valuable and—in some sense—rare.

Dick walks me around to another display case, this one filled with Hummel figurines—small German porcelains, mostly in the shape of children, first manufactured in the 1930s in so-called limited editions that numbered in the many thousands. In the 1970s, collectors— generally Americans who'd benefited from the great post–World War II economy and had cash in their pockets—started collecting. "We used to sell them for three hundred to four hundred dollars each," Dick says as he points to a 60% OFF! sign. "Now we can't discount the damn things enough." He throws up his hands. "Dolls. My wife and I used to make two thousand to four thousand dollars every weekend selling dolls in the nineties. Now they don't sell at all."

"Why?"

"Nostalgia. And for a few years [the people who loved them] had excess cash in their pockets. Mortgage paid, kids done with college. So they buy." Eventually mortality catches up, and all those mass-produced items revert to a value that's more reflective of their practical—not nostalgic—value. Which in most cases is zero.

"What's going to have value in twenty years?"

"The oak furniture that isn't selling now? We cleared Michigan's forests to make that stuff, and now it's on the third floor," he says, refer- ring to Midtown's furniture showroom. "Beats the hell out of me."

Dick introduces me to Judi Gerber, a mall tenant with decades of experience buying and selling collectibles in the American Midwest. Years ago, she used to attend farm-foreclosure auctions on a regular basis. "The farms didn't have dishwashers—and all the glass that's ruined by dishwashers," she explains. "And that good glass was very sellable." Better yet, nobody in a small town wanted those glasses, and there weren't many antique dealers competing for them. "So I could get five boxes for ten dollars, and inside there'd be a goblet that I'd sell for forty dollars."

These days, the stuff being sold out of country farmhouses isn't much different from the stuff found in suburban Minneapolis houses. Thanks to the development of the mass market, suburbanites and farmers have been buying the same stuff for decades.

"Stuff from the seventies, I thought it was popular now," I say to Linda Hemberger, another Midtown dealer with decades of experience, who's seated next to Gerber. "Age doesn't matter?"

She cackles. "Oh, my dear. We have people come into the shop with boxes of stuff they feel is worth a lot because it was Grandma's or it's a hundred years old. We have to tell them, 'That china pattern, it was included in a sack of horse feed as an incentive to get people to buy the horse feed.' If you had nothing, it was something. To millions of people."

"And now?"

"Good, not so good, great?"

Dick Richter and I slip between racks of vintage clothing and take a stairway to the third floor. The light is scarce and tinted brown, reflected off the vast expanse of wooden furniture that fills the space. There must be three hundred china cabinets, wardrobes, chairs, and tables, at least. We walk the perimeter, the aged wooden floor creaking beneath us.

Among the reasons that antique furniture isn't selling in the volumes or at the prices it once did: home ownership among young Americans is in decline, and few if any renters want a several-hundred-pound wardrobe that they'll have to move from studio apartment to studio apartment. Likewise, the advent of glass-clad apartment towers and their floor-to-ceiling windows has transformed home decorating, especially for high-end customers who once coveted big brown wooden pieces. Minimalist, modern designs often work best in those spaces—not Victorian cabinets designed to dominate a wall.

But the most important factor might be demographic: the people who treasured that big brown furniture are now downsizing and dying, leaving behind an excess of the stuff. If a young person wants a large Victorian wardrobe, it's available for free in Grandma's basement, or someone else's grandma's basement.

"Let's be real," Richter says as he waves his hand over the hundreds of third-floor pieces. "Nobody wants a fine oak dining room set anymore. And there are so many, and you can't get rid of them."

Nearby stands Dale Kenney, a hulking eighty-year-old furniture dealer. He greets us with a scowl. "I'm getting out of it," he declares as he weakly shakes my hand. Kenney is a former Northwest Airlines mechanic who got into the antique business gradually, after his mother gave him some furniture to sell several decades ago. When Northwest's mechanics went on strike, he started devoting more time to the business. "We've been in it so long, I'm buying stuff back from twenty, twenty-five years ago. People are getting old." He points to an elegant wooden shaving stand. "That piece. Used to get two twenty-five for a shaving stand. Now it's just clutter. And nobody wants a drop-front desk anymore because it can't hold a computer."

I wander around his inventory. Solid oak tables that once might have been treasured and passed on as a store of a family's wealth are marked below the price of a new iPhone. Laid across one of Kenney's oak chairs is a beat-up and dusty vinyl shoulder bag with a Northwest Orient Airlines logo printed across it. After World War II, Northwest Orient pioneered the business of flying between the United States and Asia. When I moved to China in 2002, I flew Northwest Airlines (it dropped "Orient" in 1986), and since then I've flown it and Delta Airlines (which acquired Northwest in 2008) hundreds of times over the Pacific. Over time I've developed a hobby interest in an earlier, arguably more luxurious era of trans-Pacific travel. The beat-up bag is marked at thirty dollars. "I'll take this," I tell Dale. "Do I pay downstairs?"

Nine thousand miles away, Azalina Zakaria stands beside three card tables in the murky lower level of the Amcorp Mall in Petaling Jaya, Malaysia. Wearing a red headscarf and loose black clothes, she stands with her hands crossed as she watches customers walk from booth to booth, enjoying the weekend flea market, Malaysia's best and biggest. Her tables are a hodgepodge of die-cast toy cars, old black-and-white snapshots and postcards, plates, cups, steel bowls, a typewriter, old coffee cans, and a plastic Mickey Mouse figurine.

As my four-year-old son examines her die-cast cars, I pick through a stack of old snapshots that appear to have been taken decades ago. Mostly, they depict a single six-member family in a rural setting. In one image, they stand tightly together in front of a small house with rubber trees in the background. To somebody, somewhere, this image is more than a curiosity. It's family history. "Where do you find these?" I ask her.

"My husband and I travel around Malaysia. We'll go to old neighborhoods in Johor, Segamat, all kinds of places, and knock on the doors and ask if they have anything to sell. We have a shop in Old Town," she says, referring to the crowded old Petaling Jaya town center, a few miles from the Kuala Lumpur border. "We keep most of our furniture there."

That grabs my attention. In addition to the small furniture vendors who bring their heavy pieces, weekly, to the flea market, the lower level of Amcorp Mall is home to two shops specializing in antique wooden furniture. The bigger of the two pushes its best pieces to the front of the store for the weekend. Today those pieces include several wooden dressers, vanities, wardrobes, and pharmacy cabinets, as well as a massive carved bar. I've always assumed demand for the pieces is weak, just as it is in Stillwater, but the low rent at Amcorp allows the dealers to rationalize the business. "People are interested in it?"

"They love it," she says. "That's why we sell it. The problem is finding it." She points to a small wooden cabinet holding a gramophone. "I can't afford to get this in Malaysia. It goes for two thousand to two thousand and five hundred ringgit [$490 to $610]."

"So you get it door-to-door?"

"Cannot. We import. If I buy a shipping container full of old furniture from the U.K., it costs around a thousand ringgit [$245]." She nods across the room at a stack of wooden furniture, anticipating my next question: "Theirs is all imported, too."

Never did it occur to me that the dim confines of Amcorp Mall's lower level—home to a supermarket, several small restaurants, and a handful of vinyl record shops—is a hub for globalized secondhand. "How much do you import?"

"As much as I can afford."

I think of the third floor at Midtown Antiques and its stale oak furniture made from Michigan's forests. "Do you ever buy American pieces?"

She smiles and shakes her head. "I don't know anyone."

I open my phone and show her pictures from the third floor, and her eyes widen.

Two hundred miles away, Kenny Leck leans over a bowl of noodles in one of Singapore's old shophouses, the colorful, narrow two- and three-story commercial buildings that line the streets in older parts of town. He's thirty-nine years old and the owner of BooksActually, a small bookshop widely acknowledged to be one of the best in Asia. BooksActually also houses a small antique shop focused on local relics, located in the back of the store.

Kenny is of modest height, with disheveled hair and a face that's a combination of irritated and happy to see you. It's sometimes hard to tell one from the other—until you begin chatting with him. Kenny, if he can spare a moment, is endlessly hospitable and a great conversationalist, especially when it comes to his beloved city-state.

"In Singapore, it's hard to get people to embrace secondhand," he tells me. Economically, Singapore's diverse population is dominated by its ethnic Chinese population, of which Kenny counts himself a member. "In Chinese culture, there's shame if you use secondhand. Means you're not doing well." He shakes his head. "Hand-me-downs. At Chinese New Year, it's all about new clothes."

It's a mindset that's infused Singapore since its bitter separation from Malaysia in 1965. At the time, nobody would've expected the small city-state to surpass its far more populous, resource-rich neighbor. But that's what happened. In the space of just sixty years, it's gone from a rough tropical backwater port into a global banking and shipping center, a regional hub for multinational corporations, and a research and development center for some of Asia's most innovative companies. Government is clean and efficient; quality of life is high.

But achieving so much, in so little time, takes its toll. In successful pursuit of an advanced economy, Singapore bulldozed much of its history. Villages disappeared into public housing projects known as HDB flats (for Housing and Development Board), cemeteries became temporary resting places (to make room for the next wave of dead), and the objects and ephemera of a less developed time—everything from obsolete power cords to black-and-white televisions—aren't just obsolete; they're symbols of an old-fashioned mindset to overcome.

"I've seen so much change in the last twenty years," Kenny says with a hint of exasperation as we eat lunch in a Chinese restaurant housed in a traditional shophouse. "I remember the dining room table we bought twenty years ago. It lasted for years, until we moved our house and wanted something new." He lifts a knot of noodles into his mouth. "So much is being thrown away in Singapore now. The other day somebody threw away an Ikea pine side table in our neighborhood. Nice table. I didn't pick it up because I have no space for it."

Kenny is not the sort to pass on a perfectly good piece of furniture. "I'm kind of a hoarder," he admits. "Pencils, rulers, office things, other things. Also bricks."

"Bricks?"

"Singapore made bricks at one time. They built our country, and they're everywhere now, propping doors, that kind of thing." He grows animated. "We made the A1 brick and many others. You can see the brand on the older bricks. But now we import them. I collect the old ones."

Rarely does a hoarder find practical use for a house full of stuff, much less classic bricks.* But after Kenny opened BooksActually in 2006, he looked around and realized that, even with the books, the space was empty. "So I brought in some of my old stuff," he says, like antique slide rules, and placed them around the store as decor. Soon, customers were taking an interest. "People would ask if it's for sale," he says with a laugh. "They won't buy a book, but they will buy a wooden ruler."

Books are a tough business, no matter where the store is located. So when Kenny saw that his young customers were interested in buying

---

* For the record, I am aware of at least one additional brick collector in Singapore. She is in her midtwenties and immersed in the city's literary and art scene.

pieces of Singapore's everyday history, he dove into the business of digging up more. Singapore's government regularly redevelops HDB flats and relocates families to new ones. In the process of the move, much gets left behind.

"So that's how I started my *karang guni* work," Kenny explains, using a local term for a rag-and-bone man who scavenges the waste of others. In Singapore, like elsewhere throughout history, rag-and-bone men are at the bottom of the social hierarchy. Kenny doesn't care; condemned HDB flats are a museum of the things his city-state once coveted. "It's a dirty job, digging through trash," he tells me. "But you wouldn't believe what I find. Photo albums from the 1920s—why throw those away? I pick them up and sell them."

Later, as we ride in a taxi past high-end boutiques and hotels, I ask Kenny why anybody in go-go Singapore would care about stuff pulled from low-income HDB flats.

"Nostalgia," he says. "That's what makes it work. Lack of history. We only go back to 1965. We just don't have enough history, so people are looking for a piece. Lately it's typewriters for hipsters. All driven by nostalgia." He takes a recent iPhone from his pocket and opens a browser. "Polaroid cameras," he says as he lands on a Google search page. "Eight, nine years ago, no value. Now they'll cost you two hundred dollars." He shows me an image of a compactible Polaroid first manufactured in the 1970s.

"My dad had that model," I tell him. "I wish I still had it."

The taxi stops beside a closed-off street jammed with individual vendors of used goods. They sit beneath plastic tarps and restaurant umbrellas with goods spread out before them. I see piles of clothes and shoes, stacks of old DVD players and suitcases, temporary display cases covered with shiny objects, and—here and there—electric teapots on the beat-up boxes in which they were sold years ago. One man has a pile of crutches; another has boxes stacked six feet high and covered in black plastic garbage bags. It looks informal, cheap, a bit dirty—and wholly unlike Singapore.

Kenny pays the fare and leads me slowly up the street. "Years ago, my dad told me that if I lose something, it'll turn up tomorrow at the Thieves' Market," he explains. The people sitting on folding chairs beneath the tents and umbrellas don't look like thieves. Most are elderly and look no more threatening than the residents of the average elder-care facility in suburban Minneapolis. If anything is being stolen, it's not by them. Singapore's Thieves' Market is now known as the Sungei Road Flea Market. It's a transit point, the place where things Singaporeans lose, sell, or give away acquire a new owner. "You had garage sales," Kenny tells me. "We didn't have garage sales. *This* is our garage sale."

As we stroll, a motorcycle slowly maneuvers down the street with two garbage bags of stuff tied to the back. "New inventory," Kenny says. We stop beside a small table covered in old cellular flip phones. Until recently, many were still usable. But Singapore is phasing out the cell service that they required, and so they've become obsolete. The old man in a tank top behind the table pushes an old Motorola at me. "Good one," he says.

"For what?"

"Collecting."

Kenny and I continue walking. "Sungei Road used to be twice as big. But the real estate is too expensive." He points to a newly built subway stop across the street. "In a couple of months this will all be gone." We pause at two card tables set out beneath a blue tarp. They're covered in old digital cameras and obsolete flip phones, with a couple of tambourines and bags of children's books. Among them, Kenny spots a ziplock bag filled with vintage children's superhero playing cards, which, he says, "will be popular with Gen X types." He buys five packs for twelve dollars and moves to the next table, where he buys five packs of vintage "school reward pins" for excellent performance in social studies class, glee club, and other events that evoke nostalgia. "The margin is better than books, man!"

We continue strolling. "The migrant workers are the big buyers here," he explains, referring to the Indonesian and South Asian immigrants who power the city's construction projects and service businesses. "Buying clothes and phones and shoes and other things they actually use." We pause at a far end of the market, where piles of beat-up shoes are laid out on tarps beside stacks of old jeans. Two Indonesian workers dressed in blue construction-crew uniforms are rummaging through the shoes. One holds four pairs. "They'll bring them back home to Indonesia to sell," Kenny says. Nostalgia-inducing school pins and obsolete phones won't be on the shopping list. That's the secondhand market for the wealthy.

Later, at BooksActually, Kenny leads me into the area behind the cash registers, where most of his antiques for sale are on display. One wall is covered in glasses and bottles that—due to their shape or brand— invoke nostalgia. A small wooden box is filled with "vintage buttons" priced five for $1.50. Kenny points to a crate filled with cassettes of Indian music made in the 1980s. "When I first started doing *karanguni* work, I didn't take cassettes. I mean, who's going to take these? But I had space, so I started taking them. Now they sell." He picks up *Best of Lata Mangeshkar Vol. 2.* "Some of these mean a lot to people."

He reaches into the box for another one but suddenly notices an unattended customer at the cash register and excuses himself. I watch him slide behind the counter, and then I look beyond him, to the books piled high atop the table in the center of the store and the book-lined walls that seem to lean in toward it. As with the cassettes, some of the titles will mean a lot to people in a future in which screens are even more common. Some might even be rare, and remind people of a Singapore in which BooksActually was a hub for an emerging movement to reclaim the past for the present. But in time what matters from the past will shift, and most of those books, too, will begin to linger in cultural irrelevance, their pages turned and yellowing.

For a moment in the 1990s, the internet seemed poised to make the secondhand economy a respectable and even dominant part of the U.S. economy. Much of the credit goes to eBay, one of the first, and certainly the most successful, of the online auction sites. Founded in September 1995, it grew as rapidly as any business, ever. In 1997, it hosted two million auctions. By the mid-2000s, it enjoyed hundreds of millions of registered users and a multibillion-dollar market capitalization that exceeded so-called old-economy manufacturers of new things like cars. One early researcher into internet addiction claimed that in the late 1990s "online auction addiction" accounted for 15 percent of all internet addiction cases (cybersexual addiction was number one). But folks enticed by rarity and the promise of riches hidden in closets grew bored when the transparency of the internet revealed that things weren't so rare, after all.

"You had this one piece you thought was really rare," explains Dick Richter. "At first there was a rise in prices, and then they settled down. And it sucked us down with it." As the allure of the treasure hunt faded, so too did cases of online-auction addiction. Facebook, Twitter, Netflix, and other forms of entertainment captured more and more of internet users' screen time.

It turns out that hosting online auctions of commonplace used stuff was no way to grow a stable business. To do that, you need lots of fixed-price products that don't vary in quality. So eBay has spent the last few years turning away from its past and becoming a fierce seller of new stuff. When I reached out to the company to talk about its role in the global secondhand industry, a spokesperson declined. Doing so, he said, "would probably just reinforce perceptions of eBay as primarily a marketplace for used goods." These days, the spokesperson wrote to me, "84%+" of eBay's listings are new and fixed price.

Of course, that's not close to the end of the online secondhand market. The smartphone has enabled an entirely new generation of services focused on making it easier than ever to sell stuff—and leave eBay in the past. On OfferUp, the leading U.S.-based app for buying and selling stuff, users simply take a picture of what they want to sell and post it. During a phone interview, Nick Huzar, the CEO and co-founder of OfferUp, told me that he came up with the idea of a used-good phone app after noticing that "Goodwill moves so much so fast."

"Do you compete with Goodwill?"

"Not really. We expand the market."

"How big is that market?"

"How many stars are in the sky?"

Huzar has no illusions. "Our biggest competitor is time," he told me. If you have a garage full of stuff—from rakes to Big Wheels—it's probably not worth the time to photograph and list everything on OfferUp.

But a two-year-old iPhone? That should move immediately. The problem is, from a clutter perspective, the iPhone, the good furniture, and the other "good stuff" is a small percentage of what's packed into the world's homes. The economics of decluttering for profit rarely make sense. But the economics of selling new stuff online? According to Huzar, 25 percent of what's sold on OfferUp is new. Over time, it'll grow.

CHAPTER 5

Danshari

Jeongja Han stands beside a truck nearly full with cabinets, coffee tables, chairs, and cardboard boxes of stuff packed between them. Several flights of stairs above her, a cleanout continues. "We maybe should've brought a second [truck]," she says, lamenting her misjudgment. "We reuse a lot more now." The high price of purging personal belongings is one factor driving reuse in Japan. The other is globalized secondhand.

Han gestures at rows of clay planters in front of a building across the street. "We collect those and sell them ten for one hundred yen [a dollar]," she says. A nearby wooden bench, she tells me, can go to Africa. But the majority of the goods she collects are bound for the Philippines. "They have a deep love for Japanese products," she explains.

Japan's reputation for quality has long been a key selling point for goods manufactured there. But in a less-remarked-on and perhaps equally important development, goods *used* in Japan are also coveted. "So even if something is made in China, if it's used in Japan, people elsewhere will assume it is good," explains Rina Hamada of the *Reuse Business Journal*. And nowhere is that more the case than in Southeast

Asia, where new Japanese goods have been coveted—and oftentimes unaffordable—for decades.

Later, Han drives down a long boulevard in Yamato City, roughly twenty miles southeast of Tokyo. An iPhone in her lap calls out directions as she gossips about work. Tomorrow she'll clean out the home of a twenty-six-year-old woman who died by suicide. She was hired by the woman's parents, and as she drives, she laments that more couldn't have been done for the daughter. "There are many suicides lately," she tells me. "We often find prescriptions for antidepressants during the cleanouts."

She turns left into a parking lot across the street from a Red Lobster. High above is a lighted sign: MURAOKA. Below is a business that appears to occupy a former gas station. Exposed support beams from a roof hang over the space where I expect fuel pumps once stood, and a showroom occupies spaces that might have held a store and cashier station. A forklift drives across the space carrying a pallet that holds a small refrigerator, a high chair, and a Panasonic compact convection oven. It stops at an open forty-foot shipping container full of boxes, appliances, and furniture. In the morning, it'll ship out to the Philippines.

The owner of this company is a wiry and youthful sixty-seven-year-old named Tetsuaki Muraoka. He walks over and warmly greets Han. She's one of his best customers, a reliable source of home goods from cleanouts. They walk into the main showroom but pause at a rattan chair priced for 700 yen ($6.21) that Han sold here. Han laughs when I ask how much he paid her for it. "Almost nothing, close to free."

Muraoka's shop is filled mostly with old PCs and monitors, some dating back to the late 1980s. ("Factories want them for parts for their old equipment," he explains.) He'd spent twenty years at this site doing PC repair, thinking the business would always have a future. "Then this came along," he says, pulling a Samsung Galaxy smartphone in a pink case from his pocket. Over the last decade, demand for PCs—and PC repair—declined precipitously as users migrated to the mobile internet, so Muraoka found himself in search of a new line of business. "I knew somebody shipping used stuff to the Philippines," he says and shrugs. "I learned from him."

He traveled to the Philippines and visited wholesale markets where Japanese goods are sold or auctioned. "Buyers showed me the kinds of things they want," he explains. "And they showed me how to pack stuff tightly into containers." When he returned, he started buying used stuff from cleanouts, as well as from individuals simply looking to unload stuff. In recent months, he's even gotten into the business of doing cleanouts himself. Then, once a month, he ships out three to four tons of goods via a broker able to clear a shipping container through the Philippines' notoriously corrupt ports.

His story isn't so unusual, especially to Han. When she's not busy with cleanouts, she holds seminars on how to do cleanouts. "Older people think it's an easy job to do and a good business," she explains with a polite smile. In the future, however, it might not be so easy: the Association of Cleanout Professionals is working with the government to create an official certification that would control access to the profession.

As Han and Muraoka chat, the shipping container is sealed up. "The Filipino market won't last forever," she tells him. "As the wealth level goes up, they'll want new things. Then what?" It's happened before: Thailand was once Japan's favored destination for its used stuff. But the market has faded with Thailand's increasing wealth. "Cambodia, probably," she surmises.

A few days earlier, Rina Hamada mulled the same problem over coffee. "Whenever there's a gap between wealth and poverty, there will be a secondhand industry," she says. In her view, Japan's secondhand industry already knows that the long-term outlook for reuse, especially as an export industry, is poor. Japan is too wasteful; the rest of the world wants the chance to imitate it.

For now, Han isn't worried. The fees she gets for cleanouts make for a very good business, and business is booming, even if the underlying reasons are sometimes best forgotten. "I don't want to say I get used to it," she says. "But I get used to it."

Shigeru Kobayashi is sixty-four years old with a spiky salt-and-pepper pompadour and a barreling gait. He is dressed in shades of gray: light-gray sport coat (over a white shirt), off-white slacks, and nearly black sneakers. At the moment, he's dashing through one of the secondhand-goods storage yards that Hamaya Corporation, the company he founded in 1991, operates in Higashimatsuyama, a small city thirty-five miles northwest of Tokyo.

A small office is on the left, and an empty flatbed truck is paused on a scale in front of it. Further on, forklifts zip in and out of acres of warehouses on three sides, carrying pallets of PCs, refrigerators, and boomboxes, as well as a hulking cardboard box overflowing with electric pianos. Kobayashi points to a well-built man in a sweaty T-shirt standing inside a shipping container filled with knitting machines. He's holding a clipboard and looks as if he's checking the inventory.

"He's from Karachi," says Yuki Ohkuma, a young executive translating for Kobayashi. "One of our regular customers." She calls out to the man from Karachi and identifies me as a reporter.

He lights up. "Hamaya is excellent! I've been coming here eighteen years!" The container will ship out later in the day. But that's just a start. Hamaya operates fifteen additional locations around Japan, and in 2017 all those locations combined to export around 2,700 shipping containers of secondhand Japanese stuff to forty countries around the world. The company's website, brochures, and investor materials include photos of turbaned Afghani traders exchanging boomboxes imported from Hamaya, Cambodian families with furniture imported from Hamaya, and Madagascan children holding thermoses imported from Hamaya. The pics don't exaggerate: Hamaya is by far the biggest exporter of used hard goods (textiles are the soft goods) in Asia, and possibly the world.

Kobayashi dashes into a cavernous warehouse filled with refrigerators and washing machines stacked three high in metal cages and wrapped in cellophane. "Those are for Vietnam," he says. Then he points to several pallets of rice cookers, also wrapped in cellophane. "Vietnam, too." A little farther into the warehouse we pause by a ten-foot-high stack of metal pallets that hold knitting machines. "Nigeria, but mostly they go to Pakistan now, because the market is strong." Next to it is a cellophaned stack of vacuum cleaners. "Pakistan." And below it, small desk fans. "Not sure. Yuki?"

She takes out her phone to look up the answer, but there's no time. Kobayashi wants to show me more. An aisle is formed on the left by stacks of flat-screen computer monitors that remind me of crop rows on a breezeless day. "For China," he says. "They remove the screens and use them in other devices." Large, waist-high bags are in a corner below additional stacks of refrigerators. Kobayashi opens one and gestures for me to look: rusty hand tools including screwdrivers, hammers, and wrenches the size of toddlers. "Vietnam," he announces, then sticks his hands into the bag and pulls out a screwdriver. "Quality is too good. These should be sold in Japan as vintage."

Yuki nods and taps a note into her phone.

Kobayashi is ahead of us again, moving into a brighter warehouse filled with well-built sofas, tables, and chairs (no flat-pack Ikea here). "The furniture goes to the Philippines, Vietnam, Malaysia." Toward the edge of the warehouse are cardboard boxes filled with dozens of guitars. "Acoustic guitars go to Mali. Electric to Nigeria." He points at a pallet of car radios. "Nigeria." Then he walks over to pallets of boomboxes. "These go to Mali, but the market is softening." Stacks of stereo speakers are cellophaned and awaiting shipment. "Vietnam," he says. "But they're a little dusty and need to be cleaned off." He taps a contact on his phone and begins a conversation.

"We used to get ten thousand yen for a pair of speakers," Yuki adds. "Now it's only six thousand."

"What happened?"

"The price of new things from China has dropped," she says. "Sometimes the new is cheaper than the used." Nearby are laundry baskets and plastic milk cartons filled with fishing reels. Yuki follows my eyes. "In Malaysia we have a big buyer for fishing equipment. He'll order a thousand reels and buy the rods elsewhere."

"What about those?" I ask, nodding at pallets of chainsaws.

"Cambodia," she says. "If they're bigger, they go to Nigeria. They like big chainsaws in Nigeria, and we often argue with our customers about size."

It goes on like this for half an hour. Hamaya is a museum of the stuff the Japanese don't want, in outrageous volumes. It comes from a multitude of sources: homes, offices, manufacturers, construction sites, leasing companies, and any other corner of the Japanese economy that decides to downsize and/or upgrade. Yuki tells me that just this facility receives around 130 customers per day selling things—everything from municipalities collecting stuff from residences to small-scale traders who pick up items from residences—and reminds me that this isn't even Hamaya's biggest plant.

This was not the business that Shigeru Kobayashi planned to establish. In the 1980s, he profited greatly as a scrap-metal trader who brokered broken and unwanted goods to recycling companies that turned them into raw materials. In that business, a computer, a car, or any other object is viewed as a package of commodities. If the value of those commodities exceeds what a person can obtain for the car or the computer, it's dismantled and sold off as metal. Kobayashi likely would have stayed with it. But in the 1980s the Japanese currency strengthened, and it became impossible for Kobayashi to make a profit selling Japanese metal overseas. So he looked for a new profession and noticed traders making good money by exporting used Japanese water pumps to Taiwan.

Because the Taiwan market was already saturated with used Japanese water pumps, he looked for a developing country whose market wasn't. "I saw that Vietnam needs electrical appliances, agricultural machines, construction machines, industrial machines," he says. Quickly, he narrowed his product mix to electrical appliances like refrigerators and washing machines. "In the early days, it was easy to make money because the price of new appliances was so high. Everyone wanted one, so they accepted used."

"Was it easy to get the appliances?"

"Japanese are very wasteful, and they tend to change their appliances frequently, even if they work well. They want to upgrade."

In the mid-2010s, Hamaya's sales reached roughly $1 billion per year, and nobody is more surprised by this than Kobayashi, who expected the business to fail almost from its start. "But here we are in 2018, and we still survive," he says and laughs. Then that boyish face transitions into a sad smile. "But it's shrinking rapidly now. We know that for sure."

"Why?"

"Ten years ago, new boomboxes sold for two hundred thousand or three hundred thousand yen [$200 to $300]. The new price was high. If the price of something brand-new is high, we can sell many used ones.

But recently the Chinese appliances have become very cheap. You can get the Chinese items even cheaper than the used ones in Japan. People don't have to take the used one."

Like most entrepreneurs I've met, Kobayashi admires China's entrepreneurial spirit and ability to corner markets. He's also a pragmatist who believes that his used-goods business doesn't stand a chance against the low-cost goods that have proliferated globally over the last forty years. "In 1991, when I started this business," he says, "I saw the Chinese making new products by hand. I was in the factories. Five, seven years later they automated it. That's why I expected in 2000 this business would end. We were wrong, but the drop-off has been very quick suddenly. No country is growing for us. Vietnam is less than ten percent what it was at its peak. Nigeria is twenty percent off its peak. Philippines, twenty percent."

If Kobayashi is right—and few are in a better position to be so—the democratization of stuff that began with the industrial revolution is quickening. In the nineteenth century, household objects that once held value—like dishes, glassware, and solid-oak furniture—began to lose it. By the early twentieth century, middle-class consumers could afford multiple sets of dishes and changes of clothes. Individuals further down the income ladder were still excluded from the new and fashionable, but thanks to the excess thrown off by wealthier consumers, they could participate via secondhand.

That process accelerated when the Chinese Communist Party decided to rejoin the global economy in the 1970s. Within a few years, millions of farmers had migrated to work in new factory towns. That migration helped lower the cost of manufacturing pretty much everything, and made the regular consumption of new things possible for hundreds of millions of people. It's not just the poor who benefit, though. In Japan, the price of durable goods—a category that includes appliances

Shigeru Kobayashi examines a Chinese-made boombox bound for Mali at a Hamaya warehouse in Higashimatsuyama, Japan. Japanese-made boomboxes remain in Japan, where they fetch high prices on the vintage collectibles market.

and consumer electronics—has declined by 43.1 percent since 2001. Consumer electronics account for much of this decline—and most of those electronics are made in China.

Everybody wins, except the secondhand market.

"Our cycle is ten years—that's how long it takes for something to appear in our stream," Kobayashi tells me. "Ten years ago we could get 'Made in Japan' items that were of good quality. Now it's all 'Made in China,' 'Made in China,' 'Made in China,' and the consumers aren't as interested."

Not as interested, but definitely still interested.

Data collected by Japan's *Reuse Business Journal* shows that more than two dozen Japanese secondhand companies have opened at least sixty-three retail or distribution outlets across Southeast Asia in recent years, with the heaviest concentrations in Thailand and the Philippines.

Total exports from just those companies total at least $1 billion per year, and hundreds of millions of individual bits of stuff.

Demand is strong, driven by affluence, not poverty. Between 2000 and 2015, roughly 70 percent of global economic growth originated in emerging-market economies and developing countries like Malaysia, Vietnam, and the Philippines, according to the International Monetary Fund. Those fast-growing economies also happen to be some of the world's biggest markets for secondhand goods. Newly minted consumers, keen to shop, opt for what they can afford. And usually, that's secondhand.

Across Southeast Asia small secondhand shops are often the dominant form of commerce, especially in rural towns. Those retailers favor Japanese goods and obtain them from importers that wholesale the goods. Much of this trade is conducted on the gray market, with imports mislabeled to evade customs duties or outright prohibitions. But even if the shipments were labeled correctly, the global trading system lacks a single classification for used "hard goods," making them next to impossible to find in the databases and sources used to track new goods.

Regardless of the data, there's no question that stuff flows out of Japan aided by long-standing geographic, commercial, and cultural links. For example, Japanese companies have been a fixture in Malaysia for decades, whether as industrial companies that take on contracts to build crucial infrastructure or as retailers in the country's shopping malls. Likewise, Malaysian students have been traveling to Japan on exchange since the 1980s, often on tight student budgets. Many bring back stories (or post them to Facebook and Instagram) of surviving by shopping at Bookoff and other Japanese secondhand retailers. Collectively, these experiences enhance the already formidable reputation of Japanese goods in Southeast Asia, and lay the groundwork for what might sound absurd in the United State and Europe: a department store stocked only with used Japanese stuff.

Bookoff was late to Southeast Asia. Unlike many of its competitors, it'd perfected the art of pricing Japanese stuff to move *in Japan* and didn't feel the need to export it. But as the tide of stuff grew, Bookoff's executives started looking abroad. "Bookoff is very good at buying," explains Toru Inoue, the managing director of Bookoff's international expansion, during an interview in Yokohama. "It has an annual surplus of one hundred and thirty million items in Japan that don't sell. So we need an exit strategy." The company scouted Thailand and the Philippines but decided competition from other Japanese secondhand-goods importers was already too strong. Malaysia, often overlooked because of its higher incomes and strict licensing for retailers, beckoned. A big corporation like Bookoff was the perfect means to pry open Malaysia's market.

Bookoff's first Malaysian store opened in January 2017 in a cavernous, largely empty mall twenty traffic-choked miles southwest of downtown Kuala Lumpur. On the ground floor are a handful of restaurants and fruit stands catering to the handful of occupied offices in the adjoining towers. Amid the vacant gloom, there is a bright spot: a two-story bank of well-lit windows that extend the length of the third and fourth floor on one side of the mall. JALAN JALAN JAPAN reads the sign that stretches across the glass, butting up against Malaysian and Japanese flags. In Malay, the company name means "Take a stroll in Japan."

"The mall is a ghost town," Inoue admitted. "But it's cheap, and in Malaysia you can promote via social media. Also, Malaysians love Japanese products."

It's a preposterous pitch, but it works. On weekends and on sale days, lines stretch out the door. Inoue tells me that the store has sold ten thousand individual products and grossed 2.5 million yen (around $250,000) in a single day. Those are aspirational numbers for established stores in crowded Malaysian shopping malls. But Bookoff expects them, and it is expanding on the basis of those lofty expectations. There are currently three Jalan Jalan stores in the Kuala Lumpur area, and by 2020 there will be two more. "In fact, we have enough surplus to supply ten stores," Inoue says. "This is just the start."

Inside the front doors, Jalan Jalan Japan looks like a slightly run-down Bookoff. Racks of clothes extend all the way to the back of the twenty-four-thousand-square-foot space. But unlike Bookoff's Japanese stores, they aren't segregated by color or brand; it's just one long wash of undifferentiated (mostly) women's apparel, priced to move. Garments average around 10 ringgit ($2.50) per piece. "If it doesn't sell, I lower it to three to five ringgit [$0.75 to $1.25]," says Koji Onozawa, the dapper director of the first Jalan Jalan Japan store, as he leads me on a tour. On average, the store sells five hundred garments per day, or fifteen thousand per month. "That's far more than an average Uniqlo store sells," he adds.

To our right are cases of low-cost jewelry priced for the equivalent of a few dollars. Farther on are racks of action figures in plastic bags and Tamagotchi—palm-size electronic "pets" that were popular in the 1990s. "Now people buy them here, not Japan," Onozawa says, shrugging.

Next to the toys are two racks of heavy hemp kimonos not appreciably different from the ones I saw during home cleanouts around Tokyo. "People buy them for home decoration," Onozawa says with a bewildered shake of the head. "In Japan, nobody would do that. They don't buy them at all." Next to the kimonos are two racks of white, lacy wedding dresses.

"People sell their wedding dresses to Bookoff?" I ask.

Onozawa laughs. Prior to taking on the role of running Jalan Jalan Japan, he spent his career at Bookoff in Yokohama, starting as a clerk. "They bring all kinds of things," he offers diplomatically.

I reach out to examine one of the dresses. It's not silk, but at 40 ringgit—roughly $10 at the current exchange rate—it's good enough for someone who can't spend more. "And they sell?"

"If something doesn't sell, I lower the price."

We wander into a housewares section filled with plates, glasses, and lacquerware. "Plates sell very well," Onozawa says. "A whole set for nine ringgit [$2.25]." I wander over to stacks of red and brown lacquer bowls. Some still have Bookoff price tags on them. One is marked 216 yen ($2); when it arrived in Malaysia, it was marked down to 3 ringgit ($0.75). "If you bought it new at the mall here, it would be one hundred ringgit [$25]," Onozawa reminds me. "It's a good deal for Malaysians."

Ultimately, that's the point. Malaysia's economy has been more successful than that of most of its Southeast Asian counterparts, but its per capita household income of $4,571 in 2016 is a long way from Japan's $17,136 from the same year. As a result, many Malaysians buy secondhand if they have any hope of emulating the Japanese lifestyle that's so admired across Southeast Asia.

Income inequality isn't the only factor driving the market for Japanese secondhand in Malaysia. "Japanese families are shrinking and the homes are small," Onozawa notes. "In Malaysia, the families are big and expanding and the homes are big."

I stop beside racks of toy cars and trains. There are Hot Wheels and there is Thomas the Tank Engine. It's the same mix as I saw at Bookoff stores in Yokohama and Tokyo, with an important difference: the condition is uniformly worse in Malaysia. In Yokohama, a used Thomas the Tank Engine train is mint, barely a scratch. In Malaysia, it looks used. And as I look around, I see that the same goes for clothing. There aren't any noticeable tears, holes, or stains. But the makes aren't quite as good, the fashions not nearly as up-to-date. Japan's surplus is not Japan's best. "The products in Japan are in much better condition," I say to Onozawa.

He nods. "In Japan, we can sell the best things for more than we can get here."

We walk past racks of stuffed animals piled four high and extending for forty feet. "They sell very well here," Onozawa says. "We didn't expect that." It's a colorful mix of bears, zebras, monkeys, dolls, and cartoon characters, sold off piece by piece by Japanese parents in Bookoff's hundreds of outlets. Japan's population statistics are clear that most of these stuffed toys were owned and enjoyed in households with only one child. In Malaysia, they'll be passed between families in which women average two kids.

Not all Japan's excess lands in the trash or travels to developing countries. Some stays at home, and some moves to countries just as rich as Japan. It's a point that Shigeru Kobayashi makes as he leads me around a warehouse adjacent to the Hamaya office in Higashimatsuyama. A large Michael Jackson silk-screen painting is against a far wall, and a long shelf is packed with hundreds of rolled-up Japanese scroll paintings. Scattered around them are vintage Japanese bicycles. "Most of that is exported to the U.K.," he says. "Maybe the bicycles stay in Japan."

Yuki, in a pink cardigan despite the late-May heat, points over to a corner where perhaps a dozen thermoses and ten rice cookers are set aside. "Vintage 'Made in Japan' thermoses are very hot in the vintage markets now. So are rice cookers."

"How do you sell them?"

"We have an e-commerce section for the higher-value items. Mostly they go through Yahoo! Auctions."

Farther into the warehouse, we pause at carts piled with dozens of vintage "Made in Japan" boomboxes from the 1980s and 1990s. "These are also hot," Yuki says. "We sell them at a pop-up shop in Shibuya," she says, referring to the fashionable shopping district at the heart of Tokyo. "People love to come."

I tell her that I'd seen vintage boomboxes in Tokyo-area vintage shops.

"People are nostalgic. Also, the old boomboxes are very well made."

Hamaya's e-commerce department is up the street. It occupies two floors of a long warehouse and employs more than a dozen full-time repair technicians, each of whom specializes in fixing a given range of items, from computers to electric guitars. It has small photo booths for making professional-looking auction listings and a shipping department. It feels like the future of reuse, a path forward to making and remaking. Take what needs to be fixed, fix it, and sell it to those who appreciate it. Kobayashi, however, dismisses my revelation. "Vintage and e-commerce is only a small percentage of our sales. A few percent."

"What about Malaysia?" I ask. "Bookoff is expanding rapidly there. It seems like that's an opportunity."

"We buy Bookoff's excess stock," he says as we step into his BMW ActiveHybrid 3. "Then export it. They get so many items, Malaysia alone can't take it." He pauses. "And Malaysia has a very close relationship with China."

It's true. Low-cost Chinese electronics brands such as Haier, Oppo, and HiSense are nearly ubiquitous in Malaysia. So are Chinese-made clothes. "Are you worried that new Chinese products will eliminate the need for used in developing countries?"

"Yes." He drives through Higashimastsuyama with the confidence of a man who owns a chunk of the city's land. As he turns toward a favorite restaurant for lunch, he again tells me that the global market for secondhand Japanese stuff is in terminal decline. So he's returning to his roots in the scrap-metal business. Over the last few years he's slowly built up the capacity to recycle metals from the electrical appliances that he once exported abroad for reuse. It's an expensive business to set up, requiring advanced technology to keep the process safe and clean. Japan's strict environmental regulators won't allow it to operate any other way. "Reusing things is always better for the environment," he says. "But if nobody wants to reuse, what should we do?"

When I ask whether he thinks the Japanese are becoming more environmentally conscious, he laughs and brings up his daughter. "When she was a schoolgirl, her school sent home a questionnaire asking whether we'd prefer they use new or used textbooks. It's my daughter, so I prefer new. But later I found out most of the parents chose used." He laughs. "More and more, Japan has the *mottainai* mindset," he concludes.

"Is that good for this company?"

He shakes his head. "*Mottainai* is not good for this company. If people practice *mottainai*, we don't get things in good condition, and then we can't sell to the secondhand market."

"Wastefulness helps."

"Yes."

At night the narrow streets that crisscross Tokyo's Koenji district are mostly dark but for the lights coming from the discreet, small restaurants that dot the narrow streets and lanes, and the dozens of small secondhand shops for which Koenji is famous. It's an appropriate place for old and used things; unlike most of Tokyo, which was rebuilt into high-rises after the destruction of World War II, Koenji mostly maintains the low-rise feel of a traditional Japanese town.

But that vintage Japanese feel stops as soon as you step into a second-hand shop. The merchandise is uniformly imported used American apparel. Whistler, a store perched at a three-way intersection, specializes in finely crafted used leather dress shoes from high-end American brands like Allen Edmonds. Inside the store the smell of leather is pervasive. Vintage shoes dating back decades sell for hundreds of dollars per pair, sourced in the United States by an owner passionate about American culture. Perhaps he's more passionate than the Americans.

Still, most shops in Koenji specialize in less expensive apparel like sweatshirts, hoodies, and T-shirts. Casual button-down shirts are also popular. And things that Americans might take for granted are extolled and marked up. A simple cotton sweatshirt made by sporting-goods brand Champion is tagged as 1980s KNIT and priced at sixty dollars. A heavily worn blue cotton T-shirt that wouldn't be suitable for hanging at Goodwill sells for more than fifty dollars. As an American, I find it easy to be smug about stuff that people wouldn't dare sell at a Saturday garage sale. But spend enough time around it in Koenji and something unique emerges: a Japanese identity assembled from bits and pieces of what can't be bought at home.

Nowhere is that more obvious than at the shop shining brighter than any other in Koenji: daidai. From the street, it's a blast of yellow light that illuminates the shops beside and across from it. Inside the double doors, the colors intensify into hellacious reds, pinks, oranges, and yellows that the manager, Mio Ojima, tells me are inspired by the technicolor wash of *The Wizard of Oz*.

But Oz is just a starting point. "The theme of the shop is an overturned toy box," says Mio, a slight woman dressed in a yellow-and-green floral-print dress with a collar of knit strawberries (her Instagram profile identifies her as a "Retro&Strawberry lover"). "So when we leave and turn off the lights, we imagine it coming alive."

"Like *Toy Story*."

She nods.

Mio's dress, I note, echoes the Raggedy Ann and Andy dolls that populate much of the store. Strawberries—knit, plastic, porcelain, life-size, much greater than life-size, that bright red strawberry ring on Mio's right index finger—are everywhere. Daidai is a glorious art installation, but it's one designed to sell women's apparel. So hanging on the store's racks are floral-print dresses and blouses that—if downsized—would work equally well for Raggedy Ann.

"I fly to L.A. to buy clothes," Mio says with a wry smile. "And the L.A. people come here to buy them back." She loves the hunt. The Rose Bowl Flea Market in Pasadena is a particular favorite, and she speaks knowledgeably of U.S. thrift brands such as Savers, Buffalo Exchange ("it's just like Bookoff"), and Goodwill.

But all is not well. "Three or four years ago it was easier to find things," she says. "Five, six years ago there was more good stuff." Back then, in that almost immediate but receding past, daidai was a vintage shop selling flea market finds. Since then, daidai has been forced to remake itself. "These days we cut and sew clothes ourselves from things we buy in the U.S." She pulls a strawberry-print dustcover off the sewing machine she keeps next to the cash register. "At Goodwill I buy bedsheets and curtains and make garments from them." She walks to a rack and shows off a green summer dress with yellow sunflowers that looks as if it were airmailed from 1977. "One of the reasons that people love us so much is that we reuse things. We find beauty where others don't."

Still, Mio has no illusions about the ultimate fate of her creations. "Japanese throw away more clothes than Americans," she says. "More fast fashion. They don't donate. They just throw away." She sighs. "*Danshari*." It's a three-character Japanese word that means, in order of the characters,[1] severing a relationship with unnecessary things (*dan*),

Mio Ojima and a blouse she designed and sewed from secondhand curtains purchased at a U.S. thrift store.

purging clutter that overwhelms the home (*sha*), and achieving a sense of peace by separating the self from things (*ri*). Cleaning your home of clutter, the idea goes, also cleanses your heart and mind—regardless of where the stuff ends up.

"*Danshari* is good in some ways," Mio tells me. "But it has a dark side because people throw things away. Some customers come, and I ask, 'Where are your clothes?' They say, 'We already *danshari*.'" Her eyes widen into a shocked can-you-believe-it expression. "You should have given it back to us!"

"Why do they do that?"

"Lack of storage space," she says. "Japanese homes are small. And daidai's clothes are so unique that it's hard to keep them. Also, Japan is humid and tough on clothes."

I take a long gaze around the shop. It's as far from an Old Navy, an H&M, or a Forever 21 as a retail outlet could be. But in an affluent economy where more and newer are the perpetual promise, even art can be replaced.

"I've been to American garage sales, and my opinion is that Americans treat their things well," Mio says. "Better than we do. They donate everything hoping it's reused. Even their underwear." She drapes the strawberry-print cover back over her sewing machine.

I glance around the store again. "The U.S. influences your work a lot," I say.

She shakes her head in disagreement. "I have no influences from the U.S. It's just where all the stuff is."

CHAPTER 6

Our Warehouse Is a
Four-Bedroom House

Interstate 19 runs for sixty-three miles between the southern end of
Tucson and Nogales, Arizona, stopping three hundred feet from the
crossing into Nogales, Mexico. For most of its passage, I-19 is a desolate
desert highway that passes a handful of small towns. On the north-
bound side, U.S. border control officers run semi-permanent check-
points seeking contraband and—presumably—illegal immigrants. But
get a local talking about the highway and eventually they'll bring up the
southbound side. At every hour of the day, pickup trucks—and pickup
trucks with trailers—haul loads of secondhand goods from Tucson and
Phoenix to Mexico.

I've seen trailers behind new GMC trucks packed with cushioning
mattresses and the world of "hard goods" stuffed between them: bicycles, tables, dorm refrigerators, and boxes that I assume contain dishes,
flatware, kitchen utensils, and toys. And I've seen much more reckless
haulers: older Ford pickups dangerously overloaded with bed frames,

bicycles, and commercial refrigerators, all held together—and off the road—by bungee cords.

It's the Southwestern version of Japan's trade with Southeast Asia. But here on the border, there's no Hamaya shipping massive volumes of stuff to traders; there's no Bookoff outlet opening in Mexico City. Instead, it's a trade conducted by small-business people who, pickup by pickup, evacuate the unwanted stuff generated across the Southwestern United States to Mexico's up-and-coming consumers.

The traders are relentless, journeying back and forth over the border, sometimes daily, in search of goods. When a barrier is erected, they go around it and keep trading.

And the barriers are significant. Mexico's business community long ago pressured its government into outlawing the import of secondhand goods. To do it these days, a trader needs a license—and those are nearly impossible to obtain, especially for someone who works in pickup-truck volumes. Meanwhile, the U.S. government is increasingly determined to keep Mexicans in Mexico, even if their only purpose in coming to the United States is to buy and export the stuff Americans don't want.

Small traders find a way.

Throughout Mexico, people clothe themselves in secondhand garments, furnish their homes with secondhand furniture and appliances, and educate and entertain themselves with secondhand electronics. In many small towns and villages, secondhand stores are more common than stores that sell new merchandise. It's one of North America's most environmentally sustainable businesses, but nobody notices unless they're in it.

On weekends, a mile-long swap meet pops up on Colosio, a winding boulevard in Nogales, Sonora, just across the border from Nogales,

Arizona. Vendors set up tents and tables and hang clothes on support poles and racks rolled out to the edge of the street. Used shoes are piled up; used car wheels are stacked up; used bicycles are kept beneath the tents, just in case somebody in passing becomes greedy and brave. Children's clothes are popular; so are chainsaws and generators. There's a stand selling fresh fruit and another selling tamales. Folks stroll slowly, enjoying the Sunday.

I'd like to stroll, but I'm riding in a late-model pickup driven by Shoe Guy, a nickname for an established forty-one-year-old Mexican used-goods trader well known in Tucson's Goodwills (Shoe Guy requested that I use the nickname to protect his anonymity). He's a native of Nogales and, by his account, a thirty-five-year veteran of the cross-border trade in secondhand. Five days per week (and occasionally more), he drives between Nogales and Tucson for the sole purpose of shopping at the city's sixteen Goodwill stores. He figures he travels around fifty thousand miles per year.

Shoe Guy takes a left off Colosio and sees a friend seated in a plush recliner on the side of the road. We step out of the truck. Shoe Guy is just under six feet, with a broad, muscular body, a round face with prominent cheekbones, and a deep voice that speaks English like he walks: confident and fast. He has a carefully trimmed short beard and mustache, and he always wears a baseball cap. He's a natural extrovert, with a sharp, subtle sense of humor that often goes over my head.

Shoe Guy's friend is reclining beside a new black Ford pickup hooked to a long trailer. Beside it are four mattresses, an oversize plastic cooler, a wooden kitchen table and four chairs, a microwave, two children's bicycles, and a top-loading freezer that excites Shoe Guy. "You can get a lot of money for one of those if it's older and not made in China." The man in the recliner tells Shoe Guy that he bought the freezer at a Phoenix-area Goodwill. As they chat, I look out at the tall border fence less than a mile away. It's built from steel bars spaced at four-inch intervals, some as high as thirty feet. From a distance, those repeating spaces give it a slightly hazy look, like a mirage.

Back in the pickup, we head to the Nogales-Mariposa Port of Entry. In 2017 more than three million personal vehicles crossed it, and Shoe Guy accounted for several hundred of those trips. "I'll tell you why secondhand is big," he says, one eye on the road and the other on WhatsApp messages coming onto his phone. "In Mexico people make, like, a thousand pesos [$60] per day. And say they want a mattress. A mattress [in Mexico] is ten thousand pesos. And they'll give you credit so that you end up spending three times that." At the border, U.S. agents wave us—and the truck—into an X-ray machine that the signage swears won't be harmful to our health. "But in Tucson you get a mattress for free."

"So you sell mattresses?"

"No. Bedbugs and all that. It's kind of disgusting. I don't like it. But I can make more money doing it than anything else. Mattresses are the biggest money. In order, biggest money: mattresses, appliances, and clothes."

But Shoe Guy doesn't do big volumes in any of them. Instead, he does shoes—mostly used ones, but if he can find good deals at new-goods outlets (often using coupons), he'll get those, too. At Goodwill Industries of Southern Arizona, he's considered a big buyer (which is saying something). On the other side of the border he has a network of seven wholesale buyers, some of whom take as many as one hundred pairs of shoes at a time.

His true passion, though, is toys. "Check it out—1983 Wicket Ewok Doll," he says as he pushes his phone at me. On the screen is a furry, monkeylike Ewok from the 1983 *Star Wars* film *Return of the Jedi*.

"I bought it at Bear Canyon [Goodwill] for two dollars. Sold it for more to a guy in Monterrey."

The X-ray is complete, and a customs agent waves us into the United States. "How'd you get started in this?" I ask.

"Papa was a fruit and vegetable seller." The family had enough money for a television at home, and Shoe Guy learned English by watching it. He says his favorite shows were the 1950s American comedies *Leave It to Beaver* and *The Adventures of Ozzie and Harriet*, which idealized suburban middle-class lifestyles. When he started spending time at American-side swap meets, that TV time paid off. "There were these chinos," he says, using his catch-all term for Asians. "Koreans. I spoke English, and they hired me for four dollars per day."

"Do you speak Korean?"

"A bit."

He spent years hustling and perfecting his business skills and knowledge of the secondhand market. Meanwhile, he and his family were always on the lookout for a break. "So there was this Korean guy who loved cocaine and was in the shoe business," he recounts. The Korean asked Shoe Guy's father to lend him money, and then proceeded to blow it. As compensation, he offered Shoe Guy's father his house. "My father didn't want his house," Shoe Guy says. "So he gave us all his shoes. That was the start."

He pulls the truck up to the gate of a self-storage facility in Nogales, opens his window, and punches in a code. The gate opens and he drives up to a unit. Like the other fifty-four thousand or so U.S. self-storage locations, this one is largely devoted to the overflow of stuff from American homes. But it differs in one respect. "Everybody who rents here uses it to store the stuff they buy up north." He lifts the metal curtain door.

It holds shoes, mostly. There are shoes on two sets of shelves that go to the ceiling. There are small shopping bags full of shoes and garbage bags full of shoes. There are plastic tubs of shoes, and there are loose shoes that Shoe Guy stuffs into garbage bags for the trip back across the border. There's other stuff, too. A Wii gaming unit sits on a shelf; a mini-fridge with a boxed Lasko fan on top sits on the floor; a Vizio TV is propped on plastic tubs. And near the TV is a tub of receipts from Goodwill.

Shoe Guy loads the mini-fridge and the Vizio TV into the back of his truck along with a few additional bags of shoes, and we drive back into Mexico. Shoe Guy's customer base is growing, he says, and that's a good thing. Competition is also growing, and the small-scale second-hand traders are becoming more professional. "In 1991, swap meets were a joke. People thought we were like carneys or something, a low thing. Now everybody is doing it."

"Why?"

"Big money. In 2000, there was a big crackdown on the mafia, so people jumped to secondhand from drugs." That makes some sense. Sensitivity to fast-changing markets and a talent for moving contraband help in both professions. "Now you see people driving big pickups, spending five thousand, ten thousand dollars at a time on used goods. They went clean. It's funny. What we do is not legal but it's legal somehow."

Shoe Guy takes a right turn through an arched gate and into the walled confines of the Tianguis Canoas, the largest swap meet in Nogales. He parks on an open gravel patch in front of a small stall with corrugated steel siding. It's connected to hundreds of others that snake around this wide space, which was founded in 1990 with thirty dealers. Today, hundreds are spread over several acres.

Dining room chairs, several mattresses, and a bicyle outside of a typical stall at the Tianguis Canoas in Nogales, Mexico. In the early 1990s, the market catered to locals. Now, locals sell wholesale to Mexicans from lesser developed parts of the country.

Shoe Guy's stall holds a rowdy assortment of stuff: shoes, of course, and bins of tennis balls, baseballs, and baseball bats, as well as a plug-in Nativity scene, a dollhouse, a stack of tires, bags of action figures, several large Ninja Turtles on a shelf, pots, pans, a leaf blower, a baby walker, and a boxed Moses action figure. "Got it in Goodwill yesterday," he says. "I also found Jesus." I laugh, but he's not joking. He reaches behind Moses and reveals a Jesus action figure.

"How's business?" I ask the relative behind the counter.

"People here don't buy a lot. They say it's all too expensive to be used."

"They're too uptight," Shoe Guy says with a smirk, and then leads me around the corner and into the market. "No reason for me to be here, actually. My business is becoming wholesale. For me, the swap meet is just a chance to know new people from down south." He's talking about the used-goods dealers from cities like Hermosillo and Mexico City. But the end market isn't just the big cities. Prosperity is trickling south into Mexico's most remote areas, and they want stuff, too.

We zip past stalls with bikes, stalls with lawnmowers, stalls with bikes and lawnmowers. We pass a few stalls selling toys, and Shoe Guy sees someone he knows. "This guy buys from me," he says and pauses to shake hands with a man presiding over a table of Hot Wheels and assorted action figures.

Then we turn the corner into rows of stalls selling refrigerators, washers, dryers, dishwashers—it's a veritable used-appliance super-store. "If I bring ten washers, I'll sell them quick." But there's a twist: a new appliance is nice; a broken one is profitable. "If you get a broken machine, bring it across the border and fix it, you'll earn three times what you paid for it. Can't do that if you buy new ones. Guy I sell washers to, he'll tear them down, clean them up, triple his money."

We emerge into a paved, roofed-over section of the swap meet. It's not exactly upscale, but it's less dusty and chaotic. There's none of the ramshackle randomness of Colosio's clothing racks, where colors and styles are mixed together. Here there's organization: dresses with dresses, blue with blue, white with white; NFL jerseys are segregated by team; T-shirts are arranged by size. There's a reason for the order. "This is all new," I say.

"New pushed used out a few years ago. Chinos moved in." He nods at a middle-aged Chinese couple seated in a stall filled with what Shoe Guy claims are knockoff NFL jerseys. "Chinese bring in the new stuff from L.A. Mostly fakes and knockoffs. Everything is shit—even the good brands are shit."

I look around. Most of the stalls are managed by Chinese—some are speaking their dialects, some are watching Chinese television shows on their phones, and some are using WeChat, the ubiquitous Chinese social media service, on their phones. I approach one of the stalls selling women's apparel. The fabric is thin and rough, the stitching is sloppy, and it's priced to move. Essentially, it's disposable clothing. Wash, toss, buy another.

I've seen this kind of thing before. In the early 2000s, Shanghai's subway stations filled up with tiny stalls selling similar cheap, poorly made but fashionable clothes that copied whatever was walking down the runways. The customers were teenagers, mostly (still are), flush with a bit of cash from their parents or grandparents and keen to be consumers. Used clothes weren't an option: China banned their import (effectively, unlike Mexico), and no self-respecting, upwardly mobile Shanghainese is going to be caught wearing used. Sure, everyone knows the new clothes won't survive five washes. But that's not a problem when everybody's making enough money to buy more in a few weeks.

Is it China's fault that quality is in decline? No. Initially, at least, China's apparel industry simply manufactured to the standards set by foreign companies seeking cheaper factories. And those foreign companies were only doing what good companies always do: responding to customers. Walmart and Ralph Lauren, alike, bet that price—more than quality—moves product. As it turned out, they were correct, and nobody in Germany complained when Walmart dropped the price of its in-house George jeans from $26.67 to $7.85 in the space of a few years. Walmart's competitors—desperate to keep up on the price points that matter to consumers—made the same compromises. These days, critics of fast fashion complain that Walmart has lowered everyone's quality standards. That's probably true; but the flip side is that it's also lowered every consumer's expectations of what a new wardrobe, a new toaster, and a new set of furniture should cost. In a world where new consumers are minted daily, low-price expectations matter more.

As Shoe Guy watches me, I wander the clothing section at Tianguis Canoas. "People care if it's shit?" I ask.

"If it's a choice between a five-dollar used shirt and a five-dollar new one, people are going to buy new. People wanna party, so they want new when they go out."

"I'm pretty much the same," I concede.

We turn another corner and walk into an open area bordered by the stone walls of the swap meet. Under steel roofs, dozens of mattresses belonging to perhaps a dozen vendors are set out for sale. "Mattresses make the most money because there's no Chinese competition to undercut them," Shoe Guy explains. "It's not just Chinese doing knock-offs. Mexicans, too, in Moroleón. They're making fakes."

The future, as Shoe Guy sees it, is more formal: a shop that upgrades his personal brand, maybe distinguishes him in a nice way from the sellers of cheap fakes. He plans to open a showroom in Nogales where he can display the goods he's become adept at procuring over the border. It's not a unique idea, he says. "Everyone has shops in their houses now. I have one, too. A house full of furniture, bikes, and TVs that I use as a showroom for buyers from down south. But I'm going to do something different: open a showroom near a fashionable area with hot women."

"You can do that?"

"Everybody is getting into this business. Even people with lots of money. They don't need it, but they want it. More money. More things. It's like the mafia—you can't stop it."

Every day Anna and her sister (who won't reveal her name) drive from their Tucson home to a gray strip mall on East Irvington Road on the city's south side. They arrive before eight, then wait for the manager of the Goodwill Outlet Center to unlock the glass doors. As they wait for the doors to open, Anna tells me they're from Hermosillo, the capital of

Mexico's Sonora state, and their mother still lives there. But Anna isn't in the mood for small talk. As a handful of competing Mexican used-goods traders arrive, Anna edges closer to the door, broad shoulders telegraphing her intention to be first through it. I'm in the way.

Six years ago it was Anna's mother who was maneuvering to be the first in line. She was living in Arizona when she heard about the booming market in used American stuff back home. Hermosillo was on the economic upswing, thanks to an influx of investment from the United States and other countries. As incomes grew, so too did lifestyle expectations. Farmers who'd never had a closet full of clothes, a living room with up-to-date electronics, or a kitchen with appliances now wanted it all. New was too expensive, so affordable used goods became the means to fill the aching need. Anna's mother got into the business, and it quickly grew beyond her ability to manage everything on her own. Ideally, she'd have a store in Hermosillo and somebody in Arizona to do the buying. Instead, she was doing it all.

Anna was then working at a foreign-owned logistics warehouse, scraping by on more than she'd ever earned before. So when Anna's mother asked her and her sister to join the burgeoning used-goods business, the two young women didn't hesitate. The sisters moved to Tucson to do the buying, and their mother moved back to Hermosillo to sell from her store.

I ask Anna if she regrets the career change.

"Nope." Anna is small in stature, but her steely presence fills the space between us. She turns it to the window and squints at one hundred or so tables of stuff laid out for sale. This is no time for conversation; the doors will open soon.

I thank her and walk around to the back of the building and a loading dock. Inside, I find Abel Medina, the store's twenty-eight-year-old manager, driving a forklift. He waves his greeting to me as he drives by carrying a hulking washing machine box full of stuff topped by a vacuum-cleaner hose, a purple plastic basket, a wooden extendable child barrier, and a pair of skis.

To my right are rows of tall blue plastic "cages" identical to the ones used to stash fresh donations at the Goodwill Store on South Houghton and East Golf Links (and every other Goodwill in the Southern Arizona system). But these cages aren't filled with fresh donations. Instead, they're filled with unsold items from Goodwill stores around Southern Arizona. If stuff doesn't sell in a store after six weeks, it's delivered here or to an outlet center in Nogales for one last shot and a massive discount. It's a lot of stuff: roughly two-thirds of the used merchandise stocked on the shelves at Goodwill Industries of Southern Arizona's stores fails to sell in the store. Here it's priced to move. According to signs hung throughout the Goodwill Outlet Center:

CLOTHING/ROPA
$1.49 per lb.

HARD GOODS/CHÁCHARAS
$0.89 per lb.

GLASS/VIDRIO
$0.29 per lb.

By-the-pound works well: this Outlet Center is typically one of the top three stores for sales in Goodwill Industries of Southern Arizona's network. Yesterday, an ordinary weekday, it sold just over five thousand dollars' worth of stuff. That's good for Goodwill. Not only does it squeeze extra revenue from donations, but it also reduces the costs of landfilling the stuff that doesn't sell.

Abel stops the forklift and steps off. He's an affable presence and—at just over six feet and 280 pounds—an intimidating one, too. He leads me closer to the cages and pulls out a Tupperware bowl that looks like a small toy in his huge hands. "Toys and Legos do great if they're in good condition. Tupperware, not really. Things that don't move are things you can buy at a dollar store. You can buy Tupperware for a dollar." He points at a dining room table that's sitting just inside the doors that lead to the sales floor. "My process for furniture: if it's not moving, I'll drop it to forty-nine cents. For that price, people will come take a look."

"What about free?"

"Free? If you can't move it for forty-nine cents, you can't move it. Then it's going to the landfill."

A few feet away, another worker is watching as a cage is placed into a machine that tips it onto a table with a screeching crash. There's nothing particularly careful or elegant about the process. Nor, I suppose, should care be taken: this is stuff that's priced by the pound. The staff evens it out and then pushes the table onto the sales floor.

By the doors, two carts of clothing sit covered in sheets, looking like very big bodies bound for a morgue. Abel gestures for me to follow him and pushes one through the doors; another employee follows behind with another cart.

"Lot of our customers are here every day," Abel explains to me as we head into the brightly lit, utilitarian store. There are perhaps another hundred carts lined up throughout the space, and customers are rummaging through them, looking for deals. "Eight-to-five or whenever, that's when they come." He estimates that 80 to 90 percent of the customers are Mexicans purchasing goods bound for resale over the border.

It's a big business. Large resalers in Mexico pay groups of "pickers" to spend their days at the Outlet Center, waiting for new inventory to roll onto the floor. Anna and her sister are small-time compared with the groups who compete against them. "It can get a little tense at times," Abel concedes with a shrug of his broad shoulders. "Things get carried over from the swap meets on the other side of the border. But fortunately we haven't had an incident in over a year. And that one wasn't too bad. I just hope people buy pounds of stuff."

As the two carts are pushed to an open space already partly occupied by two carts covered in bedsheets, twenty or so customers drop what they're rummaging and encircle the soon-to-be-uncovered merchandise. Abel grabs a corner of one of the sheets and pulls it off. The pickers pounce, digging into three hundred to four hundred pounds of clothing, pulling and searching for what they know they can sell in Mexico. Sleeves and pant legs flap in the air like popcorn kernels as buyers dig, toss, and yank the stuff.

"Men's jeans don't really sell," Abel observes coolly. "They're usually worn out, and they weigh more than women's, so people have to pay more at the register."

Traders pounce on a table of "hard goods" just rolled onto the floor at the Goodwill of Southern Arizona's outlet store on Irvington Road. Almost 90 percent of the goods will go unsold.

"People are that price-sensitive?"

"Oh yeah." Abel crosses his ham-sized forearms and watches the buying frenzy with a placid smile. "What's going to sell will sell in the first twenty minutes. After that, not much. We leave the carts out about an hour, sometimes a little longer, depending on what we have for inventory." I glance around the room. Most of the other hundred or so carts lack shoppers; here and there, pickers dig in without much conviction. Most of the other pickers are seated on random pieces of for-sale furniture at the back of the store, waiting for the next rollout of hard goods (including toys, containers, and suitcases) or glassware. After two minutes, the frenzy has slowed, but there appears to be roughly the same amount of stuff on the carts.

"Doesn't look like much is selling."

"Only twelve percent of the stuff that shows up here sells. The rest heads to Cherrybell," he says, referring to the street where the central warehouse is located. By my calculation, that means that less than half the donations received by Goodwill Industries of Southern Arizona actually sell in Arizona.

A cashier waves for Abel, so I wander over to Anna and her sister. They're standing beside a shopping cart full of clothes, double-checking what they pulled and throwing back garments they decide won't sell. "Our clients don't like boot-cut," Anna says as she tosses back a pair of jeans. She picks up a red skirt and carefully folds it into a keeper pile. "This'll go for two or three dollars in Hermosillo."

Anna works quickly, extracting a pair of jeans that she examines with little more than a glance before draping them across her left arm. "Some weeks we spend nine hundred or a thousand dollars," she explains. "Some days we only spend twenty. Some, we spend four hundred." Her sister reaches for a nearby shopping cart and places it next to Anna. "You have to make double or triple what you spend," Anna adds as she drops a sequined T-shirt into the cart.

This week she's keen to pull children's clothing. The school year is starting in Mexico, and her mother says there's a run on small sizes. But she's also on the hunt for winter clothes, because cold weather isn't far off, either. And it's also time to start looking for Christmas. "Our warehouse is a four-bedroom house in Tucson," she adds. "We have room. The problem is time."

"Time?"

"The quality of clothes is going down. Used to be it'd take two or three days of work and we'd have a load to send home. Now it takes six days to find the same amount of stuff."

"I've heard that from other people."

"Everybody knows it."

Across the store, two employees have just rolled out four fresh carts of hard goods. Anna looks up as the sheets are lifted from them and the pickers pounce. "My mom's store in Hermosillo is just like this. She opens the doors and people rush in." Anna, her sister, and the dozens of Hispanic pickers who work here are their proxies.

Nobody knows how many secondhand stores and swap meets exist in Mexico, how much money the trade earns, or—most important—what percentage of an average Mexican home is filled with secondhand stuff. There's a reason for that: small-scale secondhand is largely conducted in cash transactions that can't be traced—as is much of the Mexican economy. By one recent accounting, almost half of Mexico's gross domestic product is off the books and untraceable. Secondhand, invisible but essential, is the key to what everyone is missing. You just need to ask.

Later, as I wander back into the Outlet Center's warehouse, I wonder what the customers rushing Anna's mother's store would do if they saw the carts full of unwanted stuff as they're rolled off the floor. Surely, they'd buy more than the 12 percent that's taken by the traders. If the middlewoman and -man could be cut out, those carts might be cleaned off.

But that's not how secondhand works in the real world. It costs money for Goodwill to open a store and run its sprawling social services network. It costs money for Anna and her sister to spend a day at the outlet, drive their purchases home, and then drive them to Mexico. Here and there, maybe somebody does it for charity. The reality is that almost nobody is going to dig around in old clothes and broken toys for free.

Nearby, a young man is using a snow shovel to dig up unsold hard goods from a cart that's had its hour on the outlet's floor. Each shovelful is dumped into a giant washing-machine box. I see a picture frame drop from the shovel. It holds a master's of science diploma given by Northern Arizona University in 1981 to someone named Ronald Henry DeWitt. Then it's covered by another shovelful of stuff.

When that cart is empty, it'll be filled up with stuff tipped from a just-delivered cage, and the washing machine box will be set aside until it's loaded onto a truck bound for Goodwill Industries of Southern Arizona's central warehouse. For almost everything, that's the end of the line. The unsold clothing will be repacked for export to destinations around the world. But the hard goods—toys, mixers, bowling balls, planters, and everything else that constitutes the universe of what most Americans think of as "stuff"—are done. Some might get sorted out for recycling, but most everything else is landfill-bound. There's just not much else that can be done with an unwanted plastic toy airplane, a beat-up particleboard television cabinet, or a vacuum cleaner hose missing its vacuum. If there were, Goodwill would've tried it.

It could be worse. If Mexico or the United States somehow prevented secondhand traders from doing their business—if the border were blocked, if the bans on secondhand imports were enforced—Goodwill Industries of Southern Arizona would have far fewer customers, and far more of Tucson's property would end up unwanted and landfilled. Meanwhile, the vast social services network that's funded by Goodwill's stores would shrink, leaving many needy residents of Tucson without access to education and other resources that help them obtain jobs.

Early on a Saturday evening, I'm in a hotel room next to Tucson International Airport when Shoe Guy messages me. He's just crossed the border to go shopping. "Meet at 5:45 at Valencia?" he texts. "Valencia" is shorthand for the Goodwill on West Valencia Road on the south side of Tucson. I tell him I'll be there and drive to the strip mall where the store is located.

When I arrive, he's not there. He's late, he tells me via WhatsApp, because of a traffic backup on the Mexican side of the border. When he finally pulls up, ten minutes late, I see there's another reason, too: a refrigerator strapped to the bed of his pickup. As he explains it, he was speeding north from Nogales when he decided to stop into the Goodwill in Green Valley, roughly twenty miles south of Tucson. There was no resisting that fridge. "Price was right," he says sheepishly, shakes my hand, and then leads me into the store.

"I can do ten Goodwill stores in three hours," he boasts. The secret to his efficiency is frequency. He visits Goodwill Industries of Southern Arizona's sixteen shops multiple times per week—sometimes twice a day. So if there's something new on a sales floor, he notices.

Shoes are first. We slow but don't stop at the rack. Shoe Guy grabs a pair of black ASICS. "These are retro and people like them, but the sole falls apart. See?" He shows me a small one-inch tear in the shoe and places them back on the shelf. Next, he reaches for a pair of K-Swiss and—without looking at the tag inside or at the bottom—announces, "Size seven." He shows me the size-seven tag inside one of the shoes and puts them back with a smile, grabs two pairs of Air Jordans ("China-made but I can sell them"), a black pair of Reeboks, and a pair of ballet shoes, which he hands to me to carry. We're off to the appliance section. "I'd like a washer," he says as he scans a space holding several fridges and an industrial vacuum cleaner. "Nothing." He starts moving but stops short at the sight of a heavy wooden kitchen table. "Only three chairs. If it had four chairs, I'd buy it."

"What's wrong with three chairs?"

"Nobody wants a table with three chairs. It's been here three days. Trust me, they'll never sell it."

"Really?"

"Three chairs, nobody."

At that, we're headed to the register. The cashier smiles at him. "Hey, Mr. Shoes."

He gives her a shy smile and hands over one of the Goodwill gift cards he prefers over cash. "Cash slows you down," he explains to me. The total is $34.96.

I follow him out the door and to his pickup. Inside, he tosses the bag of shoes behind the passenger seat, and soon we're driving up Interstate 10. "Do you ever shop the outlet?" I ask.

"I don't like the outlet scene. Everybody knows everybody's business." Tucson's modest skyline is in the distance, reflecting a sharp desert sunset into our eyes. "And I don't like to waste time. The thing is, when I find something, I buy it. I'm not like this" —he takes his phone and turns it in his hand, pretending to examine every crack in the glass (at seventy-five miles per hour). As he does, a WhatsApp message appears on the screen. He glances at it, then places the phone into his lap. "Gotta buy new, too," he says.

"You do?"

"If you don't spend money on new stuff, the world doesn't work. Go to restaurants, pay people, buy stuff! We all have to spend. Otherwise everything falls apart. Socialism."

I tend to agree with him. But I'm curious to see where this goes. "How about the environment?"

"I'm eco-friendly, pro-animal—what do you say?—rights. The other day I hit a javelina on the highway. I felt terrible. But now I'm good with Jesus: I was in a highway gas station bathroom, and I saw a man pass out, grabbed him before he fell. Good with Jesus. But still, you gotta buy stuff and help people live."

Shoe Guy pulls up to the Goodwill at West Ina and North Shannon Roads. Just as he did at West Valencia, he dashes through the door and around the store. He picks up another pair of black Air Jordans midflight and checks them out as he moves along the shoe rack, looking for more. There's a size-thirteen pair of Nike basketball shoes. "Nice," he sighs. "People are big enough for these. Indians in Sonora. But they want sandals. They have wide feet."

We walk past a rack filled with new Halloween decorations. "If it's Christmas, I'll buy right away."

"Even if they're new?"

"Sure. Where do you get used Halloween stuff?"

We're approaching the appliances when Shoe Guy spots a doughnut maker. "If I knew someone who made doughnuts . . ." He stops to think. "But if you made doughnuts, you probably wouldn't buy this." In the toy section, he spots a plastic bag containing three *Lord of the Rings* hobbit figurines, a *Star Wars* TIE fighter, and a Harry Potter action figure. The price is $2.99. "I can make money on that." He also grabs a bank that looks like a brown M&M. "Everyone likes M&Ms."

As we whip through women's clothes, he stops at a table of shorts and grabs a pair of the very shortest. "Hollister, size three. This is for skinny white girls. Mexican girls are bigger."

I raise my brow.

"Seriously," he says. "You gotta know your market."

It's been less than five minutes, and we're already in line for a register. Before we get to the front, a cashier looks up with a smile. "How's it going, Mr. Shoes?" He looks at the pair of Nikes, the M&M bank, and the bag of toys in his hands. "I need more stuff."

It goes like this for the next ninety minutes. We drive from Goodwill to Goodwill, crisscrossing Tucson, following a route he's made thousands of times. In the stores his routes are just as well-worn: shoes to furniture to appliances to toys, more or less, depending on the layout.

It's usually a successful tack. Tonight, though, there's not much to buy. "This was bad," he says with a shrug as he drives me back to my rental car in the parking lot on West Valencia. "Probably better on the weekend. Tonight was bad, though. Really bad. Should be better this weekend."

"You'll be back?"

"Yeah."

"You'll do something else, too? A movie."

"Nah, too busy."

Shoe Guy doesn't share much personally. He has family in the area and often stays with them. He also likes dogs (he keeps rescue dogs), Bruce Lee, and being recognized by Goodwill cashiers. But that's mentioned only in passing. Instead, the one subject that comes up more than stuff is the volume of time he spends alone. "Hard to have someone if you live like I do, driving around buying stuff, back and forth. I live on the road. I'm free."

CHAPTER 7

Frayed Below the Stitch

Erich Schmidt's windowless office is down the hall from Goodwill Industries of Southern Arizona's e-commerce department, where the most valuable donations—the good stuff—are diverted and sold online (recently, a painting that looked like it was run-of-the-mill went for $24,000). It's around the corner from a warehouse that serves as a busy transit point for the hundreds of thousands of donations that enter and exit Goodwill's system every year. The fortyish blond expatriate Minnesotan choreographs it all via a fleet of trucks that ride waves of items to and from stores, landfills, recycling plants, and the global market in unwanted stuff.

Schmidt, Goodwill Industries of Southern Arizona's vice president of operations, grabs his computer mouse and pulls up spreadsheets. One shows the daily totals of stuff accumulated at donation sites. Another shows the routes that Goodwill trucks will drive that day and what they'll carry or pick up. For example, one truck will be dropping off "product" at a store on Midvale that doesn't get enough donations, before picking up excess donations at another store in an affluent neighborhood. "People call me up from the stores and say, 'I need wares!'"

He laughs. "Oh well, I'll tell the donors!" But he's not joking, entirely. Goodwill chooses its store and donation sites in part on where it expects to receive donations that can feed into stores that don't receive enough. When Schmidt dispatches trucks, he's bridging social and income inequalities.

We walk out to the warehouse. On the right are stacks of computers and monitors that didn't sell in the stores or the outlet. Goodwill sends them to Dell for recycling. Just beyond the computers are three coffee tables that look new. "These are from our Youth Restoration Program," he explains. "The participants fix them up from pieces that were donated but weren't going to sell and were otherwise landfill-bound."

The program started in 2014 and focuses on eighteen- to twenty-four-year-olds who've been through the juvenile justice system or who haven't had much employment experience or the opportunity to develop "soft skills" (like interacting with co-workers). Schmidt, like everyone else at Goodwill Industries of Southern Arizona, adores the program, and he eagerly introduces me to the coordinator and one of the young men finishing up a beautifully restored table. "This one is going to the home show," Schmidt says. "They love us there. People show up and ask if we can restore their stuff, too." He smiles wistfully. "But we're focused on what comes here."

Youth Restoration hearkens back to Goodwill's earliest days, when the mission in Boston employed the city's indigent in collecting and repairing clothes. But just as that program didn't put an end to clothing waste, neither can Goodwill Industries of Southern Arizona's Youth Restoration Program make a dent in the furniture bound for Tucson's—and America's—landfills. The program restores around four thousand pounds of furniture per month; Americans tossed out twenty-five billion pounds of furnishings in 2015. Schmidt points to a pile of furniture near the loading dock. Like everyone else at Goodwill, he hates waste—especially because it costs money to landfill. "It's not bad stuff," he says sheepishly. "But we just don't have room."

"Could you do more restoration?"

He shakes his head. "Our focus is our youth and the mission. Doing more would mean many, many more people, and more space, and more money. This isn't a business. It's a youth program. We want to help them get work. A program like this costs money."

Schmidt isn't dodging the question or the responsibility. More than anybody I've met in secondhand, he's the most visibly tortured by the flood of stuff. Stationed at the intersection of supply and demand, he's also the most realistic. And the fact is, even if every Goodwill and Salvation Army in the United States undertook its own version of the Youth Restoration Program and ran it at triple the size of Southern Arizona's, the collective effort wouldn't swallow 1 percent of the furniture being tossed out across the United States. It would also lose mountains of money, imperiling the social service missions of both organizations.

As we watch one of the young men work a plane across a stripped table, I tell Schmidt that Ikea's head of sustainability recently told a conference that consumers in the West have likely satiated their appetite for new home furnishings, a phenomenon he calls "peak curtains."[1]

Schmidt scoffs. "If the world has enough home furnishings, what's all this stuff doing here?"

We walk out to the loading dock where a truck has just arrived from the Irvington Road outlet for unloading: large boxes of unsold clothes, large boxes of unsold wares, large boxes of metal for recycling, large boxes of cardboard and other paper for recycling, and large boxes of plastic bound for the trash. Some boxes are tipped into larger dumpsters. Plastic waste and the unsold wares go into one bound for landfill.

I lean over the loading dock, peer into it, and see rolled-up carpets, bowling balls (always, bowling balls), board games, broken plates. Steel is dumped into a dumpster bound for a scrapyard. It contains a tangle of bed frames.

Schmidt stops beside a box containing scrap metal and pulls out a newish frying pan. "If I had a spare guy to sort, I could sell lots of this stuff in the store. People ask about this all of the time—can't we do it? But it's a cost-benefit thing. And devoting labor to it doesn't make sense financially."

We stand at the edge of the dock and gaze to a fence line where boxes and bales of items bound for the "salvage market," the term the thrift industry uses for export markets, are stacked and awaiting shipment. There are boxes of shoes, boxes of stuffed animals, and boxes of books. And, in the greatest volume, there are five-hundred-pound bales of used clothing. These looming, multicolored cubes are packed with items donated with the best of intentions. But the best of intentions, alone, can't sell clothes, and more than half the apparel that arrives at Goodwill is unsold. Schmidt's address book is filled with Pakistani, Indian, and Nigerian traders who call him regularly in search of product.

"Everything is based on textiles," Schmidt tells me. "In a good month, we export four hundred thousand pounds." The benefits are twofold. First, the clothes are used rather than landfilled. Second, exporting to traders who pay for the clothes is cheaper than sending them to the landfill. In recent years, the salvage market was a Goodwill "profit center." But that's changing quickly as more and more used clothes flood the global markets, driving down the prices. "Right now, it still costs us less to ship to overseas [because the clothes are sold and generate revenue] than to ship to a landfill."

That raises a question: "Would you landfill clothes?"

He shakes his head vigorously. "It'll remain a cost for us, and that's a mostly good thing. Someone overseas can always use it. For us the big question is where is all this gonna go, because there's so much of it."

And it's growing.

Used Clothing Exports occupies a series of rooms at one end of a generic single-story office building on Tomken Road in Mississauga, Ontario. It's a few miles from Toronto and oceans away from the billions of emerging-market consumers who rely on secondhand clothes. But it's here in Mississauga that perhaps as much as one third of the used clothing generated in Canada and the United States is sorted, priced, and shipped by so-called graders. It's one of the world's biggest hubs for the purchase and sale of used clothing. Yet outside the secondhand industry, the fewer than twenty companies that constitute it are largely unknown.

Inside the office, Mohammad Faisal Moledina serves me milk tea and samosas at his desk. He's a handsome man in his midforties, with well-coiffed, carefully tended hair and tired eyes. He wears a shiny gray suit. His mother-in-law is arriving from Dubai later, he tells me, and preparations have been stressful. Seated to his right, at an identical desk and chair, is his father, Abdul Majid Moledina, the princely, portly bearded man who founded the company. These days, father and son have the same title on their business cards: director.

Mohammad takes a call, so Abdul beckons for me to come around his desk to look at his computer screen. He's scrolling through a website showing images of workers—they look South Asian—sorting through hills of used clothing. "You should go there," he says. "Panipat."

It's a town in northern India that's home to the world's largest concentration of clothing recyclers. "Have you been?" I ask.

"We have Pakistani passports."

"Right," I say with a cringe. The Moledinas emigrated from Pakistan to Canada decades ago, but historic tensions between Pakistan and India make it difficult for citizens from their respective countries to visit. Despite these awkward facts, the Moledinas are doing just fine. Every year Used Clothing Exports buys sixty million to seventy million pounds of used clothes from charities and companies in North America (Goodwill Industries of Southern Arizona has been a client) and sells them onward to "graders," who sort, price, and pack them for sale around the world.

Mohammad continues his phone conversation, so Abdul decides to surprise me. He reaches for a pair of jeans on a shelf and places them on a desk. The tag reads, 501 ORIGINAL. QUALITY NEVER GOES OUT OF STYLE. But this apparent pair of Levi's is actually tagged LIVE'S.

"Do you see it?" Abdul asks.

"Yes."

"In Pakistan, they refurbish these."

"Refurbish?"

He picks up a leg and points to the hem. "See how it's uneven and frayed below the stitch? That was done in a factory. They imported these used from somewhere, washed and dyed them, and then fixed the flaws." He reaches for a men's dress shirt in clear plastic wrap and a pair of men's green khakis. "Same with these," he says. "Then they export them to dollar stores." He tells me the name and location of a store in Mississauga that sells garments like these.

"Seriously?"

His laugh is deep and confident. The joke is on me, the naive representative of the developed world's consumers. And I feel gullible. Pakistan is one of the world's largest importers of used clothes, home to thousands of secondhand traders and tens of millions of secondhand consumers. Surely there are sharp-eyed entrepreneurs among them who can spot the garments that can be transformed into "new" from the billions that can't. In fact, it's far more likely that such entrepreneurs exist in developing countries like Pakistan, where secondhand is a way of life, than in wealthy regions, where the law is likely to view "new" as "fraud."

Mohammad finishes his phone call and announces that we can go to see a clothing grader. He ushers me out of the office and into his Mercedes-Benz. It smells of cigarettes and is cluttered with stuff that he has to clear off the passenger seat. "I hope you don't mind, but we're going to a small plant, maybe fifty employees."

"What's a big plant?"

"Three hundred employees and twenty million dollars monthly in turnover. Two hundred thousand pounds per day."

Officially, around four million tons of used clothes are exported around the world every year. Unofficially, the trade is much larger. In India, where the import of secondhand clothes has been banned for more a decade, imported secondhand clothes are available everywhere, including markets visible from the seats of government in Delhi and Mumbai. In West African cities like Accra, Lomé, and Cotonou, imported secondhand-clothing stores and stalls are typically more common than stores selling new clothes.

Mohammad notices his fuel gauge is low and pulls into a gas station. While fueling, he lights a cigarette and takes a phone call; I watch as he ashes into a trash can next to the pump. Then we're on our way, and he's pointing out where the various textile-grading houses are located in Mississauga. "Back there," he says, gesturing at a warehouse behind a Tim Horton's. "One of the bigger ones."

"Why are all these clothing graders in Mississauga?" I ask.

"It's an immigrant-friendly city." And for decades, Canada has been an immigrant-friendly country. Toronto, as Canada's biggest city, attracted many of those immigrants. But when Toronto became too expensive, neighboring Mississauga beckoned. Neither Mohammad nor anyone else with whom I've spoken agrees on who the first immigrant with secondhand-clothing experience to settle in the city was. But everyone agrees it was either a Pakistani or an Indian with a decades-old family connection to the business. At some point in the 1970s or early 1980s, that South Asian immigrant trader met an African immigrant keen to export used clothes home.

Mississauga's long, cold winters also helped, ensuring that the area's summer clothes are worn briefly, and lightly. As a result, secondhand summer clothes from Canada (and northern Europe) are priced at a premium in the hot countries that are the biggest consumers of secondhand clothes. That price premium gives Canadian clothing graders and traders an advantage when competing for clothes elsewhere. Combine this advantage with large numbers of immigrants looking for low-skilled jobs, and Mississauga becomes an ideal—if unlikely—location for a global recycling hub.

Mohammad lived in Pakistan and Dubai, and he says he prefers Canada. "Life is real here." In Pakistan and Dubai, he claims, people are too worried about status. "Here, if I wear a Rolex or a nice suit, it's because I like it."

That brings to mind a question. "Do you wear secondhand clothes?"

"I don't. Nothing against it, I just don't."

Over the years, critics of the globalized secondhand-clothing trade allege that it undermines textile industries in developing regions, especially in Africa. It's a potent claim that has intuitive power. Africa is the largest market for secondhand clothes globally, and has been for several decades. Meanwhile, its textile industries have declined precipitously since the 1980s. In the Democratic Republic of the Congo, for example, textile production dropped by 83 percent between 1990 and 1996. In Nigeria, Africa's most populous country, a textile industry that employed as many as two hundred thousand in the 1970s has dwindled to almost nothing. In Kenya, home to some of the world's largest secondhand-clothing markets, a textile industry that employed as many as five hundred thousand people in the 1980s now employs fewer than fifty thousand.

Geographers and other academics have created a small industry to prove the claim. Of these, the most prominent is Garth Frazier, a Canadian academic. In 2008 he analyzed used-clothing trade data compiled by the United Nations and concluded that used-clothing exports explain "roughly 40% of the decline in African apparel production and roughly 50% of the decline in apparel employment."[2] Frazier's claim has migrated well beyond the academic journals and is now regularly cited in mainstream media, by anti-globalization activists, and, most notably, by the kind of well-meaning sustainable-clothing advocates who'd ordinarily cheer for mass use of secondhand over new products.

There's no question that secondhand is often a replacement for new (not nearly enough, in my view). But quantifying those replacements is extremely difficult, even in developed countries where tax and trade data allow for analysis. In developing regions like sub-Saharan Africa, where governments struggle to compile reliable data and statistics, it's almost impossible.[3] Countries that are known to be major importers of secondhand clothing—like Benin, Togo, Ghana, Tanzania, and Mozambique—have sporadic trade data of any kind. Most of the data they have is focused on the kinds of goods that attract additional overseas investment and aid (that is, new stuff). And obviously, they don't have data on the considerable volume of secondhand clothing smuggled between African countries (especially between tiny Benin, a global secondhand smuggling hub, and Nigeria).

Simplistic explanations built on what seem like logical correlations—used must undermine new!—don't do justice to the complex, very human reasons that individual consumers make specific choices. It's true that Africa's textile and new clothing industries underwent a significant decline beginning in the mid-1970s. But that period also encompassed an era in which Africa's cotton production declined just as precipitously as its textile manufacturing, thanks to land reforms, political frictions, war, and—most recently—climate change. It also encompasses an era of economic liberalization that opened up Africa's economies to competition from Asia (the same region that undermined the North American and European textile industries). By 2005, exports from fast-growing Asian textile and clothing manufacturers to Africa were growing even more rapidly than they were to Europe and the United States. The resulting competition devastated African manufacturers and lowered incomes across the continent.[4]

Nonetheless, incomplete trade data alone doesn't do justice to these phenomena. Instead, the individual seeking out what actually happened to Africa's textile industry must go there and meet the people who live with it. Since the mid-2000s, Ghana's labor-union leadership has blamed two related phenomena for the decline of the country's once-thriving textile industry: pirating of Ghanaian brands and styles by low-cost Chinese firms and the large-scale evasion of Ghanaian custom duties by East Asian exporters.[5] They have a point. For example, production of kente cloth, the colorful Ghanaian fabric once exported around Africa and the world, employed thirty thousand people as recently as the 1980s. Since then, Chinese counterfeits have flooded the market and devastated producers (Ghanaian kente manufacturers employ fewer than three thousand today).[6] At Ghanaian markets, buyers can expect to pay far more for locally produced, and so naturally opt for low-cost Chinese imports. The situation for Ghanaian kente producers is so dire that a government-sponsored initiative to encourage people to wear traditional Ghanaian clothes on Fridays is widely derided as a jobs program for the Chinese.[7]

If you view used clothing as an extension of Western colonialism, East Asian entrepreneurialism is a far less satisfying explanation for why Ghana's textile industry has declined by 80 percent over the last few decades. But it's a better one.

Of course, given a choice, most Africans—like people everywhere—would prefer new. But all consumers make a rational decision about value and what they can afford. Secondhand, in most cases, wins.

Mohammad Faisal Moledina takes a hard right on Dusty Drive and pulls into the almost-empty parking lot of Maple Textiles's large yellow warehouse. Next door, Mohammad notes, is another South Asian–owned clothing grader. But we're here for Maple Textiles, and he walks to the door with the confidence of an important customer. We're met at the door by Yusuf, a gangly member of the family that owns the company.

Inside, the offices are empty, and the largest room is dim, with just a desk, a few chairs, and two tables. We pass everything quickly, as Yusuf recounts that he's spent two decades living in Uganda, Angola, and Congo, working in the used-clothing business. According to him, and to Mohammad, those experiences are a competitive advantage. "I know how to choose the clothes that Africans want."

Yusuf opens a door and we walk into a three-story warehouse and an explosion of colorful textiles that dozens of workers sort and stuff into cardboard barrels and boxes. A black conveyor belt runs through the middle of the space, between the far gray cinderblock wall where hundreds of neatly packed, fifty-five-kilogram bundles of sorted clothing are stacked almost to the ceiling. The fifty-five-kilogram

The sorting room at Maple Textiles, a medium-sized secondhand clothing trader outside of Toronto. The region is one of the world's hubs for the secondhand textile trade.

bundle is an industry standard embraced around the world, made in machines that compresses loose clothes into cubes (occasionally leaving a sleeve hanging loose). Thanks to all the fabric, sound is muffled and buffeted. Voices go dead.

Maple Textiles is a lot of clothes, that's for sure. It's also a lot of different kinds of people: South Asians, Sikh men, two Spanish-speaking women, Africans, several women in hijabs. They eye me warily and turn away.

We walk between the barrels and boxes, toward the conveyor belt, which is slowly running clothes delivered in large, loose five-hundred-pound bales. The clothes are pulled and graded into smaller—and finer—categories. "First we sort into boxes," Yusuf says. "Then our more experienced employees sort into barrels." He pulls a pinstripe Abercrombie & Fitch dress shirt from a box. "This is B-grade because of the yellow collar, and it needs to be washed. So it'll go into a B-grade bundle and be sold for less."

We stare into a barrel of clothes that Yusuf calls "number three." Most are torn and feel thin and cheap. "That's sent for rags," he says. "Wiping rags."

Mohammad pulls a green velvet evening dress from a box. It looks expensive and as if it has never been worn. "What about this?"

"Tricky," Yusuf says. "The dress looks great, but it's too heavy for Africa's heat. B-grade, too."

It occurs to me that I've seen this before: the grading process is basically a more detailed version of the sorting and pricing that I witnessed in the back of the Goodwill on South Houghton. Only instead of grading for Tucson's secondhand customers, Mississauga grades and prices for Africa and other developing markets. And Africa's, it turns out, are more discerning.

We walk over to a stack of neat clothing bales that have been sorted and await shipment. Each bale is covered in cellophane and affixed with a yellow label that displays a bar code and a category: LADIES FASHION T-SHIRT.

"What's that sell for?" I ask.

"Maybe sixty dollars," Yusuf says. "And then whoever buys it will sell each of the T-shirts for fifteen, twenty cents. If they're lucky, there'll be something in there that they can sell for more and that'll make the whole bale worth it." For the next five minutes, Yusuf points at bales and explains the markets. A bundle of baby clothes sells for an extravagant dollar per pound because they're in high demand but generally aren't donated to charities. "People hand them down to others, or they're too soiled." A bale of hospital uniforms, mostly made up of washed scrubs, goes for fifty to sixty cents per pound. "The low end of the business is getting harder because of China," he says. "They're starting to export their old clothes to Africa. Hard to compete with that, and all the new clothes they send, too."

"China is sending used clothes to Africa?"

"Of course."

I should have known. China is the world's biggest consumer of new apparel. If the Chinese start throwing away at the same rate as Americans, the price of secondhand clothes is in trouble. The flood has already started: according to the United Nations' imperfect data, China is the world's fifth biggest exporter of used clothes, behind the United States, the U.K., Germany, and South Korea, and ahead of affluent countries like Canada, the Netherlands, and Sweden. Because China's export data is often flawed, or distorted by smuggling, the numbers could be much higher. Either way, traders around the world complain that growing supplies and shrinking demand are lowering prices.

But China's rising affluence isn't the only shift that threatens Mississauga. Back in the car, Mohammad tells me that Canada's increasing labor costs, partly driven by a law that raises the minimum wage, are pushing the grading businesses to Pakistan. "It's the difference between three hundred dollars per month for a grader and fifteen hundred dollars per month. If the price of the clothes was rising, it wouldn't matter. But the price is falling."

It occurs to me that somebody will have to pay for that shipping; and in the case of less valuable items, it won't make sense to export them at all. I think of Tucson and Erich Schmidt's salvage yard. "That'll mean less reuse, won't it?"

"Maybe," Mohammad says slowly.

*   *   *

At Maple Textiles, bales of sorted secondhand clothes will soon be loaded into shipping containers and bound for markets in Africa.

Wide avenues cross Cotonou, capital of the small West African nation of Benin. Single-story storefronts are obscured by tire tubes, automobile exhaust manifolds, mufflers, automotive wax, and other car accessories devoted to servicing the city's thriving used-car trade. Bars with outdoor seating serve Pils, a beer made in neighboring Togo, and skewers of meat. And here and there, handful of stores sell new home goods like bedsheets and curtains.

Turn off one of the boulevards and the smooth, paved road usually gives way to a dry dirt one and shops and stalls selling or sorting recently imported secondhand goods. The secondhand-clothing businesses grow particularly dense in a section of town known as Missebo, on the west side of the Cotonou Canal, which cuts the city in half. Shirts, dresses, and other garments hang from fences erected around stalls or on storefronts; shoes hang loose, like fish from hooks. All around, bicycles with trailers, trucks with trailers, and men with strong backs carry fifty-five-kilogram bales of clothes down the street.

I am here with Michael Ogbonna, a fortyish Nigerian who makes his living in Cotonou's enormous used-car markets on the east side of town. By some estimates, more than three hundred thousand used cars from around the world are imported into this dusty port town annually. Some are bought by locals. But the majority are destined for Nigerians who don't want to pay the high duties on cars (and other secondhand goods) directly imported into Nigeria. So budget-conscious Nigerians travel to Cotonou and pay someone like Michael to help them buy a car and clear it through the porous and corrupt Benin-Nigeria border crossing east of town (on a normal day, someone crossing the border can expect to spend several hours, pay off five or six people—and still come out ahead).

Nobody knows for sure how much commerce moves across the border between Benin and Nigeria. The World Bank estimates that it could exceed $5 billion annually. And secondhand goods are almost certainly the biggest piece, almost entirely due to Nigeria's harsh restrictions on secondhand imports, including cars, computers, televisions, and clothes. Second place? Most likely counterfeit Chinese textiles worth as much as $2.2 billion annually.[8] By most measures, in fact, Cotonou is Nigerian in all but name. Everyone—even those in the government—acknowledges that more than half the population at any given moment is Nigerian and engaged in some aspect of the illegal cross-border trade. Some of Cotonou's Nigerians are longtime settlers, having fled Nigeria during the country's civil war in the late 1960s and never returned. And others, like Michael, go back and forth; his wife and children live on the other side.

Thanks to Nigerians on both sides of the border, Cotonou's export business runs day and night (and the Beninese government, knowing a good thing when it sees it, does little to regulate the trade). But occasionally the Nigerian government will intervene, and the trade will slow for weeks or months. That's one of the reasons Michael is working with me as a paid translator and fixer; two weeks earlier, Nigeria imposed new restrictions on the movement of used cars, all but halting business at the Cotonou car markets (it would pick up again a few months later). He is a tall man with a round, bald head and eyes that squint as if he's always scrutinizing a deal. He's well read on current events and vocally opinionated. Obama, he considers a failure; Trump, a "real man." And secondhand goods, he insists, are better than new.

As we walk, he pulls at his shirt. "This is secondhand." He tugs at his pants. "These are secondhand." He takes out a Samsung phone from Verizon. "Secondhand," he huffs. "Americans are trained. They're trained. Something new, they get rid of the old one. Put it out for recycling, don't even care. Give it away. Maybe a charity makes a little money for the office."

I glance down at his feet. He's wearing a pair of new brown suede shoes. Yesterday, he was wearing a pair of old Nike running shoes. In between, I paid him.

"Why do Nigerians want secondhand?" he asks rhetorically. "Because it's durable. The Chinese things we import? They break, wear out!" He stops and cycles through photos on his phone. "Look," he orders, and shows me photos of racks of used clothes and shoes—I spot a Goodwill logo on the wall behind them. "They load up containers of this stuff," he exclaims. "You could make huge money in Nigeria."

I want to tell him it's not so easy, that the prices associated with those racks far exceed what can be obtained in Cotonou (the stuff that fails to sell off those racks is another matter). But when he looks around

Missebo, his eyes superimpose a Goodwill store where everything is nearly free for the taking.

"Hey! Hey!"

A compact, wiry man is waving to us from his perch on a red plastic chair beside three bales of clothes. Behind him is an open warehouse door revealing dozens more bales.

"Today is Thursday," Michael reminds me, dismissing him. "Tuesday and Thursday are the days that everyone puts out their bales to market."

But the man in the door is determined to meet us, and he races over. He is Mr. A (he asks that I not use his name, for fear of trouble with the tax authorities), a secondhand importer, grader, and wholesaler. His smile is toothy and underlined by a mean tuft of a goatee. He assumes I'm a Western exporter of secondhand clothes and speaks to me in English. Michael says something to him in Igbo, the native language of the East Nigerian ethnic group that dominates the secondhand trade across West Africa. Mr. A smiles and invites us to have a seat in front of his shop (later I ask Michael what he said, but he won't tell me).

As we settle into plastic chairs, Mr. A offers me a bottle of cold water. "I've been in this shop five years," he says by way of introduction. I glance into the warehouse, where two women are carefully examining two bales of clothes amid an inventory of at least two hundred additional bales. Mr. A tells me that he purchases five shipping containers of clothing per week—when the Nigerian currency is strong. "But now less, due to the economy."

"What kinds of clothes?"

"We are interested in importing durable clothes, not cheap ones. If someone in the West has worn something and it comes here, it's probably durable."

"Even if it's made in China."

"Not everything from China is bad. Just what the Chinese send to Africa is bad. They save the good things for rich countries."

It's a common sentiment among secondhand-goods traders in Africa, and there's some truth to it. China's manufacturers long ago mastered techniques for manufacturing similar goods to sell at a profit at different price points. A fashionable shirt, one made to the quality standards expected in the United States and sold for $29.99 there, can be made for much lower quality standards (lower thread counts, for example) and can sell—profitably—for $2.99 in Cotonou. The quality of the fabric and the stitching won't be nearly as good. But it will be new and fashionable, and for many consumers that matters more than durability.

"What about used Chinese clothes?"

"So much inferior. I don't import it. This is what I need." He reaches for a clipboard with two pieces of paper. The top is labeled PROFORMA INVOICE and details a load of 480 bales that he's just imported, spread over 64 categories. Under HOUSEHOLD ITEMS are 10 bales of bedsheets and 10 bales of curtains; under CHILDREN ITEMS are 18 bales of children's T-shirts and 2 bales of boys' track suits; under LADIES ITEMS are 3 bales of ladies' polyester-silk skirts and 10 of ladies' cotton skirts. Some categories are even more granular.

"Canadian clothes are good," he tells me. "But I don't want the big sizes, and I don't want winter. What I want you can get at the Salvation Army, the Goodwill. I have a guy in Canada, a Beninese. It's easy."

On December 10, 1974, the *New York Times* published a curious article under the headline DECLINING QUALITY IN CLOTHES: THE MAKERS AND SELLERS TELL WHY. The author, Enid Nemy, opened by noting a now-forgotten mid-1970s grievance:

An increasing number of consumers are complaining about a deterioration in quality—food doesn't taste the same, automobiles don't last as long, appliances collapse, the list is endless.

The fashion industry is no exception.

At the time, the United States was the source of most goods consumed by Americans. Hong Kong, then under the jurisdiction of the United Kingdom, made and exported some garments (including, reportedly, garments smuggled from China). But the overall total was too small to impact U.S. manufacturers and consumers. The notion that China, still bogged down by the violent Cultural Revolution, might one day disrupt the global economic order was preposterous.

Nemy didn't point fingers at others for what she characterized as a plague of "poor fit, inferior fabrics and shoddy workmanship." Instead, she provided room for four American apparel manufacturing and retailing veterans to explain it. Their conclusion, as summarized by Nemy, was that "quality generally has been declining since World War [II] and that what had been expediency at the time had now become a way of life."

She reported several factors accounting for the decades-long descent: a lack of product inspectors, "a dwindling supply of skilled labor," a shift to piecework (making collars only, for example, while another factory makes cuffs) rather than whole-garment manufacturing, and—most notably—the relentless march of fashion. Paul Heller, then president of the Carr Buying Office, a company that purchased goods on behalf of hundreds of shops and department stores around the United States, spoke of the latter in terms that will be familiar to contemporary critics of fast fashion:

HELLER: There's no question that our poorest quality comes from the hot fashions fad manufacturer. No doubt about it. And yet there is, particularly in young junior areas, an enormous consumer demand for this type of fashion.

Are you saying that a good deal of the fault is due to consumer acceptance of poor quality?

HELLER: No question. She is the final arbiter. And for every garment that is returned there may be 10 others that should have been returned but the customer manages to live with it because she wants that look on her back. She loves the dress.

The global dominance of China's textile manufacturers didn't happen for another fifteen years. Arguably, fast fashion wouldn't happen for another twenty. But viewed from 1974, it's difficult to argue that China's "cheap" clothing is a recent phenomenon. Rather, it's an evolution in customer tolerance that began with the industrial revolution. Thanks to technology, improved logistics, and entrepreneurial know-how, China—and East Asian manufacturing in general—has managed to do it better than anybody else.

Will Africa's consumers be the first to turn against the deteriorating quality of clothing? Probably not. Chinese textile exports to Africa have been growing for decades, and several African countries, including Rwanda and Ethiopia, are eager hosts to Chinese apparel manufacturers. Secondhand clothes remain dominant, thanks to the sophisticated ability of traders to match garments to African tastes and pricing. But if the history of mass-produced clothing is any guide, that advantage is a temporary one.

Mr. A leads me and Michael down a dirt road surrounded on two sides by shoe vendors and a handful of clothing warehouses packed with bales. Along the way, we pass two men pulling handcarts piled with garbage and watch a garbage truck dump its full load into the middle of the street. "People pay the driver so they can sort through it," Michael tells me. "Then they have to reload it when they're done." At the end of the street is a channel to the ocean, piles of garbage, and more garbage trucks.

Mr. A tells me that his biggest challenge is sorting the containers of clothes that he imports. The graders in North America and Europe do a good job, but he needs to do his own sort for his Nigerian customers. "A full container, I can sort it in a day and a half or two days."

At that, he leads us to a two-story warehouse with five truck-sized doors. Two are open, though they're barred by individual locked gates. On the front of the building is a small sign: STE LEXCO ANNEXE. Mr. A speaks softly to someone on the other side of one gate, who nods and unlocks it for us.

Inside, it's dark and stifling. The only light comes from windows high above us, its beams falling through clothing fibers onto five-hundred-kilogram bales of used clothes imported from around the world. There are perhaps fifty men here; most are shirtless, and their faces are obscured by pantyhose wrapped around their noses to filter out the textile fibers thick in the air. They are muscular men glistening with sweat, their shoulders and arms toned from the exhausting act of digging through the weight of giant bales of clothes. As my eyes adjust, the room appears mostly black and blue, thanks to the volume of denim.

Jeans are stacked up to the high windows, and workers sort them into smaller piles. I watch one man sorting; branded Levi's get piled atop the edge of a cardboard refrigerator box. He has two other piles, but I can't tell what the distinction is. He dips his hands into the pockets of jeans as he sorts, pulling out whatever he finds. As I'm about to walk deeper into the warehouse, I see him pull a small container of dental floss from a pocket. He turns it around in his hand, examining it, then drops it into a box of other pocket detritus.

One thing is immediately obvious to me: this warehouse in Missebo is in the same business as those in Mississauga, and in Goodwill's back-of-the-store sorting areas. Working conditions are far worse, of course. But the knowledge necessary to work here is much greater. There are no signs on the walls telling people what brands are worth sorting into which pile. Instead, the Nigerian men who toil in Ste Lexco Annexe must have a combination of instinct and base knowledge for what makes a marketable garment in the cities, towns, and villages of West Africa.

Mr. A gestures for me to leave. The warehouse manager is visibly uncomfortable with my presence. As we step outside, the daylight and the unpolluted air make me light-headed. "Is that typical?" I ask Mr. A.

He nods. "More than one hundred sorting and grading warehouses in Cotonou."

"People don't mind it?"

A typical sorting warehouse in Cotonou, Benin, staffed by Nigerian day labor familiar with the secondhand clothing market back home.

"Why should they? Most of the warehouses employ one hundred and fifty to two hundred men. When a container arrives in Cotonou, word gets out through our social networks, and people come to work." By "social network," he doesn't mean Facebook, but rather physical social networks that have been accelerated by text messages sent via the cheap feature phones everyone in Cotonou seems to carry. Hours are fairly standard: seven or eight A.M. until noon, and then one thirty P.M. until five or six. A day's pay is around ten thousand Central African francs, or sixteen dollars. It's good money.

"I started as a sorter," he says. "Many years ago."

I look him up and down. His compact physique is quite different from the long, strong bodies I saw inside. But surely, if you are going to be a trader in secondhand clothes, it helps to have spent hours sorting through the clothes that arrive on Benin's shores.

"We are picky in Africa," he says. "We don't want garbage. We want fashion. We want quality. Not your garbage."

"Do people send garbage?"

His mouth stretches into a mean, toothy smile. "Not if they want to be paid. They learn what we will take. We are not a dump."

That's an opinion at odds with fashionable Western perceptions and critiques of the secondhand-clothing trade. Instead of viewing it as an exchange of goods driven by African demand, Western critics tend to view it as an exchange between the savvy and the ignorant. Take, for example, Whitney Mallett, a documentary filmmaker who wrote about the secondhand-clothing trade for the *New Republic* in 2015.[9] She describes visiting a New Jersey grading plant with Michael Zweig, the plant's manager:

> By far, the most common labels here that I see are Forever 21 and H&M, fated for the cheap pile. "Nobody is stupid enough

to buy Forever 21 second-hand," notes Zweig. No one in the
developed world, anyway.

Mallett's "no one in the developed world" isn't just bigoted. It's blind
to how much value is created when less affluent people are given the
opportunity to parse the goods of the wasteful affluent. The grading
warehouses of Cotonou exist because sorters and graders in New Jersey
(or Mississauga) don't know enough about Nigeria and the tastes of its
consumers to sort clothes for them. That doesn't make New Jersey's
clothing graders stupid. It just means they're underinformed compared
with their developing-world counterparts. In Cotonou, a clothing buyer
doesn't need to see a Forever 21 tag to know it's cheap; a simple pinch
of the fabric will send it to the heavily discounted pile. Somebody might,
in fact, buy it; but nobody will overpay.

Just ask Mr. A. He's standing in the back room of another sorting
warehouse. This one belongs to him. It's roughly the same size as the
one we visited earlier, but brighter and largely empty. A few fifty-five-
kilogram bales are pressed against the far wall beneath a sign that says
TINIES, and—higher up—a U.S. flag that hangs upside down. On the
opposite wall, under the sign TROUSERS, are a dozen to-be-sorted
bales; and next to it is the sign B/W, with two graders working through
piles of women's blouses recently released from imported bales. "They
separate the lighter ones from the heavier ones," explains Mr. A. "The
prices are different."

"How do you tell?"

"Feel!"

He gestures for me and Michael to follow him into a room behind
the six-foot-tall baling machine. It's filled to the ceiling with heavy-duty
plastic bags of clothes. He pulls a clear one filled with bras toward us.
"It only has forty-eight kilos in it," he says. "We're waiting for more so

we can make a fifty-five-kilo bale." He pulls out a very modest-size red lace bra of no particular distinction (to my eyes, at least). "This won't sell. In Africa, we have fashion," Mr. A spits. "No African woman will wear this." He pulls out a silky pink negligee and sneers. "In Europe, they might wear this. But here? No way."

Five Star Rags is housed in a brown brick building beneath a flight path into Toronto Pearson International Airport in Mississauga. It's in an industrial neighborhood, with buildings that could cover city blocks, parking lots that could house neighborhoods, and at least one strip club, located just around the corner. As I step out of my rental car, a jet roars overhead; the rumble makes me feel like I'm experiencing a low-grade earthquake.

I pull open the glass front door and walk into the stripped-down reception area that I've come to associate with Mississauga's low-profile clothing graders. Amid the dim light and empty room, there's an unexpected flash: a receptionist in a bright blue sari. "Ashif will be with you in a minute. Excuse me," she says and picks up the phone. "Five Star Rags." Pause. "What country are you calling from? Zambia? Your name?"

Like most of Mississauga's South Asian clothing graders, Five Star Rags has a decades-long, globe-spanning, and family-connected history. This plant opened in the 1990s and is run by the brother of the owner of a Five Star Rags in India's Gujarat state. Family members work in East Africa, home to the company's biggest markets, as well as India and Canada.

One of them, a portly, fortyish man, emerges from the office beside the receptionist's desk. He has a firm handshake, a friendly presence, and the slow walk of someone who has seen more trouble than Five Star

Rags can ever present to him. "I'm Ashif Dhalwani," he says. There's not much in the way of small talk. He simply leads me through an adjoining door and into the sorting warehouse. It's a big one, perhaps two and a half times the size of the Maple Textiles warehouse. "I started working here in 1998," he says. "Before that, I went to college and lived in Mombasa."

"Were you born there?"

"Uganda. That's where I learned the business." He waves his hand over the colorful scene spread out before us. "You've seen this kind of thing before." True, but Five Star Rags is far bigger than anyplace else I've visited. Multiple conveyors move clothes from one type of bale to another and into bins, where the various garments are sorted. In this bigger warehouse, sorted clothes are dumped into large bays to await shipment. According to Ashif, Five Star Rags sorts 120,000 to 150,000 pounds of clothing per day. He reaches into a box and pulls out a flannel shirt. "This is polyester, and grade B because there's a flaw somewhere, a hole probably. It's dumped."

"Dumped?"

"You can't recycle poly, and nobody wants to buy it for use as a rag." He shrugs. "We have to dump it." The destination isn't in Africa or another developing country. Instead, it's the far cheaper option: a local landfill or incinerator.

Ashif leads me to two boxes filled with children's clothes. "Light children's clothing," he says, and points to the other. "Medium children's clothing." Next to them is a barrel of fleece pullovers. "They won't get used in Africa," he says. "But they'll get used. Maybe as rags for the auto industry. Or as stuffing for furniture. We sell to both."

A pile of blue jeans runs six feet high against a far wall. "No market for old jeans."

"They aren't Levi's?"

"No."

"What are they?"

"Cheap stuff from Costco. Frayed and not fashionable. The fabric is too rough, and nobody can use them as rags or anything else. There was a company that invented a process for recycling them. They went under. So these get dumped."

In my experience, nobody in the secondhand-clothing industry likes to talk about the end of clothes. But there is an end. The only question is *when*. The lives of some garments can be extended as wiping rags or as furniture stuffing. But an oily rag at the oil-change service center will eventually land in a disposal bin. For now, at least, the recycling of textiles is expensive and at the edge of the technologically feasible. "We need more textile recycling," Ashif says to me. "Long term, reuse is dead. China is undercutting us."

Ashif says that even the good-quality textiles sometimes fail to find a market these days. That makes him work harder. For example, Levi's that once had a vintage market are now shipped to Bangkok, where workers cut away the buttons and zippers to be sold to the makers of fake Levi's.

And nobody is dumb enough to *over*pay for secondhand Forever 21. "Africa is not a dump yard anymore," he tells me. "It used to be you could take the good stuff and send it to South America and the rest to Africa. But that's back when the markets were in the villages. Now it's in the cities, and thanks to urbanization and social media, people know quality."

We wander out of the warehouse and into his office. A large map of the world hangs on the wall his desk is pressed against. In recent weeks, the seven countries of the East African Community, collectively the largest secondhand-clothing market in the world, have been touting a planned ban on the import of secondhand clothes. Ashif smiles when

I bring it up. "There is no way that Africans will stop buying used clothing unless they start walking around naked."

"But if governments start blocking—"

He shakes his head. "There's always a way."

Later, as I drive away, it occurs to me that even if Ashif's customers find "a way"—like a porous border crossing—what's ultimately in store for secondhand clothing is a dump, and perhaps a recycling technology yet to be invented. Eventually, this most sustainable of industries will be out of fashion.

CHAPTER 8

Good as New

The two-story cutting room at Star Wipers fills with a soft, mechanical hum. Roughly twenty middle-aged women and a handful of men stand at workstations circled by six-foot-tall plastic bins full of used clothes and sheets. In the middle, Amity Bounds, one of the last professional American rag cutters, grabs a pink hoodie with a sparkly print across the chest that reads JUSTICE LOVE JUSTICE. Like her co-workers, she stands six inches from a tea-saucer-size blade that spins at chest-level, behind a guard with three small gaps. With a butcher's precision, Bounds slips the hoodie into one of the gaps, cuts off the hood, then slices it twice so that it lays flat. Next, she cuts off the zipper and tosses it into a waste bin; she cuts off the sparkly print ("it's abrasive and no good for wiping anything") and tosses it, too. The remaining sweatshirt offers little resistance; she slices once, twice, three times, transforming it from garment to rags.

"It took me a year to learn all of the products and learn to cut them," Bounds volunteers as she tosses the sweatshirt fillets into a barrel filled with fresh-cut rags.

"How long have you worked here?" I ask.

"Ten years."

Few consumers, anywhere, have heard of the wiping rag industry. But it bails out everyone. Approximately 30 percent of the textiles recovered for recycling in the United States are converted to wiping rags, according to Secondary Materials and Recycled Textiles: the Association of Wiping Materials, Used Clothing, and Fiber Industries (SMART), a U.S.-based trade association. And that's probably an undercount. The 45 percent of recycled textiles that are reused as apparel eventually wear out, too. When they do, they're also bound for the wiping rag companies.

Nobody counts the number of wiping rags manufactured in the United States and elsewhere every year. But anyone who knows the industry acknowledges that the numbers are in the many billions, and growing. The oil and gas industry, with its network of pipes and valves, requires hundreds of millions of rags per year to wipe leaks, lubricants, and hands. Hotels, bars, and restaurants need billions of rags to wipe everything from glasses to tabletops to railings. Auto manufacturers need rags to wipe down cars as they come off the assembly line; repair garages need rags to clean off dipsticks after oil changes; car washes need them to apply wax. Painters need them to wipe brushes, spills, and drips. And the healthcare industry demands endless numbers of rags to keep hospitals and clinics clean and sanitary. If these businesses can't reuse clothes and sheets, they'll opt for disposable paper towels, synthetic wipes, and new cloth rags, complete with all their environmental and financial costs. (For years, the disposable-wiper industry has marketed its throwaway wipers as an efficient, modern upgrade from traditional rags.*) Decades before environmental organizations

---

*   For example, Kimberly-Clark, a U.S. manufacturer of personal care products, markets its professional-grade Wypall disposable rags in a campaign titled "Who Would You Hire?" In one advertisement, a handsome, well-dressed Wypall representative engages in a tug-of-war with a short, fat, sweaty, and greasy man in a soiled tank top, who represents rags.

and governments encouraged reuse, recycling, and circular economies, the wiping rags industry had mastered the art.

Todd Wilson, the wiry, fifty-eight-year-old vice president of Star Wipers, stands beside me, watching Amity with rapt attention. "Did you see how many multiple cuts she did?" he asks with excitement. "Every time she runs it through the blade"—he stops to compose himself and then declares loudly: "Our competition doesn't do that!" Todd is one of the wiping rag industry's most passionate boosters. And Star Wipers, located in Newark, Ohio, forty miles east of Columbus, is one of the last American companies that—in his estimation—does rags "the right way."

Like most people who don't make money from cutting rags, I long assumed that the "right way" was how it was done at home. My mother would take old T-shirts and tear them into rags for polishing furniture and wiping down sinks. Our house wasn't unique. For most of human history, rag making has been an act of household thrift so common that few consumers think of it as recycling, sustainable, or green.

What transformed this act of household thrift into an industrial process were the factories and machines that created the industrial revolution. Maintaining and repairing those machines required rags to apply or wipe up grease and oil. In industrializing England, the most abundant source of those rags was the growing surplus of used, unwanted textiles made by those very machines. An industry emerged to collect and deliver them to the rag makers, and by the late nineteenth century, British rag makers were as industrialized as the textile mills, with buying networks as complex as those used to distribute clothing to the growing retail industry. Rag making soon went global: by 1929, the United States was the leading rag-making nation, home to at least twenty-six wiping rag companies with industrial laundries that ensured the cleanest rags possible. Thousands of people were employed in rag-cutting factories.

The need for rags hasn't gone away over the last century. Star Wipers has 110,000 square feet of space in Newark, much of it devoted to ware-housing the rags that it packages and ships around the United States to distributors who know—intimately—what kind of user needs what kind of rag. Still, it's a labor-intensive business, and as with textile manufacturing, much of the industry has migrated to Asia over the last three decades. Those who remain, like Star Wipers, need good reasons to stay in the United States. "It's about quality," Todd tells me. With as many as twenty-six rag cutters working at one time in Newark and another thirteen in the company's North Carolina plant, Star Wipers is likely the largest U.S. rag cutter left (there are companies that distribute more rags than Star Wipers, but most of those rags are imported).

Yet, despite the vast global demand for stuff to wipe stuff, most consumers have no answer if someone asks, "Who will be last to use your hoodie?" The end of clothes has become nearly as mysterious as the end of life itself.

Todd Wilson and I sit across from each other at a long conference table in a windowless conference room. It's lunchtime, and we're eating sand-wiches and chips from the Subway up the road. Behind me is a door that leads out to a giant laundry machine that looks a bit like a giant green metal caterpillar. It handles multiple individual loads at once, without mixing them. And not all those loads are used clothes. "The washer exists to make a new T-shirt feel like an old one," Todd explains. This makes sense when I think about my own laundry. A new cotton T-shirt, generally, doesn't feel as soft as one that I've had and washed for years. "Now think about it," Todd says. "That soft T-shirt is going to do a better job of absorbing liquid than one you've just pulled out of the pack."

As a result, buyers of clothes intended as rags typically pay more for used T-shirts than new ones. And when they can't get used ones, they spend money to launder new ones so that they feel like used ones. For example, every three weeks Star Wipers receives a load of castoffs from apparel makers in Bangladesh that must be run through the washer before cutting.

"That's upside down to me," I concede.

"You haven't spent much time around rags," Todd says with a smile.

Rags have been in Todd Wilson's family since the 1970s. Back then, his father, a manufacturer of components for card-filing systems, acquired a small rag company that became his dominant holding. In 1998, Todd and a partner formed their own rag company, named Star Wipers, and in 2005, it and Todd's father's company were acquired by the same buyer. Today, Star Wipers has 160 employees, additional operations in Pennsylvania and North Carolina, and a rag sourcing network that extends from Brownsville, Texas, to Kandla, India. In 2017, it sold around fifteen million pounds of rags, primarily in the United States.

Todd attributes the company's success to two factors. First, he cares. As he says to me repeatedly during a several-hour-long visit, "I love rags!" Second, he is a stickler for quality. "A rag is a tool," he explains. "No different than a screwdriver. Different tools for different applications. You have to make the tool and make it well." A janitorial service doesn't want to buy rags with sequins that scratch the furniture; an oil and gas company doesn't want a polyester rag that's going to discharge static electricity and set off an explosion; a maid service doesn't want a colored rag that's going to bleed dye onto a countertop. Lately, Todd finds that ensuring quality is getting harder. Wilson pulls out a copy of the January 1963 issue of *The Bulletin*, the official publication of the National Association of Wiping Cloth Manufacturers (NAWCM). Toward the end is a full page devoted to "Specifications for Purchase of Rags for

Conversion into Wiping Cloths." There are eighteen specifications by grade, including ones for White Wipers, Colored Wipers, Underwear Wipers, Mixed Wipers, and "Blue Overalls and Pants (Blue Denim)":

> Shall consist of 100% cotton material up to 12 oz. per sq. yd. Minimum area of pants leg when opened shall be 2 sq. ft. with a minimum width of 12 inches. Shall be free of coveralls and jackets. Shall be free of greasy, oily, painted, cement stock and skeletons.

The good news is that skeletons are no longer a threat to turn up in clothes purchased for wiping rags. The bad news is that the days of recycled 100 percent cotton wiping rags are pretty much over, and so are the days when wiping rag manufacturers could rely on industry specifications. The problem is that clothes and textiles simply aren't as well made as they used to be. A shirt that falls apart after a few washes can't be transformed into a rag suitable for wiping down a freshly washed car or a restaurant table. Cheap fast fashion isn't just hurting thrift shops; it's hastening a garment's trip to the landfill or garbage incinerator.

"Go try to buy a hundred percent cotton shirt today," Todd says with exasperation. "Even when it says 'a hundred percent cotton,' you can't be sure." This isn't idle conspiracy mongering. In recent years, manufacturers have incorporated more and more polyester into clothes to meet consumer demand for ever-cheaper clothing. But they haven't always done so honestly. Fabrics labeled 100 PERCENT COTTON often aren't; and cotton-polyester blends often contain more polyester than the tag claims. Star Wipers first noticed the change in the millions of pounds of linens it purchased from laundries serving healthcare facilities. Sheets and blankets that used to be cotton-polyester blends were turning up as 100 percent polyester. That's a problem. "A hundred percent polyester wiping rag is not going to do the same thing as a poly-cotton blend," Wilson explains to me. "It won't absorb as well." That's the least of it. Polyester might melt in the presence of certain solvents, heat, or—worst of all—emit static electricity.

At Star Wipers, a sorting and grading operation pulls the all-polyester blankets before they're cut and packaged for customers. But back in 1963, those blends wouldn't have made it through the factory gate. The NAWCM's "Specifications for Purchase of Rags" specifically prohibited "silk, wool, rayon, and other synthetics" from rags purchased as wipers because of absorbency concerns. Today, just as clothing consumers are willing to accept lower quality in exchange for lower prices, so too are many wiper buyers. Todd tells me that many customers have accommodated themselves to cotton-poly blends. But not all of them: "Today if people can't find what they want in a reclaimed wiper, they'll look to a new one." Paper towels are always an option; so are synthetic towels that offer greater absorbency than reclaimed poly-cotton wipers. It's a quirk of the global economy that the most direct beneficiaries of the rise of fast fashion might be paper towel manufacturers.

Todd loves rags made from reclaimed textiles. But he can't simply ignore the declining quality of used textiles. So, in recent years, Star Wipers has started to manufacture a new, 100 percent cotton wiping rag from yarn grown and manufactured in North Carolina. "We can follow it from field to here," he tells me. The environmental impact of that new rag is steep compared with that of a reclaimed one (growing cotton is highly water intensive). But that's the price of a lower price.

Star Wipers' 100 percent cotton rag is known as the STB—short for Simply the Best—and around the wiping rag industry, that is a widely acknowledged statement of fact. "It's not our biggest seller by any means," says Wilson. "But if a customer wants that consistency and is willing to pay the premium for it, we make it available." It's not good enough; it's as good as new.

Morning traffic fades as Nohar Nath's driver navigates the leafy streets of South Mumbai. In the near distance I see the spindly glamour of Victoria Station, the city's landmark train depot. The car stops just short of it and waits as we exit in front of the Empire Building, a handsome and prestigious colonial-era office building.

Nohar is forty-five, tall, lean, and handsome. He springs up the stairs, showing hints of the athleticism that earned him a spot on India's national golf team in his teens. He could have turned professional, he tells me. "But I was honest with myself. I would've been one of those guys missing the odd cut and finishing fifteenth or twentieth or twenty-fifth. It wouldn't have been enough to satisfy my ego." Instead, he earned an MBA, spent two years as an international banker, and joined the Kishco Group, the eighty-year-old family textile-trading business. The India operations are based in four offices at the Empire Building; it also has offices in Bangladesh, China, and the United Arab Emirates.

We slip into a narrow, windowless conference room, and an employee enters with milk tea. Nohar leans back in an office chair and quickly acknowledges that life as a banker is more prestigious than life as a used-textile trader. "I've had situations in the industry—I might buy waste worth a million dollars. And somebody might buy virgin raw materials from some guy for ten thousand dollars. But that guy who buys virgin product for ten thousand dollars is far more important psychologically in their mind than the guy buying waste for a million dollars."

The Kishco Group was founded in 1938 and over the decades grew into a global trader of textile products and waste. These days, it buys used textiles from Goodwills and other charities, thrift store chains, and graders across North America and Europe, and resells them around the world. Nohar knows Mississauga; he has entertaining stories about doing business in Mozambique. He is an occasional speaker at recycling conventions, and for good reason: On average, Kischo trades around two thousand shipping containers full of textiles—mostly waste—per year. "It becomes more like a commodity business," he says. "We're just paying for it and getting paid for it."

Later, Nohar invites me for lunch at the Bombay Gymkhana, an exclusive members-only athletic club that dates back to 1875 and the headiest, wealthiest days of the British Raj. It's a throwback: the bar and dining room face a neatly manicured ground used for cricket, rugby, and soccer, and guests cast lazy glances at the groundskeepers as they prepare the facility for a weekend tournament. "My family's membership extends back decades," Nohar tells me. "I'd come here after school and play sports, which is how I became so good."

Nohar directs my attention to the crowded, bustling streets beyond the placid fields and fences of the Gymkhana. Clothing stalls extend for at least a quarter mile down the opposite side of the street. Some clothing looks standardized and new, some is fake (the Real Madrid jerseys, certainly so), and much is the telltale hodgepodge sold by used-clothing vendors around the world. "We call it Fashion Street," he says with a wry smile. "Vendors mix used with the new, and nobody knows the difference."

India has a long, fraught relationship with secondhand clothing. The country's textile and apparel manufacturers spent decades lobbying to keep it out of the country for fear that lower-income Indians would prefer cheap used garments to new (they do if the price is competitive). Still, Fashion Street is filled with imported secondhand garments, and if those don't suit a buyer, there are dozens of other places in Mumbai where imported secondhand clothes can be purchased. They're smuggled through ports around the country and inducted into a complex network of buyers and sellers just below the surface of India's formal economy.

Yet, in a curious twist of trade, India's absolute prohibition on imported secondhand clothes has a notable loophole. For decades, India has granted sixteen companies the right to import secondhand clothes into Kandla, a port town of fifteen thousand people located five hundred miles northwest of Mumbai. Thanks to those licenses, Kandla is now one of the world's biggest importers of secondhand clothes (and quite possibly *the* biggest).

But there's a catch.

To ensure that Kandla's clothes don't compete against new, domestically manufactured clothes, the Indian government requires that every garment that arrives in Kandla depart from Kandla. As a result, Kandla has become a global hub for the grading, processing, and re-export of clothes. The city's handful of hotels are filled with North American and European exporters, and African importers. Indian brokers move between them.

In another curious twist of trade, the prohibition of trading Kandla's clothes into India has a spacious loophole. According to the law, "mutilated" clothes, which can't be worn and can't be sold as garments, can be sent northeast to Panipat, the town that Abdul Majid Moledina of Used Clothing Exports in Mississauga was eager for me to visit. Located fifty miles north of Delhi, Panipat has been for three decades the place where unwanted woolen clothes from the world's wealthy countries go after nobody wants to wear them anymore. That's a lot of clothes. Unlike summer clothes, which flow to developing countries in warm climates, winter clothes typically lack a reuse market. According to Nohar, Panipat at its peak could import close to a thousand shipping containers per month of secondhand woolen clothes. "You will see," Nohar tells me as we eat. "The business is changing. In a few years, Panipat as we know it won't exist anymore."

In developed countries like the United States and Japan, the recycling bin has become a comfortable counterpart to the trash bin. Bottles and cans go in one; plastic wrappers, broken dishes, and paper towels soaked with spills go in the other. Most Americans, like most Japanese and Europeans, don't complain about the sorting process and have even come to think of it as a civic duty. The few communities—mostly in the United States—that have added textiles to their curbside recycling programs have found that residents generally give their shirts away as easily as they give away their beer cans.

It wasn't always this way, of course. Because clothes and other textiles were scarce and expensive, traders thrived by bartering and trading them. But in the early nineteenth century, traders encountered a demand-side problem: the woolen clothes being manufactured on industrial looms throughout Europe couldn't be easily reused once their upwardly mobile owners didn't want them anymore. Unlike cotton and linen, which are ideal for making paper and stuffing cushions and—in wartime—bullet casings, wool has short, coarse fibers that are ideal for nothing but their original use. In a sense, they were the fast fashion of the early nineteenth century—useless and growing in abundance.

One solution was to grind up the used wool for use as fertilizer (it's an organic product, after all). But those who wanted to reuse wool *as wool fabric* had to wait until 1813, when Benjamin Law of Batley, England, devised a way to remake it into a cheap, coarse fabric that came to be known as "shoddy." The process is straightforward and familiar to anyone who's ever pulled apart a failed piece of knitting: rip it up and reuse the fibers in a new garment. Law developed processes to do this on an industrial scale, and soon shoddy was found in low-cost blankets and other garments marketed to the poor and—significantly—the military.

For the next century, shoddy was a highly profitable business, especially when supplies of virgin wool were short during wartime. By the late nineteenth century, trade in waste woolen clothing had gone global, with much of it flowing to the shoddy mills of northern England and the industrializing East Coast of the United States. But shoddy was not destined to remain an Anglo-American industry for long.

"In 1981 Panipat was just coming up," Nohar Nath tells me as we sit in the back seat of a car driving us from Delhi's airport to visit some of Kishco's clients in Panipat. "Just a small town with some hand-loom factories coming up, and some home furnishing factories coming up. And people just experimenting with the idea of recycling."

At the time, Prato, Italy, was where most of the world's shoddy was made. The industry had moved there before World War II, attracted by cheap labor and the region's history of working with wool. But Asia was starting to emerge as a textile-making rival, and several savvy Mumbai entrepreneurs saw a future for recycled textiles in India. The Indian business started in Mumbai, and labor pressures—strikes and rising wages—pushed it north to low-cost Panipat.

Because of labor pressures, Kischo, which had been a yarn manufacturer for decades, sold off its yarn making business in 1981. But it still had customers who wanted wool. So rather than leave them in search of new sources, Kishco fulfilled their orders with wool from other mills, many of which were moving to Panipat. It was a fortuitous shift. "We could take an order from our regular buyers and place the order with Factory A, B, C, X, Y, Z," Nohar explains. "And we didn't have any of the problems associated with owning a factory."

As Panipat's shoddy mills grew, so too did the need for a used-clothing supply to feed them. India, a low-income country, didn't waste nearly enough clothing to feed Panipat's mills. So Panipat's mills asked Kishco if the company could find used woolen clothes abroad and import them. Nohar's father contacted embassies and followed up in person at sources of used clothing in the wealthy developed world. Soon, waste textiles once bound for Prato or the dump were making their way to Panipat. At its peak, in the mid-2000s, Panipat had perhaps six hundred factories making shoddy, and it was—and still is—the biggest recycler of wool clothing in the world.

But it's not a business that lasts, no matter where it's located. The problem is straightforward: nobody really likes shoddy. It's coarse, it smells musty, and the number of colors and patterns it can hold are limited (and drab). For years, the leading consumers of Panipat's shoddy were disaster-relief agencies like the Red Cross, which purchased shoddy blankets for use in relief operations following earthquakes and other disasters. It's been a spectacularly good business. In the early 2010s, Panipat's manufacturers were making one hundred thousand blankets per day, roughly 80 percent of which were exported for use in disasters. The remainder were sold either to the Indian military or to consumers as the "poor man's blanket." But that's no longer the case.

In the mid-2000s, Indian incomes were increasing and low-income Indians were in a position to buy something better than shoddy. Around the same time, Chinese exporters of petroleum-based polar fleece entered the Indian market with blankets that felt, looked, and smelled better than shoddy. The fleece blankets were also durable and light-weight, making them ideal for relief operations and home use alike. They were also cheap. Over the last decade the price of a Chinese polar fleece blanket imported into India dropped from around $7.50 to roughly $2.50. "Compare that to a two-dollar [shoddy] blanket," Nohar says with a shrug. "The potential client goes to a store and naturally prefers virgin."

The dusty urban hustle that is Panipat spreads out before us, and—as if to avoid it—the highway vaults over the town. Beneath the overpass, traffic barely moves, jammed by unsynchronized stoplights that stay red for long minutes. Small shops line both sides of the street; at least half are devoted to selling mobile phones and service. Everything is shades of gray, except for the flashes of color provided by the occasional truck-load of baled used clothes.

We turn from paved roads to dirt roads cratered with deep potholes that—if not avoided—could disable a vehicle. Factories are everywhere, but the gates are closed and there are few signs of what goes on beyond the ten-foot-high concrete walls that surround them. Children play in front of some of them; parents sit on stoops, chatting; and occasionally a pair of women sort through a pile of clothes.

Around a dusty corner our car stops in front of a steel gate. The driver honks the horn, and a moment later the gate slowly rolls open to reveal a courtyard filled with a rainbow of color. There are piles of blue woolen clothes, and piles of orange; piles of red woolen clothes, and many, many piles of black. Scattered amid the piles are women draped in saris brighter than the waste, sorting through sweaters, blankets, and bolts of unused cloth. They are surrounded on three sides by ware-houses and the humming of machinery.

Nohar gestures for me to follow him through the office door, where we're met by a male secretary who leads us into the office of the rotund company director, Ramesh Goyal. He wears a wool sweater beneath a flannel sport jacket; his arms are crossed, and he's crabby because of production problems. The secretary nods at something said in a language I don't understand and rushes out.

"Ramesh Knitting Mills is a very old customer," Nohar says by way of introduction. But Goyal isn't interested in talking about the history or the future of shoddy. He likes fleece. In 2016, he installed a polar fleece line that accounts for a growing percentage of his overall production.

Nohar folds his hands into his lap. "Polar fleece is replacing wool," he says to me, more than to Goyal. "And that's a big problem for us. Polar fleece can't be recycled into new fibers, and it makes a terrible wiper. No absorbency."

Goyal doesn't care. Prior to installing fleece production, Ramesh Knitting Mills made 7,000 kilograms of yarn and blankets per day. Two years later, its overall production has increased to 12,000 kilograms per day. Of that, 8,000 kilograms is new polyester fleece made from petrochemicals; the remainder is shoddy yarn and blankets made from winter clothes. "Many Indian companies realize that demand has arrived for virgin," Goyal explains.

It's an environmentalist's heartache. But there's not much that an environmentalist can do to change the economics. A growing excess of used clothes in cold-weather countries combined with a drop in demand in Panipat has changed the business of used wool. Nohar says that ten to fifteen years ago the price of secondhand wool hung around fifty cents per kilogram. Today it's fallen to fifteen cents per kilogram, with no reason to believe that the demand, or the price, will ever rise again. Soon, that will pose a problem to exporters of secondhand wool clothes already drowning in an excess of supply. "Watch—in two to three years, recyclers in Western countries will pay people to take clothes," Nohar predicts. "The cost of landfill versus sending here will justify it. In the E.U., especially, consumers will definitely prefer to pay to send it here than the landfill."

Ramesh Goyal suggests we have a look at production, so we walk out of the office and into a warehouse where a dozen women sit on the floor around a six-foot pile of black woolen blankets. The scene might as well be lifted from the nineteenth century. Herman Melville, in his 1855 short story "The Paradise of Bachelors and the Tartarus of Maids," offers this description of the young women cutting clothes at a New England paper mill: "Before each was vertically thrust up a long, glittering scythe, immovably fixed at bottom . . . To and fro, across the sharp edge, the girls forever dragged long strips of rags." Women with scythes work all over Panipat. They are mostly older than the ones Melville describes—I'd guess over forty for the most part—and they work in relative silence. Some work on black wool; others on orange. I see piles of blue in other warehouses.

Sorters at Ramesh Knitting Mills in Panipat, India.

Color segregation matters. Goyal leads us into a room where a male worker feeds pieces of orange into the far end of a crude, twenty-foot-long, chest-high machine driven by exposed chains and gears. In turn, those gears power spiked wheels that tear the wool garments into their individual fibers inside steel drums. At the far end, a thick orange fuzz emerges and fills up two large alcoves that branch off the room. Even the slightest breeze caused by someone walking past can send it flying into the air. Everywhere, orange fuzz.

Next door is a larger room in which bags of black shredded wool await their turn at the adjoining yarn mill. At the far end, a worker is dwarfed by a pile of black wool at least ten feet high and fifteen feet long. He stands in front of another equally crude but far bigger machine, feeding black clothes into it. "Twenty, twenty-five percent of every load is black these days," Nohar says. "It's a growing percentage."

A worker in Panipat is surrounded by piles of shredded black wool produced from imported secondhand clothes.

We turn a corner into another room that hums with the manufacture of yarn. Gears and belts are exposed, drops of oil and grease stain the floor, hundreds of spindles spin, and yarn fills them up in an orange haze. Nohar reaches into a bag of gray wool yarn and pulls out a roll. "The shirt you are wearing was made from yarn with a one hundred thread count," he says, nodding at my Bangladesh-made, U.S.-bought flannel. Then he turns back to the shoddy. "This has probably a ten to twelve thread count. Good for blankets, a rug, or a towel or some jacketing materials."

But who will want it?

In the last decade, two thirds of Panipat's shoddy mills have gone out of business or consolidated into bigger companies. Of the perhaps two hundred remaining factories, at least fifty make polar fleece blankets. From Nohar's perspective, that's the future. "It's not as if the price of production is coming down. The costs are fixed. But fleece is coming down, still."

Ramesh Goyal leads Nohar and me from his shoddy mill to a clean and airy warehouse where polyester thread spins from hundreds of spools with a gentle hum and comes together in raw, milky-white sheets of raw polar fleece. I pause at a nightstand-size control console encased in steel. It's the ZY301 High Speed Warping Machine, manufactured by Wuxi Zhongyin Textile Technology Co. Ltd., of Wuxi, China. Panipat's shoddy manufacturers, long undercut by China's polar fleece manufacturers, are now buying the equipment that—until recently—outcompeted them. Thanks to labor that's cheaper than China's and abundant nearby sources of petrochemicals, Panipat's fleece makers enjoy lower costs than China's. Goyal tells me that they've even started exporting.

Sumit Jindal is the fourth-generation member of his family to run Jindal Spinning Mills in Panipat. He is short and slightly rotund, and his smartphone plays the opening chords of Nirvana's "Smells Like

Teen Spirit." He and Nohar Nath have known each other for years, and he's happy to offer a late-afternoon tour of the family's shoddy factory. "We were one of the first to Panipat," he tells me. "We started in 1973."

Jindal Spinning Mills is typical of a large Panipat shoddy mill. Clothes are sorted by color, cut on scythes, ripped and torn to fibers, and spun into shoddy. Toward the back of the factory complex, a handful of mechanical looms chug away, weaving shoddy into drab-looking blankets with occasional mechanical clanks. The blues are shallow; the reds are dull; the greens remind me of house plants denied the sun. But it's the equipment that stands out. It is ancient, creaking, and European-made. It heaves, and—here and there—it leaks.

"We have to buy secondhand machines for the recycled blankets," Jindal says. "We import them from Europe. But they're slow, especially compared to new machines."

A worker stands with an Italian-built, near-antique shoddy loom at Jindal Spinning Mills.

I think of the fleece line we saw across town. "Why not buy new?"

He smiles at me with pity. "The new technology can't handle recycled fibers." They're too coarse. So, for now at least, the shoddy industry—and wool recycling, in general—is mired in the past. The competition from fleece all but ensures it will remain there.

"How many blankets can you make in a day?"

"We can make forty thousand recycled blankets per month," Jindal tells me.

"That's a lot, no?"

He leads Nohar and me up a stairway. "The relief agencies want fifty thousand delivered today. When they call, I have to explain how long it takes us to make, how difficult it is to get them from here to port. If a supplier like us can't go fast, we're expected to keep a stock. But then we have to ask what happens if the relief agencies change their quality standards or specs? What if they go from one-ply to two-ply?"

We reach a long room covered in a vinyl floor printed to look as if it's hardwood. In places, it peels away to reveal concrete. At the far end, hundreds of shoddy blankets are piled against the walls, and a man sits at a sewing machine, stitching nylon edging on them. Farther along, women are packaging the blankets for shipment.

"We had someone in Germany that wanted six hundred thousand blankets immediately," Jindal recalls. "We'd need eleven months to do that." He shakes his head. "China can do it, and over the last three years all of the relief agencies, the Red Cross, the UN, they've switched to polyester blankets."

Jindal, like others, has refocused on the domestic market. Last year, he sold five hundred thousand shoddy blankets locally. But he's not counting on shoddy for his future. He, too, has started making polar fleece.

"Are you worried the shoddy trade will eventually end?"

"The trade won't end in Panipat. The whole world depends on Panipat. They can't dump it in the sea." He smiles as he says this, as if it's the most obvious thing in the world.

It's getting late in the day, but Nohar and I have one more stop. From Jindal Spinning Mills, we ride to a nearby two-story warehouse where we're greeted by Puneet Goyal, Ramesh Goyal's son. He leads us up a set of stairs and into a hazy factory in which sunbeams cut sixty-degree angles from windows to floor. Below them, the milky-white rolls of polar fleece are loaded into screen-printing equipment that extends for several hundred feet through the room. As Nohar and I watch, the raw fleece moves through the printer in blanket-size intervals. Along the way, a mechanical arm sweeps over and prints the outline of flowers; another arm prints a blue background; another fills in the flowers with red. From raw blanket to print takes perhaps one minute. Hundreds of blankets can be printed this way in an hour.

Chinese-made machinery churns out rolls and rolls of polar fleece blankets. Production is an order of magnitude greater than shoddy blanket production.

"The designs come from a factory in China," Puneet tells us as we're shown additional lines where the designs are baked in, the blankets are cut and washed, and the fleece is pricked and pulled so that it stands up in the fashion characteristic of polar fleece. "We also have an in-house designer. There are hundreds of designs we can have. But a recycled blanket can only have a few designs."

I glance at Nohar. He isn't saying much as he follows the screen printing, the washing, the cutting. But his mouth is pinched—I can't tell if it's because he is deep in thought, has a distaste for the strong chemical smell in the air, or is concerned for the future of his used-woolen-clothes trading business. We stop at the end of the line and see piles of thousands of blankets with different designs: flowers, tiger stripes, geometric abstractions, checks, squares, and squiggles. The blankets are soft, warm, tough. If I'm ever in a natural disaster, I sincerely hope that the Red Cross skips the shoddy and sources polar fleece to keep me warm.

Nohar starts asking about exports. "Where are you sending this material?" Kishco has markets around the world, and these fleece blankets might appeal to some of the customers who buy shoddy and other goods.

"Dubai, South Africa, the Middle East, mostly."

Nohar Nath, shoddy trader, nods. "Get me some samples and swatches. Let me work on it."

Toward the end of the Friday afternoon shift at Star Wipers, Todd Wilson stops beside a cart piled with cut-up white sweatshirts. "Now here's what I'm gonna tell you about this product," he says to me. "This is reclaimed white sweatshirt. For us to keep up with demand, we have to buy it offshore. There's not enough in the States." The problem, for those who view it that way, is that it's typically cheaper to cut sweatshirts into rags in India than in Ohio.

None of the cut-up fragments of sweatshirt through which Wilson is rummaging were used in India. Rather, they were likely made in South Asia, exported to the United States, and worn until they were donated to Goodwill, the Salvation Army, or some other thrift-based exporter. When they didn't sell there, they were exported again, to Kandla most likely (or perhaps Mississauga, en route to Kandla), cut up, and exported again—this time to Star Wipers in Newark, Ohio. Each step of that journey makes perfect economic sense, even if the totality of it sounds ridiculous.

In fact, it's the future.

Middle-class consumers in Asia already outnumber those in North America. Soon, their unwanted secondhand stuff will exceed that which is generated in more affluent countries. If those clothes don't sell, they can always be cut into wipers (assuming the quality is sufficient). And those wipers, sourced from clothes worn and cut in developing countries, will make their way to the United States. A secondhand trade that once flowed in one direction—from rich to poor—now goes in every direction.

Todd Wilson accepted that dynamic years ago. In 2016 he traveled to Kandla to teach a local rag-cutting firm how to cut rags to Star Wipers' exacting standards. It wasn't hard to find a partner. Demand for wipers from factories, hotels, and restaurants serving India's booming economy has been strong for years, and the reclaimed textiles that might have once stayed in the United States are now flowing there. Todd just wants to be sure that those rags are cut to a standard that he can import as his own.

That's not easy. Workers in Newark are taught to cut shirts and other garments so that they get around ten wiping rags per pound. "But the industry standard is around five rags per pound," Wilson says, referring to big, sloppy cuts that make an old T-shirt look like a pair of oversize wings. "And that'll be the death of us as an industry. People will feel like they're getting a better deal buying new rags. So you have to find the people cutting the rags the way you want them." His cut, the Star Wipers cut, looks like what most people think of as a rag.

That may seem trivial—maybe even comical—to someone outside the wiping rag industry. But it's absolutely critical to anyone who wants to see the life of secondhand clothing extended for as long as possible.

Wilson is unswerving in his optimism about the future of reclaimed wiping rags. But that doesn't stop him from dropping an occasional joke at the expense of the industry. Toward the start of our interview, he told me that during a recent industry convention, a fellow trade association member reported that he had good news and bad news about the industry. "The good news," Wilson recounts, starting to laugh, "is that nobody wants to get into this business."

CHAPTER 9

Enough to Sell

It's a rainy Monday rush hour on Highway 169 in Golden Valley, Minnesota, and the parking lot in front of the Empty the Nest thrift shop is relatively empty. It's similar inside the store, which is usually swarmed with people shopping for sport. But that's during the weekends. On Mondays, everything is 40 percent off, but many customers assume that the best deals disappeared over the weekend (they didn't) or appear to be shopping for only what they need, not what they want.

Sharon Fischman, the owner and founder, is at the front in conversation with a man she introduces to me as Shane the Truck Driver. He wears a cowboy hat, jeans, a jean jacket, and cowboy boots with spurs. He is in the midst of conveying some interesting news: the Perkins restaurant across the street has just closed permanently, and he has permission to pull the restaurant's sign from the dumpster where it now rests.

Sharon glances briefly into her store. It contains thousands of objects cleaned out of dozens of homes. More are on the way, via clean-outs that are scheduled weeks and months in advance. To make room for it all, Sharon will soon begin her painful weekly cull of unsold inventory. But first there's the matter of that sign. "I'm going dumpster diving," she tells me.

Shane and I follow her out the door and across the street. Sure enough, there's a dumpster in the Perkins parking lot and it holds a ten-foot-long, five-foot-tall green plastic PERKINS RESTAURANT & BAKERY sign. "I want it," she declares. Then she turns to Shane. "Do you think it'll sell?"

Perhaps there's a griddle aficionado somewhere in the western suburbs of Minneapolis who craves a pancake-house sign to fill up a basement wall. Or perhaps not. Shane smiles skeptically. "It's kind of a beast, Sharon. I don't even know where you'd put it in the store."

She turns back to the sign with pursed lips. It's barricaded into the dumpster by perfectly good tables and chairs from the restaurant (I recognize them from a lifetime of eating at Perkins). Merely creating a channel to extract the sign will be a brutal task. "Yeah, maybe. Maybe I can send my staff over to pick up some of this furniture. Let's ask."

Shane the Truck Driver examining perfectly good furniture discarded by a Perkins restaurant in Golden Valley, Minnesota.

We walk through the restaurant's open door and find the remaining employees, including the now former manager, seated around a table drinking coffee and looking morose. Sharon says a friendly hello—she was a regular—and asks for the chairs and tables. The manager says she can have the metal shelves in the walk-in refrigerator, too, just so long as everything is gone "before the higher-ups come tomorrow." We also get a few leftover brownies that Sharon asks me to place in my pockets and give to her staff when we get back to the store.

When we're ready to leave, she hesitates and turns back to the manager. "Doesn't Perkins want this stuff?"

It's a reasonable question: Minnesota-based Perkins has nearly four hundred restaurant locations in the United States and Canada. Surely the furniture can be used in one of them? The manager shakes her head. "Perkins is closing five stores this year, and there's no room in the warehouse for it. So we're putting it in the dumpster."

Back at Empty the Nest, Sharon busies herself selling the furniture she already possesses. Empty the Nest manages to sell 80 percent of the goods it acquires in home cleanouts in the store (a small percentage is also sold online). That's an extraordinarily high number for the thrift industry, where selling even 50 percent of inventory is aspirational. Nonetheless, Empty the Nest's unsold 20 percent isn't a trifle. It takes up space and weighs tons.

As the late afternoon inclines into evening, Sharon attaches a sticker gun to a belt loop and begins moving methodically through the store, identifying that which won't sell. This weekly ritual, this cleansing, runs into Tuesday. She places a green sticker on a white leather sectional sofa; later, an employee will post the sofa on OfferUp, the online flea market. She places a pink sticker on a heavy oak table with a deep gouge in one corner; soon, the crew will load it onto a truck bound for Bridging, a furniture "bank" that distributes household goods to people transitioning from poverty and homelessness.

"How do you decide?" I ask.

"Partly it's based on gut and knowing what sells. Partly on how long things have been here. And I'm also making calls based on what's coming in," she says, referring to the home cleanouts. "I've seen [pictures of] what we're getting." In fact, a truck full of fresh cleanout property is parked against Empty the Nest's loading dock, ready to be unloaded, priced, and displayed.

Sharon stares up at a tall, solid-wood television cabinet. "This has been here two months." As she contemplates what color sticker it deserves, a customer approaches to say that she'd like to buy the white sectional sofa tagged for OfferUp. Sharon beams; last-minute reprieves are rare. She excuses herself to schedule a time for the sofa to be picked up, and I wander around the store, pausing to flip through a pile of black-and-white snapshots for sale out of a wicker basket. What were once "family photos" are now anonymous "vintage photos." I wonder if family members ever find their relatives in these baskets.

Sharon admits to worrying about how to keep up with the demographics of America's retiring baby boomers as they shed stuff into the secondhand economy. A few months earlier we had a late-afternoon breakfast at the now-closed Perkins. Toward the end of the meal, she recounted a recent meeting with her staff. What, they wanted to know, should be done with soiled and torn women's clothing found in the course of a home cleanout? Should it be boxed up to be sold at Empty the Nest—where it almost certainly won't sell? Donated to the Salvation Army? Thrown away?

"So, my heart says don't throw it away," Sharon explained. "But reality is it costs money for Empty the Nest. We pay for the boxes, we pay for the time and the transportation to get it donated. And are [the charities] going to be throwing it away, too?" If she's going to run a profitable business that employs people and offers cleanouts and resale, the answer should be clear. But it's painful.

Sharon isn't alone in the struggle. At Goodwill, at the Salvation Army, at church and synagogue flea markets, near the bitter end of every garage sale, some version of the question asked by Sharon's staff is muttered. The sought-after answer—"take your unwanted used item to this innovative, sustainable solution at no cost to yourself, and it will be reused indefinitely"—almost never exists. Meanwhile, the growing flood of stuff means that the economics of creating—much less sustaining—that innovative, sustainable solution are becoming harder. Consumers in need of reassurance that their stuff is wanted and useful must, at some point, accept the idea that every object dies.

"I have a theory," I told her. "Over time, as Empty the Nest grows, you'll throw away more."

"So that's the struggle," she answered. "The throwing. The throwing away."

"People really want to know their stuff is reused."

"Exactly!"

"It's primal."

"Yes, it is. And I want to walk my walk."

So what is to be done?

In one important respect, nothing. Sharon and the rest of the existing secondhand industry, whether it's Goodwill or rag makers, are sustainable and profitable already. Their models of reuse predate the environmental movement, the decluttering fad, and the oncoming flood of unwanted stuff from baby boomers. They don't need to be reinvented, recalibrated, or regulated. If anything, they should be encouraged and studied.

Nonetheless, Empty the Nest and its counterparts aren't sufficient to solve the bundle of emotional, financial, and environmental challenges posed by humanity's avalanche of unwanted stuff. Other answers are needed.

Recycling—the process of turning old stuff into new raw materials for making more new stuff—is a good one. But as I wrote in *Junkyard Planet*, recycling is imperfect, especially as an environmental solution. First, nothing is 100 percent recyclable, no matter what the manufacturer might say (for example, half of the roughly thirty metals in the average smartphone are basically unrecyclable). Most complex objects—from smartphones to sofas—are a combination of recyclable and nonrecyclable components, and the financial and environmental costs of extracting the former often make landfilling or incineration the more responsible option.

That's not the only problem. A book manufactured from recycled paper uses less energy and fewer raw materials than one made from virgin paper pulp. But it still requires an expenditure of energy and raw materials. In fact, by easing consumer concerns over the environmental impact of consuming, and lowering the overall cost of raw materials (recycled raw materials compete directly with virgin), recycling can actually contribute to *more* consumption.[1] There's a reason that "recycling" is the third "R" in the familiar "Reduce, Reuse, Recycle" environmental mantra: it's the third best (or worst) thing you can do with stuff. When a consumer brand like Coca-Cola advertises the recyclability of its products, it's not promoting sustainability. It's helping sustainably minded consumers assuage their guilt.

Another increasingly popular solution (in affluent countries, at least) is located further up the "Reduce, Reuse, Recycle" hierarchy: minimalism.

Rather than live a lifestyle in which shopping is sport and homes are cluttered with stuff, minimalists pare down their possessions to the bare necessities and seek entertainment away from Amazon and the shopping mall. Many of the cleanout professionals I met during the course of reporting this book admitted to adopting some degree of minimalist practice after regular exposure to the pervasive excess of stuff. Jill Freeman, the professional sorter who works with Gentle Transitions in Minneapolis, was straightforward when I asked what her home looks like: "We don't buy stuff. We don't bring things home. We already have everything we need." It's an approach that she tries to impart to others. She explained to me that rather than give physical gifts for weddings and other occasions, she prefers to give cash or "experiences," like restaurant gift certificates.

I'm sympathetic. Though I've never been much of a shopper, the experience of reporting this book—days spent in thrift shops and attending home cleanouts—made me reassess my own consumption and hoarding. The things that I value, I quickly realized, generally aren't valuable to anyone but me. Once I had that understanding, I started letting go and curtailing what I was buying in the first place.

It'd be nice to think that lots of Americans, in particular, would have the same epiphany (perhaps by reading this book?). Certain trends are positive. For example, the smartphone has given billions of people around the world a reason not to buy a camera, a television, a home stereo, a laptop, DVDs, CDs, cassette tapes, videotapes, or photo albums (in a generation, paper snapshots will be as relevant as painted portraits). Yes, dematerialization, as the phenomenon is known, will leave behind lots of obsolete, hard-to-recycle smartphones. But compared with piles of VHS tapes, CDs, DVDs, vinyl records, snapshots, landline telephones, VCRs, and other smartphone-replaced stuff that turns up—mostly unwanted—at Goodwills, it's genuine progress.

Nonetheless, neither the smartphone nor the popularity of minimalist lifestyles or other individual-based consumption choices can overcome two immovable facts. First, despite being the subject of best-selling how-to books around the world, minimalism (and the Japanese "art" of decluttering) hasn't made much of an impact on the world's stuff. Arguably, it's increased it by giving folks an incentive (empty house!) to buy more. Second, consumption-based economies and lifestyles aren't going away—even in affluent economies where environmental consciousness runs high.

For example, in the early 2010s, sociologists, economists, and marketers noticed that millennials—a generation born between the early 1980s and late 1990s—were buying far fewer cars and homes than their predecessors. According to this popular narrative, millennials were instead embracing the new sharing economy and services like Uber's ride shares and Airbnb's home shares. Rather than buy stuff, they preferred to buy experiences like travel. The optimistic interpretation, widely disseminated in mainstream media, suggested that the willingness to share rather than own was inspired in part by climate change and growing environmental consciousness.

However, recent studies suggest that the millennial penchant for sharing over ownership is actually about a shortage of money. High urban rents, backbreaking student loans, and the long shadow of the 2008 financial crisis have crimped millennials' ability to make the big purchases their parents considered a rite of passage. Put more money into millennial pockets and they, too, will acquire stuff. Indeed, a 2018 Bank of America survey of two thousand adults found that 72 percent of millennials consider home ownership a "top priority," and ranked it over travel, getting married, and having children.[2] Another consumer survey found that, despite their embrace of ride sharing, 75 percent of millennials who don't own a car aspire to own one.[3] Meanwhile, across the Atlantic, an ongoing European Union research project into the sharing economy finds that millennials are "interested in sharing platforms only when platforms offered a more cost-effective alternative to traditional services."[4] In this way, at least, millennial consumers in Europe and the United States aren't that much different from their resource-poor developing-world counterparts. Both sets aspire to consume.

That doesn't mean humanity is helpless against the rising tide of unwanted secondhand. But it does mean we need to be more creative with the kinds of questions we ask about that tide. For example, when viewing a home that's cluttered with stuff bound for the dumpster, the question shouldn't just be "What do we do with it?" It also needs to be "How do we make sure homes fill up with stuff that can eventually be resold at thrift stores?" Jill Freeman reframed the problem for me over coffee: "If you want to have an estate sale, it isn't about having enough stuff. It's about having enough to sell." Put differently: Goodwill simply isn't capable of selling a used shirt that pills after two washes; Empty the Nest can't move—much less sell—a set of Ikea shelves made from particleboard held together by glue.

From that perspective, the crisis of stuff didn't cause Grandma's house to fill with property bound for the dumpster. Rather, it's a long-brewing crisis of quality.

The remaining chapters of this book will examine steps that can be taken to reverse this crisis of quality and ensure that more stuff flows into the secondhand economy. Think of it as a program to boost the fortunes of thrift stores, rag makers, and other stalwarts of used stuff.

Only the first two steps—initiatives designed to boost product longevity and repairability—require direct intervention by government. And those interventions are relatively minimal, intended to encourage consumers and manufacturers to act in ways that they already consciously or unconsciously think is in their best interests. One of those interests is lowering the cost of ownership for stuff ranging from refrigerators to sweaters. Nudging consumers to buy longer-lasting, more durable, and repairable products is one method to do that. Along the way, such nudges will produce more inventory for the secondhand market—meaning less stuff overflowing our homes.

The third and final step might be the most difficult. It asks consumers, journalists, corporations, and government regulators to embrace the idea that what they view as waste, others view as an opportunity. As I'll show in this book's final chapter, prejudices—sometimes racial, sometimes economic, always ignorant—have a stubborn and long-standing history of inhibiting reasonable people from seeing the possibility of secondhand goods in circumstances different from their own. Overcoming a crisis of quality means accepting that there are people who can see quality where you don't.

Obviously, no single solution—or combination of solutions—will be enough to prevent homes from filling up with unwanted stuff. Thrift stores will continue to throw out goods. Cleanout businesses will struggle to find homes for collectibles that are no longer collectible. Fashion will transform the most durable of garments and the sturdiest of dining room tables into wastes of space that nobody wants. But amid the pessimistic piles of stuff, entrepreneurs are finding ways to make a living from the leftovers. They are making business plans, employing friends and family, and investing themselves and their capital into a secondhand economy that already exists, and one they're gambling is just around the corner. I think they're onto something, and they could use a little help from all of us to achieve it.

CHAPTER 10

And It Lasts Forever

The pedestrian border crossing at the southern end of North Morley Avenue is the busiest point in sleepy downtown Nogales, Arizona. I watch a mother and her young daughter carry two small duffel bags through the TO MEXICO gate. Thirty seconds later, a gnarled old man in jeans and a denim shirt returns from Mexico carrying nothing.

Most of the buildings along Morley are two stories, and none look as if they were built recently. There's a duty-free shop, a perfumery, some ATMs, and a few old department stores converted into dollar stores catering to border traffic. I stop into a store with stacks of knockoff Levi's in the windows and wander aisles of low-cost, low-quality China-made tchotchkes, clothing, and even snack foods.

Goodwill is located a few blocks north, precisely at the point where the town's commerce begins to fade. It occupies a single-story building at one end of a parking lot bordered by a half-empty strip mall and a Pep Boys automobile-parts shop and service center. Inside is a smaller and slower version of the Outlet Center sixty-five miles north on Irvington Road. At nine forty A.M., six customers slowly rummage through thirty-two carts, piled mostly with clothes. Nobody seems to be in a hurry; competition, if it exists, is taking the day off.

I wander the store, stopping in a corner where two carts are filled with Goodwill donations that didn't sell and will soon be landfill-bound. Among other items, I count three bowling balls, an empty Miracle-Gro sprayer, a cracked child's booster seat, a no-brand vacuum cleaner, a TurboTax 2005 box, a beat-up briefcase, a rolled-up rug, and many, many sport water bottles with fitness club logos written across them.

Meanwhile, on the opposite end of the store, the Thursday auction is about to begin. Three employees stand by with clipboards, chatting in Spanish with three middle-aged women. These are the regular attendees, and—according to Lupita Ramos, the store manager—they buy a lot for their Mexican customers across the border. Their male partners stand off to the side, hands in jean pockets, smiling sheepishly at one another beneath cowboy and baseball hats.

The first auction lots are a dozen washing-machine-size boxes of unsold hard goods, including toys, plastic pitchers, old appliances, and binders. The bidding starts at twenty dollars and moves up in one-dollar increments. Most boxes fetch winning bids between twenty-five and thirty dollars. Two don't sell at all. I peek into one of the unsold ones: at the top is a Black and Decker bread maker and three bowling balls.

Next, the auction shifts to carts piled with used child car seats. Those get my attention. Like many parents, I am familiar with the alleged hazards associated with used and expired child safety seats; they're an angry staple of online parenting forums. The manufacturers of car seats aren't shy about promoting the idea that older seats are a hazard that should be kept from the secondhand markets. For example, Graco, one of the world's largest manufacturers of child safety seats, explains on its website that "used or expired car seats can be dangerous, especially if you don't know the car seat's history." So Graco's website recommends the following:

> To help ensure a car seat won't be used after expiration, it is a good idea to remove the cover, cut or remove the harness straps, write on it with a sharpie, and place it into a black garbage bag before taking it to be recycled or disposed of.

The practical effect of advice like this is to terrify parents into destroying used, unexpired car seats for fear that they'll become tools of death in the hands of less-thoughtful parents. Retailers, keen to sell more car seats, perpetuate the message. For example, as recently as October 2018, Target offered this warning in stores and online: "Used car seats shouldn't be sold or given away, since they expire every six years and regulations change constantly." That message makes its way into thrift stores. When I asked a Goodwill donation door employee whether Goodwill accepts used car seats, he responded, "No, because people will accuse us of killing their kids."

It's a colorful answer, but it's not entirely accurate. Goodwill Industries of Southern Arizona accepts used car seats as donations but won't sell them in Tucson-area stores. Instead, they're either shipped to Nogales, where they're put up for auction, or sold online—but only if they haven't expired. In Nogales they're purchased by Mexican second-hand traders, who take them over the border. Mexican families who can't afford new can take advantage of the cut-rate pricing to protect their children.

This seems like a situation that benefits parties on both sides of the border. But as a parent conditioned by endless warnings about used and expired car seats, I must concede I was wary when I saw those used car seats waiting to be auctioned. Is it actually safe to use a used car seat? Is it even legal?

To find out, I contacted the United States Highway Transportation Safety Administration, the U.S. government agency that regulates child safety seats, to obtain a list of rules and regulations relating to expiration dates on child safety seats. A spokesperson wrote back: "There are no actual rules or regulations in the U.S. about using an expired date car seat."

Of course, the U.S. government isn't oblivious to the possibility that a child safety seat could degrade over time. Its voluminous rules for regulating and testing child restraint systems* includes detailed protocols for testing whether the seatbelts included with a child safety seat are able to withstand long-term exposure to sunlight, abrasion, and microorganisms (the belts are the only parts of a child safety seat that must be tested for durability, according to the regulations). If the seatbelts don't pass, they aren't installed. Period. There are no expirations.

Notably, those durability tests are the same ones the U.S. government requires of automobile safety belts worn by older children and adults.[†] They're also tested on a pass/fail basis. That makes sense—who wants a car with seatbelts that expire?—but it also raises an awkward question. What accounts for the expiration dates on child safety seats and the maniacal fears about used ones?

To find out, I sent a four-question questionnaire to ten of the world's biggest child safety seat manufacturers. In it, I asked the process by which they determine the safe lifespan of a safety seat, whether materials manufacturers (such as the companies responsible for the

---

*   Child Restraint Systems. 49 CFR 517.213.

†   Seat Belt Assemblies. 49 CFR 571.209.

plastics) are consulted, whether the manufacturers rely on any data or studies to determine expiration dates, and when expirations were first attached to seats.

Only two companies responded. Graco emailed to recommend that a car seat be replaced after the "useful life date" and sent me a link to public information on its website about car seat expirations. That was no help. Britax wrote back with information that answered questions I didn't ask ("Car seat lifespans have increased since the 1990s because vehicle windows are now more advanced and . . . lessen a car seat's direct contact with UV rays"), or didn't answer them at all. For example, here's the third question from my questionnaire and Britax's response:

> Has Britax conducted any studies on aged car seats that have influenced the determination of lifespan? Could it share those studies?
>
> • *Britax declines to comment.*

Enter the Minneapolis-based Target, a major vendor of child safety seats. For years, it has run a campaign in which consumers are given store credit for recycling their used and expired seats at Target stores (Target then destroys the seats so that they won't enter the secondhand market). In part, Target frames the trade-ins as an initiative to protect children. And since the program started in 2016, Target claims it's recycled more than 500,000 used seats.

As I've already noted, as recently as October 2018, Target's trade-in website claimed, "Used car seats shouldn't be sold or given away, since they expire every six years and regulations change constantly." When I reached out to Target to ask if the company could provide a source for that claim (because the manufacturers wouldn't), a company spokeswoman replied by referring me to a car-seat-industry-sponsored website:

Car-Safety.org.* Within hours of that email, Target changed the language on its website to read: "According to car-safety.org, car seats expire every six years . . ."

I figured that a major, publicly held company like Target wouldn't lie to a reporter about something that could easily be verified. I also figured that Car-Safety.org would have links to studies showing, for example, increased risk between a used car seat and a new one. But I was wrong! Target's new language was nowhere to be found on the Car-Safety.org site. In fact, there wasn't anything close. So I wrote back to Target and told the company so. Hours later, its website language changed again, this time to read: "According to car-safety.org, many manufacturers recommend that car seats expire around the six-year mark." That's a grammatically suspect way of accurately conveying what the site actually says: "Six (6) years is the general recommendation." But anyone trying to locate data supporting that recommendation will be disappointed. Car-Safety.org—like the manufacturers who support it—just makes unsubstantiated claims.

Is Target purposely conveying false and unverifiable information to parents? I'm fairly certain the reason Target is so cavalier with its language surrounding car seats is that the company—like many parents—simply assumes data exists to substantiate the expirations that manufacturers print on car seats. Of course that assumption is lucrative, insofar as it helps promote the sale of more car seats at Target. Company

---

* Among other notable characteristics, Car-Safety.org is home to a forum where participants one-up each other with accounts of how they keep their expired car seats from entering the secondhand market. My favorite comes from a user named southpawboston: "best to take a sledgehammer to it or a sawzall and cut it to pieces, then write all over the broken pieces 'EXPIRED—DO NOT USE—UNSAFE'. then dispose in trash bags so as not to advertise the seat." The advice, as outlandish as it sounds, is really just a tarted-up version of the advice that Graco offers on its website.

management, with conventional wisdom on its side, isn't likely to concede it's wrong.

But I believe in giving the benefit of the doubt.

So I went back to Target to ask if it could offer another source for its claims about the dangers of used and expired car seats. The Target spokeswoman, clearly irritated to hear from me again, suggested that I read a *Consumer Reports* article.[1] I did, but that didn't answer my questions either. Rather than further aggravate Target—which didn't appear interested in a serious discussion about misleading marketing practices—I reached out to *Consumer Reports* to see if they had any data substantiating car seat expirations. They never responded.

And then I happened upon Sweden.

Since 2008, the Scandinavian country has managed to halve its highway fatality rate, and it even has a program to eliminate highway fatalities entirely by 2050. To help achieve that goal, Sweden has some of the best and strictest child safety seat laws in the world. And they've paid off: child auto fatalities have been reduced to almost zero. It's no exaggeration, and probably an understatement, to claim that Sweden is the global auto- and road-safety gold standard.

I figured that if anybody could give me an honest, data-driven answer to the question of whether used and expired child safety seats are dangerous, it would be a Swedish regulator. So I contacted Maria Krafft, the director of traffic safety and sustainability at the Swedish Transport Administration, who years ago had blogged in favor of used car seats and where to buy good ones in Stockholm.[2] Krafft referred me to Professor Anders Kullgren of the Karolinska Institutet and the Chalmers University of Technology, as well as the longtime head of traffic safety research at Folksam, one of Sweden's largest insurers. Like auto insurers everywhere, Folksam has a financial self-interest in ensuring that passengers are safe (danger equates to payouts and financial losses). In fact, during the early 1990s, Folksam manufactured its own line of child safety seats. If used car seats are a hazard, Professor Kullgren would know. He shared his thoughts via email:

> We have the same experience in Sweden. Manufacturers of child restraints (and other safety equipment such as bicycle and motorcycle helmets) tell their customers to buy a new product after a certain period of time, often relatively short.
>
> We can't see any evidence to justify that from what we have seen in real-world crashes.

The email continued, touching on Folksam's past as a seat manufacturer:

> We still have some seats stored at Folksam that have been used. We have not seen any changes or problems with the plastic material in those seats for this 20–30 year period of time.

That's not data, but it's more than what the world's biggest car seat manufacturers and Target are willing or able to reveal.

Professor Kullgren concluded by writing that Folksam's recommendation is that so long as a seat hasn't been in a crash or otherwise doesn't exhibit any damage, it's fine to use. He also noted that seat designs are always improving, so a consumer buying a newer seat is likely getting a safer seat—especially if the old one exceeds ten years in age. But there's nothing illegal or unsafe in using an older one.

Kullgren's email wouldn't have shocked any of the bidders at the Goodwill car seat auction. Roughly fifty seats were up for sale, and all but three sold, all in a matter of minutes. Prices ranged from five to thirty dollars. As the seats disappeared, one of the bidders asked a

Goodwill employee when the next ones would arrive. Thinking back on the auction, I think it's too bad that Target recycled those more than 500,000 seats over the years. They would've sold, and many children south of the border would be safer because their parents had access to a secondhand market.

Since the dawn of the mass market, product manufacturers and retailers have been sensitive to the lifespans of their products. Some of that concern is in the interests of both consumers and manufacturers. For example, an expiration date on a can of soup protects consumers from eating spoiled food—and manufacturers from responsibility if the consumer becomes sick from eating spoiled food. And some of it is in the interest only of the manufacturers. In 1924, the world's largest lighting manufacturers formed a cartel that agreed to reduce the lifespan of lightbulbs as a means of boosting sales.[3]

In most cases, product lifespans tend to be utilized as negatives that encourage or require the purchase of more stuff. Your packaged cookies perished, and your aspirin expired: go buy more. Lifespan can also be *engineered* to drive sales. For example, the usable lifespan of a smartphone or tablet computer is often limited to its useful battery life. Apple is good at this. In 2017, the world's most valuable company admitted that it had secretly slowed older iPhones (via a software patch) as their batteries aged and depleted. Public outrage forced the company to apologize and explain that it had merely been trying to maintain iPhone battery performance. In France, at least, law enforcement had doubts about the excuse and initiated an investigation into whether Apple had violated the country's "planned obsolescence" law, under which it's illegal for a company to deliberately shorten the life of its products.

The French (so far) have not prosecuted Apple or anyone else for "committing" planned obsolescence. That's wise. Planned obsolescence is too much a part of consumer culture to be eradicated by law enforcement. Indeed, it's a venerable tradition. In 1955, Harley Earl, the first designated head of design at General Motors (and arguably one of the most influential artists of the twentieth century), explained that his designs weren't intended to be timeless:

> Our big job is to hasten obsolescence. In 1934 the average car ownership span was 5 years: now [1955] it is 2 years. When it is 1 year, we will have a perfect score.[4]

Earl was mostly successful. During the middle decades of the twentieth century, abandoned cars became one of the most public and pressing environmental problems in the United States, worthy of mention and action by Presidents Lyndon Johnson and Richard Nixon.[5] But Earl also seemed to underestimate the quality of his own artistry, and a consuming public's desire to own something timeless (as well as something new and disposable). The Chevrolet Corvette, a car model imagined by Earl, remains one of the world's most collectible vehicles. In 2013, one of Earl's own Corvettes sold at auction for $925,000. Presumably, the bidder didn't consider it obsolete.

It's not just wealthy car collectors who seek timeless products. Average consumers are just as hungry. In 2016, European researchers presented 2,917 European shoppers with a choice of products labeled with different expected useful lifespans.[6] In an era of fast fashion, Ikea furniture, and disposable glow sticks, the conclusions were surprising: on average, sales of products whose lifespan was labeled and was longer than the competition's increased by 13.8 percent—*irrespective of price.*

Some product categories did better than others. Lifespan labeling made virtually no difference in television purchase decisions, while it contributed to a 23.7 percent boost in suitcase sales, a 20.1 percent increase in printer sales, and a 15 percent increase in athletic shoe sales. But the most illuminating findings related to the money that consumers claimed they were willing to spend for a longer product lifespan. For example, when presented with dishwasher options, 90 percent of those surveyed said they were willing to pay an average of €102 ($115) *more* for a dishwasher priced between €300 and €500 ($340 and $567) if the product lifespan would be two years greater than the competition's.

These are jarring findings, if only because most consumers, marketing analysts, economists, and businesses journalists are focused almost exclusively on the production, marketing, and sales of *new goods*. But spend even a few minutes in a thrift shop, or at the fabric markets of Cotonou, and it's obvious that consumers instinctively value durability—and vendors price it in—over limited-use products like Ikea furniture and fast fashion. They know their long-term interests aren't served by purchasing the short-term reward; given the opportunity, they want to spend more to spend less.

In September 2017, I traveled to Chicago for Poshfest, the annual two-day conference organized by Poshmark, a fast-growing online market-place where roughly three million individuals buy and sell clothes from one another. There are hundreds of attendees, most of whom earn income by selling on Poshmark (several told me they earn in excess of one hundred thousand dollars per year doing so). When I asked sellers the brands most sought by their customers, the names were uniformly high-quality (and expensive): Lululemon Athletica, Santana Canada, the North Face, among others. These claims aren't just the subjective impressions of individual vendors, either. According to Poshmark's own metrics, Lululemon Athletica was—in September 2017—Poshmark's bestselling women's apparel brand (making it the bestselling brand on the site), and it's remained stubbornly near or at the top of the rankings ever since. When I asked Priscilla Romero, a Colorado-based Poshmark seller who has listings for hundreds of items on the app, why second-hand Lululemon is so popular, she looked at me with pity: "It lasts." Cheap athletic wear simply wouldn't be as collectible.

When I contacted Lululemon to ask whether secondhand contributes to their retail pricing decisions, they declined to comment. Fortunately, other companies are open to discussing the possibility.

In 2011, Patagonia, the maker and retailer of high-end, sustainable outdoor clothing, began an initiative to collect and resell used Patagonia garments (first on eBay, subsequently via Patagonia's own stores and website) that the company wants to see total 10 percent of overall sales by 2023.

I spoke by telephone to Phil Graves, Patagonia's director of corporate development, about the impact of used Patagonia products—the company has branded it "Worn Wear"—on sales of new Patagonia. He told me that the two markets are independent—so far. But long term, the resale market probably boosts the potential market for Patagonia's expensive new stuff. "A lot of used customers are new customers to Patagonia," he explained. "They like the message—organic materials—but maybe they lack the means to buy it. So lower prices are a way in."

For now, Patagonia's new sales are far greater than its secondhand ones. But if Patagonia items are as valuable and durable as Graves suggests, the ratio should start to shift (as it has with refurbished smartphones, which now constitute the fastest growing segment of the global smartphone market). If and when it does, Patagonia's secondhand market will resemble a much smaller version of the world's biggest and most valuable secondhand market: that for used cars.

Sustainably minded consumers don't often think of motorized vehicles as sustainable models of anything. But perhaps they should: in 2018, Americans bought 17.3 million new cars, and 41 million used ones. That's not an anomaly, either. In developed economies like the United States and the European Union, used-car sales tend to be two to two and a half times greater than new. And as short-term leasing of cars becomes increasingly popular (around one third of all new car production is leased), the size of the secondhand market expands as more cars go off-lease. That, in turn, makes high-quality, recent-model cars available to more people. And it's all happening at a time when demand for automobiles is increasing rapidly, especially in emerging Asia and Africa.

It's a little bit like Patagonia, when you think about it. Prospective car buyers can access a favorite brand for less (Patagonia gives store credit for trade-ins of old clothes—just like a car dealer does for old cars), and they can do so at the same store the new stuff is sold. Only, in the case of cars, it's called a dealership. And nothing markets a new product's durability quite like a robust secondhand market for the old ones.

For nearly as long as there have been new car models, consumers have been looking for ways to value that reliability. Systematic help arrived in 1926, when a Los Angeles entrepreneur named Les Kelley published the first *Blue Book*, a guide to the value of new and used automobiles that's grown into a global institution. From the beginning, Kelley saw the value in providing a new car's projected resale value. Kelley explains its reasoning on the company website:

Why is resale value so important? Because you probably aren't going to drive your car all the way to the scrap heap. And whether you tend to keep cars for three years or 10, your total ownership cost is going to be impacted by the amount of money you recoup when you sell it.

Total cost of ownership is so critical to Kelley that it hands out annual "Best Resale Value Awards" that car companies use in marketing their new cars. And why not? Here's Kelley's rationale for giving Toyota its 2018 "Best Brand" award:

> Durability and reliability are especially important to used car buyers, and Toyota's sterling reputation blankets its wide range of cars, trucks and SUVs (and a minivan). If you want to spend less on a new car, buy one that will be worth more when you sell it as a used car. When you buy a Toyota—any Toyota—that's what you get.

In other words: spend more to spend less. Unlike product expiration dates, this is a positive message about product lifespan that reframes the consumer experience as an investment rather than a short-term act of consumption. In many respects, it's the unspoken rationale that drove European customers to say that they'd spend more on a dishwasher.

Of course, investment isn't available to everyone. The potential buyer of a $13,000 Chevrolet Spark subcompact likely bases the purchase decision on different criteria than the potential buyer of a $50,000 Volvo S90 station wagon. But thanks to the *Kelley Blue Book*, someone with the budget for a $12,000 Nissan Versa can assess a much wider variety of models based on the overall cost of ownership. For example, as of 2019, a six-year-old plug-in electric hybrid Chevy Volt is typically

60 percent less than a new one (in fact, it's right around the price of a new Chevrolet Spark)—and the high-quality electric vehicle is likely to last much longer than a car of similar vintage built around an internal combustion engine.

Can that used-car experience be replicated in other products? Realistically, most of the objects cluttering modern homes are too cheap to inspire secondhand markets. There will be no disposable glow stick section at Goodwill, no eBay category devoted to cheap plastic picture frames or broken no-name feature phones. But as nearly three thousand European consumers demonstrated in 2016, the desire to invest in stuff, rather than just consume stuff, runs in parallel with a decades-long boom in low-cost, low-quality goods.

People have been saying "they don't make 'em like they used to" for as long as somebody else—somebody other than an immediate family member or neighbor—has been making stuff.

They aren't wrong, either. Global clothing utilization—a metric measuring the total number of times a garment has been worn, even after resale—declined by 36 percent between 2002 and 2016.[7] Notably, the biggest declines didn't come in wealthy economies, but rather in Asia's emerging economies. In China, the average number of wears dropped from two hundred to sixty-two (fewer than in wealthy Europe).

Some of the decline can be attributed to the speed of fashion and its globalization. But not all. Garments with little to no exposure to the currents of fashion aren't worn as much, either. For example, global hosiery utilization dropped by roughly 40 percent, and nightwear utilization by more than half. In other words, you probably aren't imagining it if—like me—your socks have more holes these days.

Likewise, you also aren't imagining things if your washing machine breaks more often than the one your grandparents had. A 2015 study commissioned by the German Environmental Agency found that—between 2004 and 2012—the proportion of purchases of electronic appliances replaced because of defects grew from 3.5 to 8.3 percent.[8] Similarly, the share of large household appliances (like refrigerators and washing machines) that had to be replaced within five years of purchase grew from 7 to 13 percent. If those numbers don't seem large, think of them in terms of a single manufacturer. What would the consuming public think—much less say in online reviews—about a washing machine manufacturer whose five-year failure rate increased from single to double digits in the span of eight years?

Consumers know what's happening. In 2014, a British nongovernmental organization that works with business, government, and communities released data showing how badly manufacturers of household appliances are doing when it comes to meeting consumer expectations.[9] For example, British consumers expected washing machines to last a minimum of six years. But according to survey data, a whopping 41 percent of washers purchased in 2012 replaced products less than six years old, and 82 percent of surveyed respondents claimed that the replacement was due to a breakdown or an unreliability. Refrigerators and vacuum cleaners performed even worse.

Not all—or even most—of the quality problems can be blamed on the manufacturers. Price is king for most consumers, and manufacturers are always seeking ways to lower costs so that they can meet that demand. Sometimes meeting the demand means cutting corners, as consumers of fast fashion learn when they fish out their faded garments from the laundry. But not always. The first Motorola cellphone handsets cost nine thousand dollars in the 1980s, and they didn't include cameras, GPS, voice recognition, or other features that smartphone consumers expect in phones that cost two hundred dollars. The pressure to innovate is sometimes the best cost-cutting incentive of all.

To reach the testing lab for the world's largest maker of commercial laundry machines, you need to travel to central Wisconsin and descend a stairway into a basement that smells like soap. Around a corner and then another is a room that looks like a laundromat evacuated by chemists. There are dozens if not hundreds of machines here; they all appear to be running, but the only people watching after them wear white lab coats.

I am here with Randy Radtke, global public relations manager, and Tom Friederick, supervisor of quick response engineering, at Alliance Laundry Systems. Every year the century-old company sells millions of washers and dryers to customers as diverse as hotels, laundromats, hospitals, militaries, college dormitories, industrial laundries, res-

taurants, and—increasingly—homeowners. Most of that equipment is made by 1,600 manufacturing employees here in Ripon, population 7,500.

We pause in front of a Speed Queen–branded top-loading washer, Alliance's brand for the consumer and coin-operated laundry market. It doesn't come cheap. By the company's own estimates, it's roughly three hundred dollars more expensive than what the competition puts out—or roughly a thousand dollars for an

The entry-level Speed Queen TR3 doesn't look like a trendsetter, but it sells like one. (Image courtesy of Alliance Laundry Systems)

entry-level washing machine. For that price, it certainly doesn't look like anything special. The model I'm gazing at is a steel box painted white with three knobs—for water temperature, load size, and cycle type. If anything, it reminds me of the ancient, unkillable washer-dryer set that ran for decades in the basement of my grandparents' home.

"We run it nonstop for a year," Friederick says, and opens the lid to show me water swishing around. "They're not all prototypes. Sometimes we're auditing one of our own machines to ensure we're keeping up standards. Sometimes we're prototyping a single part. It varies." Nearby, a machine is running with a green piece of tape affixed to the control panel. Someone has scrawled across it: NOISEY/MED. SPIN.

"What's that mean?"

"Might be an older machine with prototype parts in it."

In the testing lab, they go to extreme lengths. "We'll put hockey pucks in the dryers," Friederick tells me. "When they come out, they look like charcoal briquettes." Sure enough, I hear a chorus of thumps in the dryer testing area. Then we turn a corner and encounter something louder: every four seconds, a mechanical arm opens and slams the doors of a washer-dryer combo. According to a mounted counter, I witness slam 54,472. Elsewhere I see a washing machine that's been running for 9,861 hours and another that's logged 3,180 cycles. At the far end of the room is a box where valves used to mix water inside a washing machine are on cycle 206,261.

"We also test the coin boxes for the laundromats," Friederick says. "Beat them up pretty good to simulate somebody trying to break into them."

"Can I see that?"

He laughs.

But there's a more meaningful point to be made about those coin-operated machines. Next door are manufacturing operations that sprawl over several city blocks. I'm given a tour that includes the brightly lit line where hundreds of workers assemble around 1,400 smaller dryers per day (elsewhere are assembly operations for bigger dryers, including some almost as big as my rental car). The devices look mostly identical on the line, but when we reach the inspection area at the end, I notice a crucial distinction: some have laundromat coin boxes and some don't. "There's no difference in how things are made here," Radtke explains, raising his voice over the factory din. "Machines for consumers and machines for business are made on the same lines."

That isn't just a way to save money on space and manufacturing costs. It reflects a philosophy of design. The idea is simple: upfront costs are less important than the long-term cost of ownership. A laundromat washing machine, subjected to all kinds of abuse, is bought to last. One that isn't will inevitably break down and fail to generate business.

It's a point that Mike Schoeb, Alliance Laundry Systems' CEO, makes during a video conference with me from the company's headquarters in Miami. "It's about total cost of ownership," he explains. "Service calls are really expensive. So the design criteria we use is not 'first cost,'" he says, referring to the sticker price. "That's important, but depending on the year of the survey, it's the number three, number five criteria for our [commercial] customers."

The consumer market behaves differently. First cost tends to be the most important factor to people browsing through the appliance sections at Best Buy and Lowe's. So rather than design for the durability valued by business, most consumer appliance manufacturers will work on finding a way to ensure an attractive sticker price.

After the tour, I sit at a long table in an airy conference room off the lobby of Alliance Laundry Systems' sleek new offices (next to the factory) in Ripon. Jay McDonald, the company vice president in charge of home laundry sales in the United States, and Susan Miller, the Speed

Queen brand manager for North America, join me. Both are sales-people, and they press the sale immediately, bringing up Speed Queen's strongest selling point: "Built to Last 25 Years." The message is plastered on the machines, on the brand's website, in its brochures, and—increasingly—on review and social media forums where fans of the Speed Queen brand brag about their machines. "It's not something you can just go out and say," McDonald tells me. " 'Twenty-five years.' You have to prove it."

The sad thing is, decades ago you didn't have to prove it. Take, for example, Maytag, the venerable U.S. home appliance brand (now owned by Whirlpool). In 1967, the company ran its first television advertise-ment featuring Ol' Lonely, a Maytag repairman who spends his time alone, waiting for service calls that never come. In that ad, Ol' Lonely summarizes what he symbolizes: "Maytag washers and dryers are built to last. That makes a Maytag repairman the loneliest guy in town." Appliances were pricey and expected to last. Consumers wanted reas-surance, and Ol' Lonely conveyed it so convincingly that he's one of the most iconic characters in the history of American advertising.

Then, around the mid-1990s, consumer and manufacturer expecta-tions began to shift. Low-cost factories in Asia emerged that were capable of building appliances for less than, say, Maytag factories in North America. To remain competitive, manufacturers who remained in high-wage countries like the United States lowered prices. That discounting didn't come for free. It often took its toll in quality: metal parts gave way to less durable plastic ones; sheet metal became thinner, less durable, and more capable of projecting noise. Still, consumers sort of won. Since the mid-1990s, prices on all major home appliances have declined, becoming an ever-smaller part of the overall budgets of people around the world.

But declining quality eventually catches up with manufacturers and their customers. In the early 2000s, Maytag faced growing numbers of complaints and class-action lawsuits over quality problems. It wasn't making much of an effort to solve the problems, either. Instead, it was introducing new, low-cost, and low-quality models. Dependability, the essence of the Ol' Lonely character, was no longer the most compelling reason to buy a Maytag.

Suddenly, Ol' Lonely didn't really have a place in Maytag's advertising. To help him work through the crisis, Maytag hired a marketing consultant who advised the company to embrace the notion that "the most innovative new technologies are not completely dependable."[10] The televised advertisements that followed this reinvention featured Ol' Lonely paired with a younger, more energetic apprentice who spends his time trying to figure out how to outsmart the machine's many new innovations—and in the process, annoying his boss. The apprentice didn't last very long.

Around the time that Maytag was reengineering Ol' Lonely, Alliance Laundry Systems was contemplating how to reenter the home laundry business. The company had changed hands twice since the late 1970s and, thanks to a noncompete agreement, was prevented from making equipment for homes. But that restriction was slated to end in 2004. Jay McDonald was part of the home laundry decision-making process, and he told me that the company took a close look at what kind of washing machine could be manufactured for the cheap prices that had become the going rate for models like Maytag's. According to the company's calculations, such "a machine can only be manufactured to last five to seven years."

Rather than reenter the market with a low-quality, low-durability product that competes with similar machines made by much bigger companies, Alliance Laundry Systems did something heretical: "We went back in with the most expensive product out there. Our pitch: We haven't changed anything in twenty years. It's the same product as the 1980s." He chuckles, and adds, "Oh, and we had virtually no marketing budget." It was a bet that there are consumers nostalgic for the way things used to be made, and who don't mind paying a bigger sticker price to obtain the dependability that they used to take for granted. It was a bet that there are still consumers who evaluate purchases with the same time horizons as businesses.

Those were solid bets. Alliance Laundry Systems won't share data on sales of the Speed Queen brand, but did tell me that the business has tripled in size since 2013. "We are taking market share," McDonald says. Speed Queen is also garnering attention. In 2019, *Consumer Reports* surveyed its members on their experiences with 71,038 different washers. Speed Queen was the only brand of top-load agitator washer (the type found in most American homes) to receive an excellent score for owner satisfaction and predicted reliability.

Miller, seated across from me, explains that the short lifespans of other washers—Maytag claims its washers are designed for ten years of life[11]— are precisely what creates Speed Queen's opportunity. "Our customers aren't in their twenties. A Speed Queen is their third washer. The others broke and they want one that lasts." She pauses for just a beat. "'I've found this brand,'" she says, paraphrasing the social media–driven word of mouth that's been crucial to the brand's success, "'and it lasts forever.'"

Speed Queen isn't the only company to realize that there's money to be made by reembracing dependability, and the home appliance sector isn't the only consumer sector in which a company seeks to differentiate itself on the basis of product lifespan. It's happened in apparel, too (at least, at the high end). For example, Lululemon Athletica, the popular maker of athleisure highly sought on the secondhand market, has its "Five Year Collection" of short- and long-sleeved T-shirt and V-necks. They're ridiculously expensive—$58 for a T-shirt—and it's not clear whether they're expected to actually last five years, so much as "stay fresh" for five years. But the quality of materials is mostly undisputed, and the volume of secondhand Lululemon Athletica already being traded among aficionados serves to justify both the pricing and the five-year claim.

"Consumers don't want to pay more, but they will when they see the value" is how Alliance Laundry Systems' Mike Schoeb put it to me. As products pass from first owners to second and third, that value is passed along.

Historically, it's a slow process. But thanks to the internet, it's speeding up. Apps like Poshmark enable consumers to flip their clothes after one or two wears. Similarly, an emerging "clothes sharing" industry gives consumers access to short-term rentals of recent fashions. Since consumers have the garments for only a short time, many of the consumers don't care about the quality so much as they care that the styles are up-to-date. By necessity, though, the clothing-sharing companies are very concerned about quality, indeed: a garment that breaks down after a few "shares" isn't going to be as profitable as one that lasts for dozens.

Nonetheless, as admirable as this business model might be, it isn't nearly sufficient to make a large or immediate dent in the crisis of quality impacting apparel. And other products (washing machines, for example) are simply too big and unwieldy to be flipped or shared in developed economies (secondhand appliances are crucial in developing economies).

So what more can be done?

One option is for governments to become more directly involved in regulating the durability of products. To some extent, they already are.

Minimum safety standards in cars, child safety seats, electrical appliances, and other products are common and necessary.

But stepping beyond safety to require, for example, that Maytag make washers with the same quality standards as Alliance Laundry Systems is more ambitious—and more problematic. For one thing, Alliance Laundry Systems probably wouldn't like it. After all, the company's booming consumer business (and its pricing) are built on the idea that consumers should be able to choose a better machine among many that are inferior. Second, and even more important, consumers who can't easily afford Speed Queen would be the ones who suffer if governments started imposing durability requirements that raise the price of stuff. That's not only unfair; it'd probably result in a backlash against the social and environmental goals that inspired durability requirements.

Finally, regulations requiring minimum durability standards would inevitably chill the quest for innovation in new and existing products. Forcing companies to get it right on the first go will convince many to skip the innovation and development process altogether, and just keep making what they're already making. For most of humanity, the argument that progress must stop in favor of dependability won't fly.

The better approach is simpler: companies must be transparent about the lifespans of their products and attach a sticker or tag (physical in stores, and virtual for online) to their products informing consumers of just how long they're projected to last, based on verifiable testing. The requirement doesn't necessarily have to be a government regulation in order to have an impact. A voluntary program in which industries agree on durability standards and how to label durability would work just as well (and perhaps even better).

Of course, there are many ways to measure lifespan. For some product categories, like washing machines and other home appliances, timeframes can be measured in years. For apparel, it might be a grading system that takes into account a range of factors, including colorfastness, resistance to abrasion, and durability in a home washer (these standards mostly exist, by the way). For more complex products, like laptops, fairness might dictate that manufacturers reveal the expected lifespans of replaceable parts, starting with batteries. For smartphones and other short-lasting consumer electronics products, the timeframe should incorporate the months or years that the manufacturer plans to support the product with security and other software updates.

Lifespan labeling isn't a new or radical idea. For the last few years, governments of countries in Europe and the European Union have explored requiring lifespan labeling on certain product classes. And in the United States, upholstery manufacturers have long relied on "fabric wearability" codes to set transparent, universal standards for furniture durability. These days, most quality furniture makers include a tag disclosing long-term wearability (even though many consumers may not be aware it's there or what it means). Similarly, ASTM International, an organization that develops voluntary technical standards, has dozens of standards related to textiles. For example, swimwear retailers might look to "Standard Performance Specification for Woven Swimwear Fabrics" when ordering woven swimsuits from a manufacturer.

Will lifespan labels work? So far, the two most robust studies (both conducted in Europe) have shown modest but tangible effects on consumer buying decisions.[12] But those studies, for all their merits, focused only on the most immediate impacts. The more meaningful impacts will occur as manufacturers rethink how they design, manu-facture, and market products.

Child safety seats are an excellent example of how transformative this rethink might be. At the moment, seat manufacturers have no incentive (or regulation) requiring them to reveal or compete on the durability of their products. And so long as parents can't evaluate a seat in terms of how long it will last, manufacturers can get away with suggesting that the devices are, effectively, hazardous on expiration. Lifespan labels would eliminate that practice by forcing manufacturers to compete over lifespan—and build accordingly. Logically, the seat advertised to last ten years will outsell the one advertised to last six.

Of course, not every product category will benefit equally from lifespan labeling. If the apparel industry were to adopt a lifespan- or durability-grading system for its products—and that's an "if"—the impact would likely be smaller. Customers who shop fast-fashion brands are unlikely to encounter the high-durability labels of Patagonia. Even so, the society-wide impact of such labeling shouldn't be underestimated.

Encouraging consumers to think more seriously about the financial, environmental, and personal costs of their consumption would be a major step in addressing the crisis of quality and the environmental and social impacts of too much stuff. Better yet, it would spur businesses to seek economic incentives to design and market better products. Today's secondhand economy, faltering in search of quality, should have more than it can handle.

CHAPTER 11

A Rich Person's Broken Thing

Fifteen miles north of Tamale, the capital of Ghana's Northern Region, Ibrahim Alhassan, master television repairman, is crouched over the back of a twenty-five-year-old television picture tube. He has a soldering iron in one hand, a circuit board in another. As he explains it, the set's manual volume and channel controls are broken. So he's replacing it with a board that he's jerry-rigged specifically for this purpose, and which will give the owner remote control—as well as volume and picture controls. The total repair bill is five dollars, not including parts, which are hard to obtain in the Northern Region and can push the price to seven or eight dollars. It's a good value. Around here, a secondhand tube television of similar vintage starts around fifteen dollars.

Alhassan's shop is located on a dusty red-dirt road that runs the length of a residential portion of Savelugu, a farm town of around forty thousand people. Most of the buildings are made from mud walls; some are round, with thatch roofs; some are square and topped with corrugated steel. Television antennas poke up from almost every building, except for the town's main mosque, which is topped by golden cupolas. Many residents have mobile phones, but they're primarily feature phones used to communicate via text message, and—for some—engage in basic mobile banking. Broadcast television and DVDs remain the primary form of screen entertainment, and Alhassan ensures that the shows go on.

"DVD players are popular," he explains as he works. "I receive lots of those." He's a handsome fifty-year-old, slightly unshaven, his eyes red from (I assume) staring too long at circuit boards. But fatigue doesn't wear away his good mood and easy smile.

"You fix DVDs, too?" I ask.

He turns to Wahab Odoi Mohammed, a Ghanaian American trader of used U.S. electronics, and says something to him in Dagbani, the language of this region. Then he turns back to me and says, "I'm in electronics. I know boards and voltage meters, so I can do it."

"How many televisions do you fix per day?"

"Five per day, depending on the problem."

Tamale, a town of, officially, 350,000 people, has more than a hundred TV-repair businesses, with many doing far more than five repairs per day. Conservatively estimated, that's *hundreds* of second-hand televisions repaired weekly in this sparsely populated section of West Africa. In the big cities of Ghana and Nigeria—the most affluent parts of West Africa—the electronics repair shops are more common than Starbucks in Manhattan. Conservatively estimated, that's *thousands* of secondhand televisions repaired weekly. Multiply that across developing West Africa, and that amounts to tens of thousands of secondhand televisions—most imported from Europe, the United States, and East Asia—repaired weekly.[1] For anyone worried about resource conservation, that's a rate of reuse that far exceeds that in San Francisco, Amsterdam, Tokyo, or any other developed area that prides

Ibrahim Alhassan outside of his television repair shop in Savelugu. It's a central gathering point in the neighborhood, often filled with friends, relatives, and fans.

itself on sustainability (and upgrades relentlessly). Turns out, product durability isn't just about making it right the first time.

Alhassan is typical of West Africa's DIY repairmen (and they're uniformly men). His family lacked the resources to pay for education beyond middle school, so he was apprenticed to an electronics repairman in Kumasi, a center of Africa's secondhand trade located roughly 250 miles south of Savelugu. Then, with the aid of his master, he set up his own business. Here in Savelugu, he has the respect of his neighbors. As we chat, one jumps in to declare, "We all have faith in him, that he can fix things."

In one respect, however, Alhassan is a bit of a throwback: he works on old tube televisions at a time when much of the world, including the bigger towns of Ghana, has moved on to using (and fixing) flat-screen televisions. "How old are the televisions you fix?" I ask him.

Alhassan leans in close to the circuit board and carefully solders a connection. He works at a thick wooden table covered with cables, tools, a long power bar, gouges, and burn marks. "As old as forty years," he says, nodding in the direction of a small Sony Trinitron awaiting his attention on the ground. Behind him, two heavy wooden doors open to an unlit space filled with dozens of televisions piled atop one another, boxes of circuit boards, and assorted picture tubes. He's been in business since 1992. By the looks of it, his collection dates back at least that far.

"The hardest thing for the television repairmen is parts," he explains. "We don't have parts stores. So if we need a part, we get it from the old televisions. I have many, and so do my friends and old apprentices. If I need a part I don't have, I see if they have it. They all have old televisions like me, and they can check if the board is still available. Then we trade, and I do the repair."

"And if you can't find the part?"

"No repair."

I hear this repeatedly in Ghana: a chronic lack of parts prevents devices from being repaired and used longer. It's a leading reason that old devices pile up in sheds, in front yards, and even on roofs (there's an old television and a cassette deck holding down part of Alhassan's corrugated metal roof).

Seated next to Wahab, and listening intently, is Robin Ingenthron, CEO of Good Point Recycling of Middlebury, Vermont. He's a gregarious fifty-seven-year-old with intent eyes and a camera. But Robin's not here as a tourist. Rather, he's doing research on West Africa's extensive repair economy. For years, he's legally exported used electronics to developing countries, including Ghana. Wahab is one of his customers, and the two men are keen to expand the trade beyond whole devices like televisions to the parts necessary to keep them running even longer.

"Do you repair flat screens, too?" Robin asks.

Alhassan examines his soldering. "My former apprentices learn the tech and teach me and my friends. We get together once per week. Learn and have a good time." He looks up from his work. "I've witnessed people with flat screens. In my opinion, flat screens don't last long."

That's certainly the case in developing countries like Ghana, where the underdeveloped electrical utilities are prone to brownouts and other problems that can damage the delicate electronics in a flat-screen television. For Robin and Wahab, that's the immediate and long-term opportunity. If the television manufacturers won't sell the parts to Ghana, they will.

I step out from beneath the metal awning that shades Alhassan's workspace and snap a photo of the televisions and parts piled up between Alhassan's home and the one next door. As I check the photo on my camera's screen, Robin walks over. "It's like the Ozarks in the seventies," he says, referring to the part of rural America where he grew up. "Bunch of old junk cars sitting around for nothing but the parts." As Robin knows as well as anyone, that "nothing" is worth something. He also knows, as well as anyone, that repairable devices are worth more.

In 1829, Lydia Maria Child, author of *The American Frugal Housewife*, offered this common-sense advice to her readers:

> Keep a bag for odd pieces of tape and strings, they will come in use. Keep a bag or box for old buttons, so that you may know where to go when you want one.[2]

In the nineteenth century, and well into the twentieth, domestic manuals like Child's offered a range of tips designed to aid women in the pursuit of household thrift. In those days, thrift wasn't a matter of choice or virtue. It was a necessity. The essentials of daily life—clothes, kitchenware, tools, furniture—were expensive and intended to last for years if not lifetimes. Repair was a way to ensure that they did. Sewing a button required less labor and fewer resources than making a new shirt. Saving random strings saved the time and money necessary to buy string on a trip to town (or order it from a catalog). In 1829, having a bag of string and a bag of buttons was common sense.

Two centuries later, that's generally not the case. As a member of Generation X, I might be among the last Americans to have memories of mothers who kept bags of buttons. And those bags of buttons typically had more to do with domestic habits passed between mothers and daughters than any need for midcentury household thrift. My mother's mother, on the other hand, knew thrift, and it traveled with her from rural Iowa and South Dakota to Minneapolis. My aunt, Rita Sandstrom, recalled it for me via Facebook Messenger late one night:

> She had a sewing kit with all sorts of supplies in it: darning eggs (which I used for fixing holes in socks—especially my dad's); many types of sewing needles, pins, safety pins, many wooden spools of thread in every color and thickness (they've been made of plastic for years now), metal thimbles, pin cushions, measuring tape, seam ripper, tailor's chalk and, of course, lots of various buttons.

Aside from hobbyists and perhaps the deeply committed knitter, that lifestyle has disappeared from America. By the time I was a teenager, the price and utilization of clothing was falling rapidly in the United States, negating the argument for mending at home. As an adult, I've hung shirts with missing buttons in the closet and forgotten them in favor of a new one.

Of course, household thrift based on necessity hasn't totally disappeared. From the beginning of the automobile age, weekend mechanics saved money—and their cars—by doing repairs and modifications at home. For car owners who had the money (and an aversion to grease), independent garages and repair centers emerged. For those with even more money, and cars under warranty, the expensive authorized service center thrived. From the auto manufacturer's standpoint, the various repair options and price points served their interests, especially as cars moved off warranty. After all, nobody is going to buy a Ford if the only place they can get the tires rotated and a new oil filter is the dealership.

The proof, if any was needed, is found in the South Bronx on a cold Saturday morning in late March. Robin Ingenthron parks his black Honda on the street beside a brick self-storage facility, and Wahab Odoi Mohammed and I step onto the street with him. A few car lengths away, a bronze Hyundai station wagon is rolled off a flatbed tow truck into a forty-foot shipping container bound for a West African port. By noon, at least two more cars will be in that container, levitated and secured by chains.

"Over here," Wahab says as he confidently strides down the narrow dirt alley beside the storage facility. It opens to a long dirt parking area filled with dozens of cars, dozens of shipping containers, with a forklift zipping between them, and a handful of bundled-up African men. "This place is ninety percent Ghanaian," he declares. "They ship all over West Africa." We pause beside a black 2017 Honda Sonata whose front end is crushed and flattened, the hood bent upward slightly, its paint cracked. "Doesn't matter," Wahab says as he lifts the hood. "The engine is okay." Inside the vehicle are boxes filled with repair parts to make the vehicle new again. Doing the repair would be cost-prohibitive in the United States. But it's no problem in Ghana, where much of the automobile repair business specializes in fixing up imported accident cars packed with parts.

"How much does a car like this cost at auction?" Robin asks.

"It depends," Wahab says. "This one maybe less than five thousand dollars. Then fifteen hundred dollars to ship. Maybe six thousand for the duty. By the time it's all done and repaired, maybe fourteen thousand. That's less than the cost of a new or used one." Wahab would know. When he has time and money, he cruises internet auction sites in search of vehicles totaled in U.S. auto accidents. They're listed by insurance companies keen to recoup some value from the loss. Among the most enthusiastic buyers are West African traders. In 2017, 48,899 used cars were exported from the United States to Nigeria, 12,434 went to Ghana, and 12,130 went to Benin.

Suleiman Jawula, a charismatic Ghanaian American, wanders over. He's a public-school teacher who runs a lucrative side business shipping cars to Africa and the Middle East from this lot. "My people, they want a car for when they go home to visit," he says. "So I help them." He and his crew can pack and ship eight shipping containers in a day—or roughly thirty cars. That's not easy. We open a container and see a car hung from the ceiling with chains, just inches from the car that's fixed by chains below it. Behind them are two more. For years, this particular method has delivered cars unscathed (beyond their preexisting accident damage) across oceans. In years past, when this lot was larger, crews could pack forty containers per day—or as many as 160 cars.

Wahab is a regular customer. When he wins a car at auction, he or Suleiman arranges for it to be shipped to the South Bronx and packed for shipment (a courier typically charges between five hundred and a thousand dollars, depending on where in the United States a car is located). When it arrives in Ghana, Wahab arranges for the vehicle to be repaired, and then he either sells it immediately or drives it around until he tires of it and a new one arrives from the United States. It's a lot of turnover: Robin loves recounting the afternoon that he had to get out of a car in the middle of Tamale, Wahab's hometown, because Wahab had just sold the car in which they were riding to a person he'd encountered on the street (the transaction: Wahab's 2015 Ford Fusion for a 2011 Chevrolet Cruze, seven thousand dollars, and some land).

"Wahab," Suleiman declares, "I have a pickup for you." The four of us walk over to a badly dented 2007 Toyota Tundra.

"How many miles?" Wahab asks, looking inside.

"Forty thousand," Suleiman answers.

Wahab looks at me and says, "He'll want around five grand for it."

Suleiman smiles.

As the others chat, I wander by myself, pausing beside a wrecked BMC Mini, a Camry, and a beat-up F-150 pickup, all of which have been packed with repair parts for the trip to West Africa. Then I come across a Chevy Equinox SUV with its driver side completely collapsed from an accident and the front end compressed from what must have been an even worse impact. I grew up in a family scrap business focused on recycling cars. On a good day, we'd crush sixty, many of which looked better than this Equinox. So far as I'm concerned, it belongs at a scrapyard. I look through the windows and am not surprised to see that this vehicle isn't filled with parts. "Wonder what the deal is," I say to Robin, who is nearby.

"Maybe they're sending it to be parted out."

"The parts are worth more money than the car," Suleiman says as he approaches with Wahab. "I have clients."

*   *   *

In 1994, the U.S. government required manufacturers to include computers for monitoring and controlling emissions in all cars and trucks. To maintain those computers, and the engine components to which they're attached, manufacturers created software. Lawmakers foresaw trouble: manufacturers and their dealerships could, in theory, use that software to place independent repair shops at a competitive disadvantage. As a result, Congress required manufacturers to make those tools available to any repair business that requested them. That was farsighted, in light of what was to come.

During the next twenty-five years, computers became increasingly critical to the operation of automobiles. Today even the cheapest of budget vehicles includes electronic controls for the engine, automatic transmission, antilock brakes, and cruise control. Predictably, auto manufacturers have tended to restrict essential software diagnostics and tools to their authorized dealerships and service centers, with negative consequences for consumers. For example, some airbag sensors can be reset only with the manufacturer's software after they fail. If an independent garage doesn't have that software, the car owner is forced to seek service at the dealership—or drive around with a broken airbag.

Auto manufacturing isn't the only industry to restrict access to repair. Many of the same anti-repair practices are common in the consumer electronics and appliance industry.

Consider the practices of Apple.

In recent years the world's largest consumer electronics manufacturer has systematically disabled iPhones that had their home buttons replaced by independent repair shops (imagine if Ford remotely disabled your car engine because your power locks were fixed at a local garage, not a dealership);[3] sued an independent Norwegian repair shop for using secondhand iPhone repair parts;[4] and sealed up its phones and

computers with unusual screws that—for a while at least—most independent repair shops didn't have the drivers to loosen.[5]

And those are just the one-off occurrences. As a general practice,
Apple refuses to make service manuals or parts available to independent repair shops or consumers (even for relatively simple procedures
like an iPhone battery switch). Why does Apple take these steps? On
January 2, 2019, Apple CEO Tim Cook addressed a public letter to
Apple's investors in which he cut the company's quarterly revenue
outlook for the first time in fifteen years. Among the reasons cited was
a steep decline in iPhone sales due to eleven million iPhone owners
opting for a temporary twenty-nine-dollar sale on battery replacements
rather than a far more expensive upgrade.[6] The company has subsequently raised the price of an iPhone battery replacement, presumably
to a level that will make an iPhone owner ask: "At that price, doesn't it
make more sense just to buy a new phone?"

How many Apple devices are left unrepaired because the company's
anti-repair (and battery replacement) practices drive up the cost of
ownership? In the world's towns without Genius Bars or Apple-
authorized repair centers, how many phones sit in desk drawers unrepaired? And what will happen to devices that break after Apple stops
providing its authorized repair centers with the tools to fix older devices
(a particularly thorny problem in developing countries that buy older,
secondhand devices)?

If today's consumers could simply treat phones, laptops, and other
devices as luxuries, this would be the proverbial "first-world problem."
But the twenty-first century is a connected age, and electronic devices
are essential to functioning in daily life. Ensuring that these devices last
longer, via repair, won't just be an environmental imperative. It's also
a common-sense imperative, the kind of household economy that

wouldn't be unfamiliar to nineteenth-century keepers of button and string bags.

Robin Ingenthron was raised in rural Arkansas by an academic father descended from newspapermen and a mother descended from—in his proud words—"true hillbillies." Ever since he was young, Robin tells me, his grandfather was teaching him "how to fix stuff," starting with cars. "The main thing that he would tell me is"—he switches into a higher-pitched, old-timey voice—"'all of this is going to be incredibly important to you, young man, knowing how to fix stuff.'"

We're seated in Robin's home office in Middlebury, Vermont. A large picture window looks out on a half acre of green lawn and then mile after mile of forest. Robin's wife, a professor of French at Middlebury College, just left for work and we're onto a second cup of Robin's black coffee.

I suggest that his grandfather's advice about repair is from a different era. He corrects me. "I think it's advice from poor people. People who are poor fix stuff. I was raised that the smartest thing you can do is buy a rich person's broken thing," he says. "The best deal you can negotiate is when the rich person doesn't know how easy it is to fix it."

The recycling business, and its relentless pursuit of value in what others view as worthless, was a perfect fit for Robin. After college, he served in the Peace Corps, worked at a small recycling company, and eventually worked his way into a job as the recycling director for the Massachusetts Department of Environmental Protection. During his tenure, he was assigned an unenviable task: set up recycling infrastructure to support a state ban on the dumping of old tube televisions and monitors into landfills. He did it by relying in part on recyclers interested in purchasing the televisions for reuse—either as whole televisions or as parts. "You just had to look at the prices that were being paid to know that TVs have value," he tells me as we drive across Middlebury to Good Point Recycling. "They aren't waste." It was a good deal for everyone. The State of Massachusetts saved money, the repair industry got parts and televisions, and consumers could feel good knowing that their unwanted devices were "recycled" in a manner that ensured the highest environmental outcome: reuse.

A few years later, Robin quit his state job and followed his wife to Middlebury, where he established Good Point Recycling as a business that, among other things, collected used American computer monitors and sent them to places where they could be reused.[7] One of his biggest markets was China, where, he learned during one visit, massive factories remanufactured those old computer monitors into tube televisions for emerging markets. He recalls a single broker in Los Angeles "purchasing fifty thousand used American televisions *per day*" for the Chinese remanufacturing industry. Eventually, many of those refurbished monitors were exported back to the United States as new devices, giving the rich man the opportunity to buy back his broken thing at a premium.

We pull up to a brutalist concrete building in a leafy industrial park that, in addition to Good Point Recycling, is home to the largest hard-cider brewery in the United States. Robin leads me inside Good Point. Forklifts zoom back and forth, loading boxes and barrels of metal and televisions and other electronics into trailers. It's a tight space filled with large washing machine boxes full of old monitors and pallets of old computers.

As we stroll, two large photography umbrellas flash. Elias Chinchilla, a longtime employee, is pointing a camera at the parts he's just extracted from a forty-eight-inch Samsung television manufactured in 2017. "Looks like it had the shit kicked out of it," Robin says of the shattered screen set off to the side. The likely story is that somebody dropped it, realized it would be more expensive to repair than to buy a new one, and left it for recycling at a local government collection station. In Vermont, Good Point has the contract to recycle those devices—and it will. But only after the $25 worth of Samsung parts (that's the ballpark guess in the warehouse) are extracted and listed on eBay. Most of his customers are repair businesses in North America, but the company ships around the world.

Robin has been recycling for years, and business is booming. "But the thing that keeps us growing while other electronics recyclers go out of business is the eBay business, the part business." Most of Robin's recycling competitors still look at a television as a package of potential raw materials. Robin sees a package of stuff to keep televisions working. He's not alone. The biggest television-parts business in North America (Shopjimmy.com) breaks down 1,000 to 1,500 televisions per day and generates tens of millions of dollars in revenues from the extracted parts.

Cannibalization isn't a new concept in the world of repair. As Robin reminded me in Savelugu, it's the side business of any auto junkyard (and sometimes the main business). Around the world, it's often the best—and sometimes the only—option to pull off a fix.

What's particularly frustrating, at least for those who like the idea of a thriving repair industry, are the lengths that some manufacturers will go to scare customers into not attempting a repair on their own. For example, it's the rare consumer who hasn't encountered a sticker warning not to open a device or the warranty will be voided.

Kyle Wiens, who is speeding much too fast downhill (actually, downmountain) on Highway 101 from his home in Atascadero, California, hates those stickers, and in recent years he's played a key role in raising public awareness of the fact that they're illegal.[8] Just as bad, from Kyle's point of view: they're an outright violation of basic property rights. "If you buy something, you should be able to do what you want with it," he all but yells as he keeps his eyes focused on the traffic he's passing. "You should be able to fix it. I mean, it's yours!"

Kyle, thirty-five, is the boyish CEO and co-founder of iFixit, a sixteen-year-old, 170-plus-employee San Luis Obispo, California, company that aspires—in Wiens's words—to be "the repair manual for everything."

The business model is a unique one. iFixit (with the help of an army of volunteers) creates repair manuals for devices that don't have them and posts them to its website, where anyone can access the information for free. As of this writing, there are more than thirty-eight thousand manuals (and counting) for products ranging from the latest Samsung Galaxy Note smartphone to the Oral-B Vitality electric toothbrush. To monetize this massive informational giveaway, iFixit sells repair parts and tools, as well as software and consulting services. In 2016 the company generated $21 million in sales.

In some respects, iFixit is the twenty-first-century analogue to Lydia Maria Childs and *The American Frugal Housewife.* Just as nineteenth-century frontier women lacked complete information on how to manage and fix their stuff, so too do contemporary Americans overrun with technologies. "How many objects are in a home?" Kyle asks as he exits into San Luis Obispo. "Is it a thousand? Ten thousand? It's an order of magnitude more than it was fifty years ago. And yet the economics don't work for there to be a local espresso-machine repair guy. So either consumers have to figure out how to repair things themselves or . . ." He shrugs.

Kyle's ambitions for iFixit are vast. "Last year more than one hundred million people visited our site in search of repair information," he says.

"We estimate that for every repair that we ship out of the building [in the form of parts], there are one thousand to ten thousand repairs just using our manuals. And we ship hundreds of thousands of parts every year." His goal is one billion repairs per year. At that point, he figures, iFixit will impact the U.S. economy as much as Home Depot has. "[People know they] can go to Home Depot, get their parts, and talk to someone who can tell them how to do the toilet. [Home Depot has] changed the fabric of American society, and that's what we want to do. We want to change the fabric of American society so that repair is a viable option for people."

To bring that goal to fruition, the company does far more than offer free repair guides. It cultivates the media. For example, every year, iFixit flies some of the company's best techs (and sometimes Kyle) to Australia so they can be among the first in the world to buy and take apart the new iPhone models. By the time consumers in the United States—Apple's biggest market—wake up on an iPhone-release day, iFixit has already posted a slickly produced guide to tearing it down and assigned a "repairability rating" to the device. By early afternoon of the release day, every significant tech publication in the world, as well as many mainstream media organizations, has run a story on the teardown and the assigned repairability scores.

The resulting coverage has not only boosted iFixit's profile well beyond what's normal for a 170-employee repair parts and tool company, but also boosted the very idea of "repairability" into the mainstream.

From the inside, iFixit's headquarters doesn't look like a former auto dealership. Polished concrete floors are divided by desks, boxes filled with parts inventory, and exposed wooden columns that support a second floor and a sweeping staircase. As he shows me around, Kyle stops at a desk covered with hundreds of neatly stacked iPhone-size boxes. Each contains a new iPhone 6 screen, freshly delivered from a Chinese manufacturer that reverse engineers iPhone parts. It's not a genuine part—only Apple has the new ones—but it's all but identical, cheaper (especially if you do the repair yourself), and one of iFixit's better-selling items. Before the screens can be listed as merchandise, however, they need to be tested: an unshaved young man in a black baseball cap unboxes each one, plugs it into a partly dismantled iPhone, and runs a set of tests to ensure that it works. The vast majority do. "We think of ourselves as a quality filter on China," Kyle explains. "We get stuff and test it."

Around the corner is a small warehouse filled with individual parts, iFixit-branded tool kits, and all-in-one tool-and-part kits for doing straightforward jobs like battery replacement. "The key to this business is being able to get the parts, good parts," Kyle says as he stops and opens a box containing a kit for changing an iPhone 6s battery. "Sometimes we get them for a while, and then we can't. Beats headphones were something that was good for us and we could get parts. Then Apple bought them and we couldn't."

Like any company that sells stuff, iFixit spends a lot of time thinking about what its customers want. Sometimes the answers are easy and obvious. Everyone likes nicely packaged stuff (even iFixit's refurbished parts are packaged attractively). But it's much more difficult to answer the bigger questions that animate iFixit: Are consumers willing to invest time, money, and effort to extend the lifespans of the objects they own? And if so, which ones?

The answers are never static and require iFixit to parse reams of data, from consumer surveys to device-bestseller lists. Sometimes the themes that emerge are dark for a company devoted to expanding repair options. For example, the sticker warning consumers not to open up their television is a manufacturer's obvious (and probably illegal) effort to bend consumer psychology toward its preferred repair outcome: none, or one at an authorized service center. So, too, for that matter, are smartphones that lack hatches for easy battery replacement, cars that can be diagnosed only with software owned by a dealership, and a $39.99 tablet computer made by a manufacturer without a website, much less troubleshooting tips. iFixit's role, in a sense, is to bend that psychology back to a place where a consumer feels empowered to take control of her or his stuff.

Kyle offers me an example in a small office on iFixit's first floor. On a workbench is an open iFixit-branded toolset, as well as several additional tools scattered about. Kyle grabs a screw head in the shape of an oval. "So I was invited to do a teardown at Barcelona Design Week in 2015," he explains. It's the sort of thing that he's asked to do all the time, thanks to the intense popularity of the company's Apple teardowns. I've been to recycling conventions where Kyle and his teardowns are promoted like feature keynotes.

Which is what happened in Barcelona, where he was provided with tools, a large audience, and the expectation that he could work quickly.

"It ended up being a coffeemaker teardown," he recalls. It started out well, but in the midst of it—with everyone watching—he came across what looked like a rivet. "I'd asked the maintenance guy for a drill to get it out," he says, and then his voice tenses with a laugh. "And then I realized it was a screw. A new type of screw!"

Who uses a screw that looks like a rivet? Somebody who doesn't want you to turn that screw. Or, as Kyle puts it, that oval screw was designed and installed "as a means of frustrating self-repair—it's anti-user." That's a problem for anyone, anywhere, who wants to repair a coffeemaker. "So we developed this driver to open it," he says, placing it back in the toolkit.

That's one way to bend consumer psychology away from the manufacturer (or, more modestly, boost the coffeemaker repair industry). But from Kyle's perspective, becoming Home Depot requires more than screw heads and free manuals. It requires the kind of social change that can be engineered only by governments and the companies responsible for making unrepairable stuff for the consumer economy.

Is it possible?

There's reason to believe that it is.

On July 31, 2012, the Massachusetts legislature passed legislation requiring automobile manufacturers to provide the same information and training to independent garages as it does to authorized dealerships and service centers. Three months later, 86 percent of Massachusetts voters supported a referendum that required essentially the same thing. Having spent years lobbying and campaigning against consumers and independent repair, the auto manufacturers realized they were on the losing side of an argument that was about to go national. Rather than face fifty different "right to repair" laws, the automotive industry entered into negotiations with the associations representing independent repair garages and auto parts makers. The result was a nationwide 2014 agreement requiring twenty-three major automakers to provide access to their diagnostic and repair information systems (for vehicles dating back to 2002) to any repair shop or owner with a computer.

A similar law or agreement that applies to makers of consumer electronics and appliances is long overdue, and would have a profound and lasting impact on the growing clutter that's found in homes around the world. Basements filled with broken vacuum cleaners and junk drawers filled with broken phones wouldn't necessarily disappear. But there would be less reason to accumulate, because devices would be, by nature, upgradeable, repairable, and resalable. It'd be an indirect govern-ment stimulus for secondhand.

For example, I own an Apple iPad Mini 2 that I purchased in 2014. I use it daily to browse news apps and to check occasional sports scores. Five years on, it continues to perform well. There is, however, one problem: after several years, the battery can barely hold a charge for twenty-four hours. Obviously, there's no battery door on an iPad. It's sealed up.

As I searched online for repair options, I learned that Apple might be the answer I was seeking. As far back as 2010, the company offered this solution to iPad customers with bad batteries:

> If your iPad requires service due to the battery's diminished ability to hold an electrical charge, Apple will replace your iPad for a service fee.

In other words, Apple has made it so difficult and expensive to replace an iPad battery that Apple itself thinks it's more economical to simply get a new iPad. When I visited an Apple store in Minnetonka, Minnesota, a Genius Bar attendant confirmed that remains Apple's practice. He told me that Apple doesn't actually replace iPad batteries; instead, for the bargain price of ninety-nine dollars, it switches out my old one with a new or refurbished one. Apple appears to be making the calculation that so few consumers actually bother to replace their iPad batteries that it's worth the hit.

But what if, unlike me, a consumer doesn't have easy access to an Apple store or its handful of authorized service centers? What if that customer lives in Mandan, the seventh largest town in North Dakota? There's no Apple store there. Apple has a mail-in option for U.S. consumers, but that requires waiting days for the iPad to get to the service center and back. It's even worse for international customers. What's the resident of Savelugu, Ghana, to do with the used iPad Mini he acquired that now needs a battery switch?

There's no official iPad Mini repair manual online. But iFixit has one, and even sells a kit to help consumers perform the repair. Through no fault of iFixit, it's a daunting job. The first problem is that Apple seals the iPad shut with adhesives that can be loosened only with repeated applications of heat (say, a bag of rice warmed in a microwave), and—in iFixit's manual—six strategically placed guitar picks to help lift the cover, carefully.

When I spoke to Kyle Wiens about iPad Mini repairs, he sighed. "That's one of the toughest. You can wreck the thing if you're not careful." That seems to be the consensus when I looked for independent repair companies willing to replace the battery: nobody wanted to do it. I also asked around in Malaysia, where I currently live, and found one repair shop that was willing to give it a try . . . for the equivalent of $150. As it happens, used iPad Mini 2s are available in Malaysia for less.

A consumer right-to-repair law would have two key provisions. First, manufacturers must be required to create and post online information for the disassembly and repair of any products that they make available for sale. Second, manufacturers must be required to sell the same parts and tools (including software) to consumers and independent repair shops that they provide to authorized service centers (and to do so on fair and reasonable terms).

Initially, right-to-repair laws would ensure that more consumers are able to access repair in their communities. That'd lower the cost of repair, especially for technology, and encourage consumers to seek options for lengthening the lifespans of their stuff.

But the more profound impact will be on the design of products. So long as manufacturers aren't required to explain if—or how—their products can be repaired, they have no incentive to make them more repairable. But the moment that Apple or any other consumer electronics company is legally obligated to make repair parts and manuals available to shops and the public, it has an implicit incentive to make those parts marketable. And they'll do that by making devices easier to repair.

Right-to-repair laws will have an even more profound impact on low-cost manufacturers (say, of the $39.99 tablet computers sold at 7-Eleven). At the moment, nothing is preventing them from dumping their unrepairable, badly made products—especially in places like Africa, which need low-cost tech. But if a country has a right-to-repair law, they won't be able to do that without first creating a service plan for the device, in the form of parts distribution and manuals. That requirement will, in short order, lead to better quality.

In fact, it's already happening.

Just off Interstate 80 in Lebanon, Tennessee, is a massive building owned by FedEx Supply Chain, a subsidiary of shipping giant FedEx, that provides business services, including product returns and recycling. I'm met there by Andrea Falkin, senior manager at Dell for North America environmental affairs and producer responsibility. She takes me past security and upstairs to a sprawling, windowless production floor that looks a bit like a mechanized Sam's Club with higher shelves, more conveyor belts, and workflow. It's here that FedEx receives returned Dell devices from around the world; assesses them for potential repair, refurbishment, and resale; and then ships them off again. "Thousands per day," she tells me. "The idea is to reuse. We financially reward FedEx for reuse, penalize them for scrapping."

Dell doesn't do it for fun. When a device arrives in Lebanon, it's already a loss. A consumer bought it and—for reasons ranging from a defect to a change of mind—doesn't want it. For Dell to recover as much remaining value as possible, they need FedEx to opt for reuse, not recycling.

Andrea pauses on the perimeter of the factory floor. "That's the parts inventory," she says, pointing at a two-story island that fills up a portion of the room and contains inventory worth, during my visit, a cool $21 million. "If you have a Dell that's out of warranty, the parts come from here," she explains. "You can go online and order it." One source of those parts is the computers arriving from around the world. If they can't be repaired, they're cannibalized, the parts cataloged and held until someone inevitably wants them. Dell makes parts available to anyone with a credit card and a shipping address (repair manuals are free on its website).

In fact, Andrea knows more than most people about computer parts. Before she joined the environmental side of Dell, she was an engineer involved in designing Dell computers. As she recounts this period in her career (she has memories of inspecting Dell parts in southern Chinese hotel rooms before they were sent for production), she smiles a lot—especially when she encounters devices in Lebanon that she helped design ("my babies," she calls them).

Which is often. At one point, she stops to point to a Dell desktop that she identifies as "circa 2005 and 2006, and we had big arguments about this." She slips her fingers beneath a latch and lifts off one side of the computer case. "You can't just build it for a man's hand; you need to build for a woman's hand too. That's inclusive design," she says and puts the case back. "We kind of have this joke around the engineers at Dell," Andrea says. "It's that you have to take apart one of our products before you get to design one." I don't get the joke, but I do get the point, as underlined by Andrea: "Taking it apart makes you ask questions. Are there better ways?"

FedEx certainly hopes so. It has a financial incentive to repair and refurbish as many devices as possible, as quickly as possible. To do that, Dell has adopted a set of design principles that make things easier to take apart. For example, whenever possible, Dell uses fasteners like screws, rather than glues and other adhesives, to hold its devices together. Devices that are adhered shut are hard to open and often break in the process; screws, on the other hand, simply unscrew.

It's not just FedEx that profits from Dells that are more repairable. Dell's customers also profit if they can fix things themselves rather than send them out for authorized service. Of these customers, the most critical are corporations, many of which buy thousands of devices at a time and evaluate their purchases in part on whether their own IT departments can service the machines. If repair is expensive because of bad design, that's an opportunity for a competitor to sell a more repairable computer that costs less over the life of the machine.

Near the end of my tour, Andrea stops near a pallet piled with perhaps fifty older Dell desktops. "These are off-lease machines, returned to Dell," she explains. "Dell made money off them for one to three years, and now it's time to make more. They're sold by the pallet."

"Who buys them?" I ask.

"Someone who needs a great deal," she says, shrugging. "Could go overseas, could go to a start-up, could go to an overseas start-up." She gestures for me to follow her to the exit. "We used to scrap them. Now we don't."

Recognizing the potential in secondhand markets led Dell to design products that can last longer *because they're profitable*. Right to repair is a means of encouraging reluctant companies uninterested in second-hand to rethink their approach, and hopefully adopt Dell's. If they don't, they'll face the consequences of falling behind competition committed to a profitable device afterlife.

That future is coming faster than many consumer electronics companies want. As of 2019, more than twenty U.S. states are considering right-to-repair legislation (unsurprisingly, Apple and many other leading consumer electronics companies vigorously oppose them). Kyle Wiens believes it's just a matter of time before one passes it, and the consumer electronics industry scrambles to settle, like the auto manufacturers did after the Massachusetts law. Europe is even further along. Several European governments (including Germany's) and the European Commission have already accepted, officially, the principles behind right-to-repair legislation. At some point in the next several years, Europe will make them law. In time, those laws will boost the second-hand markets, filling them with goods maintained well enough to be sold and resold, over and over.

CHAPTER 12

More Suitcases

The inability to envision a certain kind of person doing a certain kind of thing because you've never seen someone who looks like him do it before is not just a vice. It's a luxury. What begins as a failure of the imagination ends as a market inefficiency: when you rule out an entire class of people from doing a job simply by their appearance, you are less likely to find the best person for the job.

—MICHAEL LEWIS, *MONEYBALL*

The coastal road that runs east from Accra, the capital of Ghana, is washed tan with the dust and sand of the beach it parallels. On both sides, business thrives in small sheds and storefronts. A few advertise food—I see dried fish and signs shaped like fish hanging from awnings and roofs. But by far the chief business on this busy stretch of highway is secondhand. Used tires are stacked high in clusters; washing machines are long streaks of silver and white; office chairs, leather sofas, and display cabinets sit close to the road, beckoning passersby.

To the east are some of the world's biggest and most dynamic second-hand markets. In Togo, Lomé's used-shoe markets are famous; in Benin, Cotonou's car markets are notorious; and Nigeria is the single biggest market for used goods in Africa. But before traveling onward to those destinations, travelers must pass through the thicket of truck traffic that starts miles before Tema, the biggest port in Ghana.

I'm seated in the back seat of a sedan with Robin Ingenthron; Wahab Odoi Mohammed is in the driver's seat; and Leticia, a customs clearing agent who works with Wahab, is in the passenger seat. "You can't bring your cameras into the port," Wahab tells us as we turn left into the Golden Jubilee Terminal. "The officers don't like it."

To our right, hundreds of shipping containers are piled four and five high in a fenced-off yard, empty and awaiting shipment. Beyond them, towering cranes slowly remove full containers from a just-arrived ship. We park and walk to an office where we pay the equivalent of sixty cents to enter the container yard where Wahab receives the goods he buys and packs in New England.

"Half the cargoes are secondhand," Leticia says as we walk through the container yard gate. "It's the biggest business here." She isn't refer-ring to just Tema. In Ghana, secondhand goods are more common than new ones, and secondhand retailers far outnumber new ones. In Tamale, Wahab's hometown and the third largest city in Ghana, the ratio could be as high as 100 to 1.

It's a phenomenon that government statistics fail to record for a number of reasons. First, most of the trade is "informal" and conducted via cash and barter, which is difficult to track. Second, few developing countries have the resources to gather and publish quality data about used goods. Factory orders are a crucial metric for governments seeking investors; used television imports are not, despite their deep explana-tory powers.

As Wahab and Leticia lead Robin and me into the Golden Jubilee Terminal, the scale of the trade reveals itself. By my count, at least six hundred shipping containers are laid out, extending for hundreds of feet. A few dozen are open, and goods are being unloaded by hand. "Usually those are the people who imported," Wahab says. In the distance I see two sets of port officials with clipboards and pens in hand. They examine the contents of each container and assess duties. The fees can be steep: Wahab tells me that the duty on a shipping container full of monitors, televisions, and computers can range from seven thousand to eight thousand dollars, on top of the roughly five thousand dollars it costs to ship the container from Vermont to Accra, and the thousands of dollars he pays for the monitors.

If Ghanaians weren't hungry for used televisions, and willing to pay for them, the export business would be financial suicide for Wahab and the thousands of other West African entrepreneurs who account for most of the devices that arrive on the continent. As of 2019, the recyclable value of the metals and plastic in Wahab's average load of electronics (for example, his upcoming load of 400 monitors, 1,200 laptops, and 120 iMacs) is in the range of two thousand dollars, minus the considerable labor and time necessary to extract those metals and plastics, and the thousands of dollars it costs to buy them from Robin. It would be cheaper for Wahab to pay a New England recycler to recycle that container. Fortunately for him, Ghanaians are willing to pay a premium for imported secondhand stuff. It lasts longer and is cheaper than much of what's shipped to Ghana as new product. Drive around his hometown of Tamale, and Wahab will point out the hospital that uses his computers, the school, and the bank, in addition to the individuals. They want to buy durable stuff that lasts.

Wahab isn't alone in importing quality used goods into Ghana. In 2011, a consortium of research organizations, including the United

Nations Environment Programme, sponsored a study of Ghana's
e-waste situation (as of 2019, it remains the only study of its kind).[1]
When they surveyed electronics arriving in Tema, they found that
60 percent were in working condition, 20 percent could be made to
function with repair and refurbishment (good thing Ibrahim Alhassan's
Savelugu shop has thousands of counterparts across Ghana), and the
remaining 20 percent could not function and would go to waste (after
being cannibalized profitably for parts).

It's a good business—if you can get the stuff. Wahab says that the
quality laptops and desktops that Ghanaians covet have become harder
to buy overseas in recent years, as recycling programs in the United
States and Europe swallow up more reusable material for recycling into
raw materials. "If I bring a load of laptops to Tema," he told me, "I'll
have people rushing over from around the container yard asking to buy
them. There's so much demand."

A typical Tema stall selling a variety of imported secondhand goods, including
refrigerators, stereo speakers, and DVD players.

It's not just secondhand electronics that people covet. The first container we pass carries—among other things—the following used goods: twelve televisions, four car bumpers, one dozen children's bicycles, two baby car seats, a used propane-powered generator, and a La-Z-Boy. The container next to it holds four sofas, a crib, sixteen televisions, five large stereo speakers, a treadmill, and unopened boxes of other stuff. There are, conservatively estimated, at least two dozen other containers undergoing inspection as we stroll. And hundreds more containers are being off-loaded from boats on the water.

After leaving Golden Jubilee Terminal, we take a walk beyond the container yard. Along the streets, tents and stalls packed with used goods recently off-loaded from containers line the streets, right up to the curbs. Various tents and stalls are devoted to used refrigerators, used office chairs, used bicycles, used clothing, and, of course, used televisions, computers, and other electronics.

It's a trade that should be celebrated. It's a guarantee that somebody, somewhere, values old stuff. From an environmental perspective, it's reuse on an industrial scale, the green economy made real. Better yet, no legislation or regulation was required to create it. A globalized trade in secondhand goods evolved on its own, connecting those who have stuff with those who don't. Goodwill and Greenpeace couldn't have devised a better system if they'd tried.

So why, if I show an image of African men and women standing beside disassembled computers, televisions, or bales of used clothes to a university or recycling-conference audience (as I've done), do they recoil at the e-waste dumped on Africa? Why doesn't it occur to such audiences that small African entrepreneurs like Wahab are *importing* these devices to sell to technology-hungry folks across West Africa?

Longer-lasting, repairable products are key to promoting a second-hand future. But if the affluent people who own that longer-lasting stuff hesitate to sell it to particular classes of people—for example, West Africans—then there's really no point in creating longer-lasting, repairable products. Manufacturers might as well just make products that work only for their original owners and then spontaneously combust.

Wahab doesn't sell his electronics in Tema. Instead, he sends his shipping containers four hundred miles north (trucking fee: $1,200) to Tamale. There he divides the inventory between customers, including Steve Edison of Bugi Computers in Accra, who flies to Tamale for his share and then pays a truck to drive it back to Accra.

When I met Steve for the first time in 2015, Bugi Computers was just a single small shop off Oxford Street in Osu, a thriving residential and commercial neighborhood that's become Accra's cultural and commercial center. Then, as now, the shop's walls were lined on two sides by display cases filled with used computers and a few accessories; two thirds of the way into the shop was the counter, and behind it was a repair shop. Back then, Steve had an earnest but shy presence. He'd come to work in a white lab coat and spend most of his time in the back doing complex repairs on laptops and desktops. When customers turned up, it seemed he wanted nothing more than to get back to fixing.

Today, Bugi Computers has three shops in Osu, and Steve's lab coat has been replaced by fashionable formfitting shirts that display his gym-toned physique. When I arrive at the shop with Wahab, Robin, and Wahab's cousin Oluu Orga (who works for Wahab), Steve shakes hands, slaps backs, and banters. And why not? Ghana's economy is one of the fastest growing in the world, and Accra is home to a young population keen to own technology. Secondhand (and Bugi Computers) is the first rung on the ladder.

Wahab and Steve back away to talk business, so Robin and I examine the inventory. Robin recognizes some secondhand iMacs he sold to Wahab and points them out to me. Later, he nods at the locked display cabinets and several new, still-in-the-box Nokia phones. "Steve'll sell more and more new stuff," he predicts. "It'll take a while, but that's how it goes in every developing country. One day, it'll be Best Buy."

But not too soon. "People in Ghana, they don't want the new computers from China," Wahab says, interrupting. "If you give them a choice between a new Chinese laptop and a three-year-old used laptop from the U.S., they will always buy the used one. They know it will last." At that, Wahab asks Robin to show Steve the database of used TV parts that Good Point built in Middlebury; they're keen to start exporting the parts. I've already heard this pitch, so I step outside to the dirt lane next to Bugi. There's a small shed there, and the door is open to two young men in lab coats. They're Steve's techs, and one is removing the broken screen from a laptop that a customer just sold back to Steve. He'll replace it with a screen cannibalized from one of the dozens of laptops on the shelves above the work area.

Music plays from down the street; the smell of fried food comes from the opposite direction. Pedestrians walk by chatting on feature phones, animated at the end of the day. It's Accra's best hour.

Amid it all, a young man in his late teens or early twenties slowly moves down the street pulling a wooden cart the size of a large kitchen table. It's balanced on a custom-built steel suspension and four large car tires. It carries a few pieces of rusty sheet metal, a large steel bracket, a beat-up VCR, one large tube television, and several hollowed-out steel desktop computer cases. I stand to get a better look: there are also a handful of computer motherboards scattered on the cart's surface. The cart and its load must weigh several hundred pounds, and the young man's Baltimore Ravens T-shirt is drenched in sweat.

Throughout this hilly, sprawling city, hundreds—maybe thousands—of young men pull wooden carts just like this one, paying for the unwanted junk (rusted gutters, broken televisions, dead laptops) of the city's growing middle class and businesses. Most of these cart pullers work dawn to dusk, walking miles to pick up stuff that they can sell for reuse or recycling.

"I used to do that, oh yeah."

I didn't notice that Oluu Orga, Wahab's cousin, has been standing nearby. I look back at him. "Really?"

"After I finished school, I left Tamale and moved to Accra, then Cape Coast," he says in his soft, low voice. "Oh yeah, I did the scraps. I needed to earn money. We'd go around and collect everything."

Oluu is in his midthirties, tall, a sharp dresser. Back in Tamale, he has a wife and children for whom—in his own words—he's "always hustling" to earn money. I can't see him pulling a cart through the streets of Accra. But that's my failure, not his. "What kind of life was it?"

He shrugs and gives me a disarming smile. "I worked with my brother. Oh yeah."

It's early evening, and the shadows are growing long as Oluu, Robin, and I step out of a taxi and into a dusty parking lot across the street from a place that the *Guardian* labeled "the world's largest digital dump,"[2] CBC called "the world's largest e-waste dump,"[3] Al Jazeera called "the world's biggest e-waste dump,"[4] and PBS's *Frontline* declared the final destination for "hundreds of millions of tons"[5] of e-waste annually (a volume that, if true—and it's not—exceeds the volume of waste computers, phones, and televisions generated every year on a global basis by a factor of five, at least). Other news organizations, environmental organizations, and government bureaucracies have repeated these same statistics, turning them to flawed conventional wisdom.

More than any other place on earth, this place, Agbogbloshie, has defined the Western image of a globalized trade in secondhand goods. If, when you read the words "used computers Africa," you conjure an image of young black men tending to smoking clouds of electronics, you're probably thinking of Agbogbloshie. If the words "electronics dumping" generate feelings of indignation based on a documentary you saw or story you read years ago, odds are that story was about or at least included mention of Agbogbloshie.

But the funny thing about a place that *Time* once called one of the ten most polluted places on earth is that it doesn't look or feel that way from a parking lot across from the street. Instead, I see the famous yam market's roadside wooden stalls stocked with yams and red onions, and diesel trucks loaded down with even more yams slowly navigating choking traffic. After the yams, the most noticeable things about Agbogbloshie—at least from across the street—are a bus station that conveys Ghanaians all over West Africa, a Pepsi bottling plant, a meat market, several banks, dozens of used computer shops, used-car dealerships, and a church overseen by Ghana's most influential preacher. We are also engulfed in the dust of Ghana's dry season, and an acrid cloud of smoke that billows from the other side of the yam market.

We dash across the street, avoiding impatient, angry taxis, heaving yam trucks, and two women walking with sacks of yams atop their heads, immune to the commotion. Between onion stalls, a driveway is formed by three large concrete blocks that gives way to a muddy path sloping toward the smoke. As we enter, we pass a young man pulling a wooden cart piled with six desktop computers.

"Oh yeah," Oluu says as we walk up the path. "At first, pushing the cart was so hard for me. I'd start early in the morning and go all around Accra looking for scrap. Metal, computers—it didn't matter. Then come here and sell."

"Here" spreads out before us as the muddy path widens into a space that's roughly 650 feet long and 1,450 feet wide (accounts suggesting it's larger seem to mistake the city dump abutting it as being a part of the scrapyard). At that scale, it's not the world's biggest anything, much less its "biggest digital dump." I am personally familiar with recycling facilities in China, Europe, and North America that are significantly larger.

Which makes sense if one looks at the data.

According to the most recent data available, Ghana imported 215,000 metric tons of secondhand electronics in 2011. For the sake of argument, let's say that number tripled over the next decade (unlikely, but let's argue it), to 645,000 metric tons. Meanwhile, the UN estimates

The scrapyard at Agbogbloshie.

the globe generates 44.7 million metric tons of e-wastes annually. Which, if accurate, means that Ghana's e-waste imports accounted for no more—and likely far less—than 1.50 percent of the world's e-waste.

Still, there's not much pleasant at Agbogbloshie. To our right is a trash-strewn field where junk cars, vans, trucks, and buses are piled up haphazardly, waiting to be torn into their individual parts for resale or recycling. That's no accident: Agbogbloshie is mostly devoted to recycling automobiles and selling the parts. In fact, that's been the primary business here since the early 1990s.[6] The roughly five hundred workers at Agbogbloshie (many also call it home) crowd dirt-floored stalls, mostly hammering away at greasy automobile parts, whether axles or motors. Other workers dismantle whole vehicles using hand tools. Environmental protection isn't a concern: oil and other fluids drain off into the soil and the nearby Korle Lagoon. Human health matters even less: safety equipment is nonexistent, and the air is riven with the smell of burning plastic.

Of course, Agbogbloshie isn't just cars. We walk past an empty plastic television case, a stack of ten to twenty desktop computer cases, a pile of circuit boards, stacks of steel desktop computer cases, a small hill of rusty steel scrap, a smaller stack of still-wet paint cans, a spaghetti-tangle of burnt rubber-encrusted wire extracted from burnt tires, and three large electrical transformers (presumably from a local utility) leaking their toxic oils onto the soil. Nearby, two men pry microprocessors from circuit boards with screwdrivers and break apart aluminum window frames with hammers. Individuals who work at the site report that it recycles between thirty and fifty televisions per day.

"Is any of this junk trucked here from Tema?" I ask Oluu.

"Tema?" he asks.

"Yeah. The port. Do people bring it from Tema to dump it here?"

"Oh no. Too far," he answers (Tema is twenty miles away). "Every-thing here is thrown away by people in Accra. The things in containers at Tema are too valuable for Agbogbloshie."

"Really?"

He laughs. "When I worked here, we wanted things from Tema. That's big money. Instead we have to scrap in the neighborhoods."

As any Accra taxi driver will be happy to explain, Agbogbloshie is where Ghanaian things go after they've been used until they can't be used or repaired (some will also tell you it's a place where stolen prop-erty can be fenced). Most of that Agbogbloshie-bound junk was, in fact, imported into Ghana, then used, repaired, and reused, often for decades. What little data exists supports the claim: according to a survey of West Africa's e-waste, as much as 85 percent of the used electronics in Ghana were generated in Ghana itself, from devices that were purchased new or used in Ghana or were imported as working or repairable.[7] Computers and televisions too old for Accra make their way to smaller towns, where they last for years, even decades (Ibrahim Alhassan isn't the only repair tech in Ghana working on a twenty-five-year-old television).

It's not hard to find this information. It's available online or by taking a taxi. Yet, for more than a decade, reporters have failed to ask these questions or search for these answers. Why? It's not my place to impugn the motives of other reporters. What I do know (based on conversations with reporters) is that many reporters are sent to Agbogbloshie by editors in hope of replicating a story in the *Guardian* or on BBC. For Europeans in particular, Ghana is a short and relatively inexpensive reporting trip, and Agbogbloshie is easily accessible. Nonetheless, it's still an investment, and few reporters—especially television reporters—are going to risk calling an editor and saying, "By the way, the BBC got it wrong. It's actually an auto junkyard."

Now, to be clear: I'm not excusing anything that happens at Agbog-bloshie. As someone who grew up in the recycling industry and has covered it for years as a reporter, I can state with confidence that there's a safer and cleaner way to do pretty much everything that's done there. Meanwhile, what happens in Agbogbloshie has devastating conse-quences on the environment and human health (it's not uncommon to hear deep hacking coughs as one walks around Agbogbloshie).

But that's not the only lens through which one should understand Agbogbloshie. A wider lens that takes in a West Africa beyond Agbogbloshie—that incorporates Accra's up-and-coming middle class, its countless secondhand shops, and the port of Tema—suggests hope amid the dinge. In that picture, Agbogbloshie, a slum that's home to forty thousand people, has risen above poverty and pollution and func-tions as a perfectly circular economy where things are used and then reused—in effect, injected back into middle-class African life as refur-bished products—in ways that rich countries simply never achieve.

You just have to look for it!

Walk out of the dump, take a right, cross the bridge, and you find businesses selling goods made from junk sold in the junkyard. There are aluminum cooking pots and stoves made from scrap aluminum; steel barbecue grills made from scrap steel; new electrical transformers made from scrapped transformers; stall after stall of refurbished auto-mobile parts; and businesses that repair computers and make "new" ones from parts recovered from old computers. They are the "thirdhand market," super-low-end counterparts to Bugi Computers and the secondhand market. It's all possible because, at some point, somebody imported used stuff from a wealthier country. That stuff circulated through Ghana, round and round, until it landed here.

"How many people were pushing carts around Accra when you were working here?" I ask Oluu.

"So many. We'd all be looking for the same thing. That's how the computers come here. We'd buy them from businesses and homes."

After a year of pulling carts, Oluu moved up. A cousin (not Wahab) secured a contract with a Chinese trader interested in buying and shipping Ghanaian circuit boards back to China for recycling (the market for old boards is much stronger there than in Ghana). Oluu left his cart behind, hopped on a motorcycle, and spent his days driving around Accra buying electronics from the men with whom he used to pull carts. Oluu also picked up computers and sold them to the many repair shops around Agbogbloshie that took these machines, fixed them, and resold them. If a computer couldn't be fixed, they'd recover the parts and build a machine from those. Even today, Agbogbloshie's jerry-rigged machines remain a popular and affordable technology for students, businesses, and, in Oluu's words, "regular people." Only if a part can't be fixed (and in Ghana, skilled circuit board repair is common) is it recycled—often in China or Nigeria. Soon, Oluu was making enough money to afford an apartment of his own.

We emerge from the scrapping zone into an open space that abuts the landfill and comprises perhaps one fifth of what is known as Agbogbloshie—and 99 percent of what's written, photographed, and broadcast about it. Trash is strewn everywhere; my feet crunch it as I walk. A few hundred feet away a group of perhaps twenty people stands around three smoky, noxious fires sending black clouds of poison across Agbogbloshie. There are two groups among them. The larger one, comprising perhaps a dozen people, are Agbogbloshie scrap workers and business owners who arrive with ten-pound balls of insulated wire extracted mostly from cars. To sell that wire for scrap, they need the insulation burned off. So they pay the smaller group here, the one that tends the fires, to do just that. Every day, a few hundred pounds of charred copper are sold out of Agbogbloshie, preceded by toxic smoke.

A small wooden shed sits roughly a hundred feet from the burning. It's a kind of clubhouse for the burner crew, and Oluu and Wahab approach it confidently (they are members of the same tribal group as the burn crew). Awal Muhammad, a burly leader of this group, has a family and employment opportunities in the Northern Region, but he prefers this life. He's the boss and—to be honest—I think he enjoys the attention he receives as the face (literally) of Agbogbloshie. When photographers visit the site, he's the one whose photo is often taken next to the flames (if you've ever seen a photo of an African man burning wire, the odds are good it's Awal). If a photographer tips him properly, he'll add a bit of extra fuel to the fire to make it more photogenic, put his safety at risk and wave a burning tire over his head, or, at a minimum, ensure his crew of burners is available. These are all services provided to the producers of a 2017 video for the British rock band Placebo, who certainly got what they paid for. Placebo promoted the video on social media as being "filmed on location at Agbogbloshie, the world's largest e-waste dump."

In the years since Agbogbloshie was "discovered" by European and American environmental activists and journalists, hundreds of stories have been published about the place. I've read or watched most of them. They have a few things in common: fires, nameless young African men, the phrase "primitive recycling," and a claim that Agbogbloshie is the "largest" something. Few, if any, include data, much less images of repair. Interviews with the repair businesses around Agbogbloshie are nonexistent. Implicit in these editorial choices is the assumption that Ghanaians are incapable of doing anything with foreign technology other than burning it. That's a failure to see the computer workshops in

Agbogbloshie and around Ghana. And in many cases, it's a failure to recognize that the developed world has something to learn from the developing world about managing stuff.

What makes that failed reporting so damaging, beyond its impact on the public, is its impact on secondhand traders, consumers, researchers, and policymakers. Introduce Wahab to a government official in the United States (as I've seen Robin do), mention that he's a secondhand-electronics trader, and the presumption of guilt is palpable. "Well, there have been documentaries," I heard one official say to Robin, with Wahab present (as if he were not). No follow-ups were directed to Wahab, the Ghanaian trader. All questions were addressed to Robin, the white man who does business with the Ghanaian.

This sort of prejudice has real-world consequences for what humans can actually know. For example, in 2017 the Ellen MacArthur Foundation, a globally renowned British charity that researches and promotes repair and reuse policies, published *A New Textiles Economy: Redesigning Fashion's Future*, a 148-page report suggesting ways to make clothing more sustainable, reusable, and recyclable.[8] It was widely covered in the global media (especially the contribution that high-end British fashion designer Stella McCartney had in shaping it). Yet despite the fact that Africa—and East Africa, in particular—is the largest market in the world for secondhand clothes, the report mentions Africa a mere four times in passing and includes no African authors or contributors. A casual reader could easily come to the conclusion that—in the view of the Ellen MacArthur Foundation—Africa's used clothing traders and users have nothing to teach the world and have nothing meaningful to contribute to the future of clothing. That's not only incorrect; it's bigoted.

*   *   *

In summer 2008 an employee of the British branch of Greenpeace, the global environmental organization, and a journalist with Sky News, the British television news network, acquired an old tube television. Rather than enjoy it, the two gentlemen hired a mechanic to open the case, remove a part so that it no longer worked, and—before closing it back up—attach a satellite tracking device to the interior. Then they dropped it off at a government-run collection site that promised to recycle it safely in the U.K. or another developed country.

That wasn't what Greenpeace and Sky News hoped would happen. Instead, they hoped to track it to a developing country, and—ideally—a digital dump.[9] With a little luck and lobbying, their reporting might even result in the criminal prosecution of whoever sent it there.

What's the crime?

In the 1970s and 1980s, journalists began to uncover cases in which companies and governments in the developed world dumped hazardous waste in countries in the developing world to save on disposal costs. In response, environmental groups and interested governments drafted national and international laws and treaties to restrict and ban that trade. It was a good thing to do. But there were problems, starting with the way that some of the advocates and the resulting laws divided the developing world from the developed one. In Europe, for example, the developed countries are defined as the thirty-six countries belonging to the Organisation of Economic Cooperation and Development, the twenty-eight states of the European Commission, and Lichtenstein. These are, collectively, among the world's wealthiest nations (all but three of which—Japan, Korea, and Mexico—are majority white), and they reserve for themselves the right to recycle and reuse their waste.

Preventing rich countries from exporting hazardous waste to developing countries is a good thing. Toxic ash removed from a Swedish power plant, for example, doesn't belong in places that don't have the technology to process it. But the problems start when it's time to define what, precisely, is waste. Toxic ash from an incinerator is clearly waste. But what are we to make of a television with a missing part en route to Nigeria? Under European guidelines, if an electronic device—a monitor, a phone, a microwave—isn't tested and working, it's automatically waste (and hazardous, at that). Never mind that in Nigeria and Ghana, a nonworking television isn't automatically viewed as waste but rather as a resource to be fixed or mined for parts and sold to people who can't afford new. And never mind that Nigeria (and Ghana, for that matter) not only don't prohibit these imports but have actually opened their doors more widely to them in recent years.[10] African wishes be damned, Europe has decided that its definition—the rich man's definition of his broken thing—is what matters.

Not long after Greenpeace dropped off its sabotaged television in Hampshire, BJ Electronics, a company owned by a Nigerian trader named Joseph Benson, purchased it (along with other electronics) and loaded it into a container bound for Nigeria. Neither the Greenpeace television nor most of the other appliances were tested before shipping. So putting them on the water was, under U.K. law, instantly a criminal act. Or, in the words of the Sky News correspondent: "It's only illegal to export broken appliances from the U.K. to certain places, like Africa."

Greenpeace and Sky News tracked Benson's container to the Alaba electronics market in Lagos, the largest secondhand-electronics market in Nigeria (and probably the largest in Africa). It's home to more than five thousand small shops and—reportedly—more than one million visitors per day. Alaba's repair technicians are renowned for being some of the most talented and experienced in all Africa. They don't just fix televisions; they make refurbished televisions from parts scavenged from old ones. If a circuit board is faulty, they don't instantly throw it away; they take out their magnifying glasses, microscopes, soldering irons, and spare-parts boxes, and they fix it. Indeed, when a Sky News correspondent arrived at Alaba to search for the tracked television, he observed "fairly skilled electrical engineering work being carried out on appliances," according to documents from Benson's subsequent U.K. criminal trial.

Unfortunately, Sky News didn't include footage of those skilled tech-nicians in its report, much less inquire into whether one of those techs could fix the sabotaged television (invariably, the answer would've been yes, assuming the parts were available). Instead, it showed a Greenpeace activist paying around forty dollars for the television (roughly ten times the television's value as scrap metal and plastic) and driving it to a garbage dump.

That unidentified dump looks a bit like Agbogbloshie, minus the cars, trucks, buses, televisions, computers, and other whole electronics, and the smoky fires in which wire is burned. There are, however, pieces of broken glass, some bits of copper and circuit boards, and lots and lots of garbage. That was enough for Sky News to declare the dump the "likely" destination for the sabotaged television (before Greenpeace and Sky News rescued it).

In spite of the shoddy reporting, the four-minute segment was a viral sensation. The British government, sensitive to public outrage, indicted Joseph Benson, several of his colleagues, and BJ Electronics for waste trafficking. In 2014, Benson was sentenced to sixteen months in prison and a £142,145 fine. The U.K. Environmental Agency hailed the verdict as a blow against criminal waste trafficking, and the global press covered it—and continues to hail it—as a landmark. Among the only critics was Robin Ingenthron, who blogged furiously about the trial and verdict, rightly pointing out that Benson's crime was the temerity to ship from an affluent country to a less wealthy African one.

Few people cared—particularly the prosecutors.

Benson's prosecution was largely managed by Howard McCann, principal counsel at the U.K.'s Environment Agency. Shortly after the conviction, I contacted McCann to ask if he thought it possible Benson was actually accomplishing an environmental good. Was it possible, I asked, that Benson's goods were actually reused? And for much longer than they would've been used in the U.K.? McCann answered candidly:

> Ostensibly it might have been for re-use. We didn't have any evidence that it was going to be dumped. We make no reference to dumping, even though we know it takes place in Africa. There are waste heaps in Africa and Ghana where electrical waste can be dumped . . . It's possible, but there's no evidence that we have, that the items might have been repaired for re-use or some of them may have been cannibalized for re-use.

That lack of evidence didn't bother McCann. As he explained to me, Benson's intentions and the ultimate fate of those devices were irrelevant to the case, no matter how environmentally sound repair and reuse might be. What mattered, McCann emphasized several times, was that Benson did not recognize how the U.K. and Europe define "waste." "The items were waste materials when they left this country," he explained. "That's why we tried it." When you think about it, insisting that Africa's secondhand traders adopt Europe's definition of "waste" or risk prosecution—*in Europe*—is a kind of colonialism. Waste colonialism.

Barriers that give moral and legal standing to businesses, governments, and individuals who choose to discard their goods—electronic or not—rather than have them used by people of lesser means, aren't good for the environment, and they certainly don't help clean up clutter. Rather, they become short- and long-term incentives to buy new and cheap—especially for those who can't afford quality.

So what can be done? Is there a legal solution that ensures exporters of secondhand stuff—everyone from Joseph Benson to Shoe Guy in Nogales to Goodwill International—aren't viewed as morally suspect? Is there a treaty or law that ensures Africans who want to import and repair stuff from rich Europeans and Americans can continue to do so? Is there some way to convince reporters to start looking beyond the pile of burning wires at Agbogbloshie, and start visiting the repair shops down the road?

Before attempting to answer these questions I want to acknowledge something that I've touched on throughout this book. Generally, the globalized trade in secondhand stuff takes place between rich and poor. Due to a range of historical factors, including the lasting legacy of colonialism, income (and the state of national development) is often directly correlated with race, and thus the globalized trade in secondhand goods is typically between different races. Whether acknowledged or not, debates over whether certain countries and peoples can import or export "waste" are, at their core, debates over whether certain racial groups should have access to material goods, and whether they should be required to use and dispose of them in ways that richer, usually white countries prescribe.

As a white U.S. citizen, I'm wary of presenting solutions that might make me appear to be assuming the mantle of a white savior. But I am also a business journalist with a career spent covering the global recycling and reuse industry. In that capacity, I've learned that ignorance, racism, and other prejudices are among the most intractable barriers to the development of globalized secondhand and recycling (often known as a "circular economy"). I hope my observations and recommendations will be considered in that spirit.

Legal solutions are the easy ones. Step one is ending laws and prejudices that bar the trade in secondhand goods between countries based on their level of economic development. That approach might have made sense in the 1980s and 1990s, when Europe, Japan, and the United States were the world's largest generators of used stuff (not just electronics), and the income gaps between developed and developing countries were much wider. But in 2019, developing China is the world's largest generator of secondhand stuff—and one of its fastest growing exporters as well. "It used to be one billion people selling to three billion people," Robin Ingenthron once said to me. "Now it's three billion selling to three billion."

Laws, regulations, and treaties that fail to recognize that shift are not only archaic, but, if enforced, will create two worlds: one in which Europe trades secondhand with rich Europe, the United States, Japan, and a handful of other countries whose economies grew in the immediate aftermath of World War II; and one in which a much larger developing world trades among itself. Long-term, that's good for the developing world, and bad for everyone left behind.

My critics will point out that it's not just developed countries that want to restrict the trade in secondhand. True enough: plenty of developing countries, too, have signed on to international treaties or enacted national laws that restrict it. For example, in 2018, Rwanda imposed tariffs on imported secondhand clothes that have made them effectively unaffordable to its citizens. The tariffs were designed to boost Rwanda's once-proud domestic textile industry. Whether such an effort is desirable, or attainable, remains in doubt. In South Africa, a similar ban merely served to boost importers of low-cost, low-quality Chinese apparel, and there are signs that Rwanda is experiencing something similar. Meanwhile, the smuggling of secondhand is rife and growing throughout the country.

Rwanda isn't the only country to experience a burst in secondhand trade after banning or restricting secondhand. India bans the import of secondhand clothing, yet it's everywhere; Nigeria restricts and taxes the imports of secondhand everything, yet the consumer economy remains, in many places, secondhand. Meanwhile, the specter of corruption that haunts many developing economies ensures that the benefits of restricting secondhand go to manufacturers, not consumers. Developed-world advocates for secondhand barriers in developing countries would be wise to consider whose side they are taking. White saviors have a history of failing to save anyone.

Next, the global media has an obligation to stop stigmatizing the trade in secondhand—especially the immigrant and ethnic-minority businesses that make up most of it. Instead, it needs to recognize secondhand as a globally significant industry and start covering it as such. From Mexico to Ghana to India, secondhand *is* the consumer economy. But good luck finding any quality, consistent news coverage. On a monthly basis, more English-language stories have been written about the iPhone in India (a product with a price that exceeds most Indians' annual incomes) than have been written about recent dramatic changes in the price, quality, and availability of used garments that clothe hundreds of millions of Indians. That's editorial malpractice, a journalism designed for the affluent and comfortable, not the curious.

Worse, it's journalism that fails to see, identify, and comprehend the actual issues faced by developing countries with inadequate waste-management systems. For example, the burning waste at Agbogbloshie isn't the consequence of indiscriminate dumping by Western countries. Any reporter who visits one of Accra's homes knows that the city of 2.5 million has enough stuff to keep Agbogbloshie's fires burning for years without additional imports. Instead, Agbogbloshie's problem is one that faces many developing countries: safe, clean garbage disposal and recycling is extremely expensive, accounting for half of all municipal costs in some poor countries. As a result, roughly three billion people, globally, lack access to any kind of organized waste management. When that fact collides with the explosion of stuff, globally, places like Agbogbloshie are the result.

Media organizations (and environmental activists) that want to do something for developing countries with waste problems would do themselves and those developing countries a favor by focusing on the need for modern waste management,[11] and by not repeating stories that serve to—among other injustices—criminalize immigrant and ethnic-minority businesses.[12]

Finally, consumers and donors of stuff in the developed world need to get past their "waste provincialism." At Goodwill Industries of Southern Arizona, employees often hear from donors that they want their stuff "reused in our community." That's a good and proper goal. Taking care of one's neighbors should be a primary concern of any citizen, anywhere in the world. But it's invariably the case that one's neighbors tend to be roughly equal to you in terms of taste and, most important, income and demographics.

If that's the case, and you still want to donate your stuff, you'll need to accept that your old stuff (and the identity tied up in it) might end up in the hands of somebody very different from you. In fact, that person might not view your donation as charity: she might buy it; she might view it as a rich person unloading a perfectly good thing for cheap; and when it finally breaks, she might feel there's no better option than selling it to a guy with a cart like Olu used to pull. If that bothers you, it might be time to invest in a bigger storage unit.

In late winter I join Wahab Odoi Mohammed in the warehouse at Good Point Recycling in Middlebury as he tests piles of laptops that he'll carry back to Ghana in suitcases. The warehouse is heated, but it's still cold inside the capacious space, and Wahab is bundled tight in a bright orange down coat he'd never have occasion to wear in Ghana.

Wahab isn't new to the cold. In 2001, after completing high school, he was sponsored to live in Cape Cod, moved to New Jersey, and then Vermont. He had a steady job working as a social worker when, one afternoon, a friend who fixed used computers took him to his favorite place to buy them: Good Point Recycling. That trip sparked something in Wahab. For years, his friends and family in Ghana had expressed to him an interest in importing used electronics for sale there. In this warehouse was the chance.

"Let's call Steve," Wahab declares and dials up Steve Edison on WhatsApp. It's ten P.M. in Ghana, and a grainy face on a dark street appears on Wahab's Samsung Galaxy Note 7. "Steve!" he yells out. "Look what's in Robin's warehouse." He pans the phone over hundreds of laptops and monitors that have little value in Vermont except as scrap, or—perhaps—parts. But in Ghana, they're worth a fortune. Wahab picks up a five-year-old Dell that Steve can sell for much, much more than Wahab pays for it. "A Dell, Steve!"

Steve smiles, then catches himself. "Very nice."

Wahab picks up a beat-up Fujitsu laptop. "A Fujitsu, Steve!"

"Also very nice."

Wahab says goodbye, picks up a boxy old Samsung laptop, and points to a scratch across the screen. "Grade B," he declares. "We can fix that in Ghana with some rubbing alcohol and a fingernail. Make it look like new."

"How much will you make?"

He tells me the margin—I agree not to reveal it—and I quickly understand how used laptops can finance a round-trip lifestyle between Ghana and Vermont. But Wahab is about much more than suitcase volumes. Tomorrow, he'll be at Good Point's new warehouse in Brockton, Massachusetts, where he has enough computers and monitors to fill a shipping container bound for Tema.

Today, it's about smaller volumes. Wahab takes that Samsung and places it in a suitcase filled with ten mostly worthless-in-America laptops and piles of dirty laundry to cushion them. "It's one hundred dollars for each extra bag beyond the first two on Delta," he explains. "Already I have eight bags." He looks over at an additional pile of computers that he's yet to evaluate for shipment. "I need more suit-cases," he says. "You want to go to T.J. Maxx?"

Wahab borrows the keys to Robin's Honda and takes the wheel. "Someone back in Ghana asked me, 'How much do you spend on travel each year?' I said, 'Maybe fifteen thousand dollars.' And they're like, 'Wow, that's more money than I make in a year. Do you make money?'" Wahab scoffs angrily as he navigates expertly through town. "Of course I make money! Would I do this for free?" He nods at the snowy, frozen landscape. "That's why I get so mad when I see stories about dumping e-waste in Ghana. You think Robin would pay me to dump his computers in Ghana?"

I've been in the room when Robin and Wahab have negotiated the price of goods that Wahab buys and ships to Ghana. The men are close

Wahab Mohammed and Robin Ingenthron discussing computer parts that Wahab is shipping back to Ghana from Good Point Recycling's warehouse in Middlebury, Vermont.

friends, but you wouldn't know it based on those heated discussions. So no, I don't.

Wahab continues. "What I don't understand is why, if I buy some goods and have them in my possession, I shouldn't be able to repair and sell them?"

"People who want to stop exports say that used goods don't last very long and become hazardous waste," I explain carefully. "They're worried they'll end up in a dump, burning."

"But then nobody should be able to sell new goods in Ghana either!" Wahab says. "All the new China goods don't last very long either. They should try and stop those. Then Ghana should have nothing. That's what they want?" He pulls into a strip mall with a T.J. Maxx at one end and changes the subject. "I buy so many suitcases and they're all sitting in my house in Tamale. People always ask if they can buy them. I need to open a store." He pauses, thinks about it, then laughs. "Maybe I will do it."

AFTERWORD

The greatest hazard I encountered while reporting this book was temptation. At a Bookoff in Yokohama, Japan, I nearly scooped up armfuls of used Thomas the Tank Engine train cars for my son; at Empty the Nest in Minnesota, I was on the verge of purchasing a *Monday Night Football* board game that I'd played as a child; in Tamale, Ghana, I spotted a vintage J. Geils Band T-shirt in a street stall selling second-hand clothes; at the Amcorp Mall in Petaling Jaya, Malaysia, I inquired about an art deco dresser; at a Koenji vintage shop (whose name I failed to write down), I was tantalized by a vintage Coleman tent in excellent condition; at Alliance Laundry Systems, I briefly considered text messaging my wife that it was time to buy a new washer.

Mostly, I resisted. Mostly. At the Goodwill Outlet Center on Irvington Road in Tucson, I purchased an Angry Birds board game and a pair of corduroys, both for my son. At a Goodwill on University Avenue in St. Paul, I purchased a Chutes and Ladders game, also for my son. Then there was that vintage Northwest Orient Airlines shoulder bag that I bought at Stillwater's Midtown Antique Mall (described in chapter 4) and subsequently gifted to my cousin Bruce. And I can't forget the handful of porcelain refrigerator magnets in the shape of vegetables that I purchased at Singapore's Sungei Road Flea Market. Meanwhile, my wife—who accompanied me for some of the reporting for this book—also bought stuff. In her accounting: a "few" books for herself, a handful of toys for our son, an REI-branded shirt, and a Lululemon top for $3.99 (incredible bargain!)—almost all of which were found at the Goodwill up the street from the house we rented in Tucson.

We don't regret any of the purchases. It's good stuff. And except for two notable items, I don't regret what I *didn't* buy.

It's mid-afternoon on Saturday, and the donation door at the Goodwill on South Houghton and East Golf Links is nearly blocked by the flood of stuff. I stand inside, relieved by the air-conditioning, and watch as cool Michelle Janse walks through the barricade of stuff with pivots worthy of an NBA All-Star. She's carrying a stack of books on top of a stack of magazines. "We're getting a lot of books the last two months," she tells me. "Digital age, you know, phones." She drops them into a washing-machine box labeled RAW BOOKS.

Raw books? I look into the box anticipating a frenzied stack of hot romance. Instead I see a two-foot-deep frozen whirlpool of coloring books, cookbooks, recipe binders, several romances (*The Remnant: On the Brink of Armageddon* catches my eye, and feels apt), and dozens of stray fashion magazines. It's depressing but nothing I haven't seen before. At Bookoff's Yokohama warehouse, dozens of boxes like this are bound for recycling plants daily.

Muscular Mike Mellors and another employee start to push furniture into the warehouse. They don't have to say anything: I know I'm in the way. So I retreat toward the furniture that's priced and ready to be moved onto the sales floor and stop at a long table covered in gray plastic storage totes. Each is labeled with a price: $0.99, $1.99, $2.99. Next to the table are carts filled with "wares," the Goodwill term for used stuff that isn't electronics, clothing, media, or furniture. Employees are ordinarily stationed here to sort and price the wares from the carts to the totes (it's all-hands-on-deck at the donation door as Saturday rush hour hits). The totes will then be taken to the sales floor, and the merchandise placed on shelves.

I lean over the $2.99 tote. It holds a set of matching blue plates held together with a rubber band, a neatly folded Texas state flag, and a set of six steak knives in their original packaging. Next to the $2.99 tote is a much fuller $0.99 tote. Among other things, it holds a dish rack, a wooden meter stick, a Tupperware bin, a glass vase, and—in the corner farthest from me—two small porcelain cats roughly the size of a hand. One is black and one is white.

I hesitate and feel my throat catch. "Sasha and Julian," I think, recalling the names of my mom's beloved cats who passed a few years before her. These two porcelain cats—precisely these two porcelain cats—used to sit on a side table in her living room in Minnetonka, inanimate reflections of the real cats lounging on the floor.

I reach into the tote, pick them up, and turn them in my hands. I don't know what happened to my mom's porcelain cats. It's possible that during one of her moves they were lost or perhaps landed in a relative's basement. It's likely they eventually ended up at a Goodwill or a Salvation Army. It doesn't really matter, though. I know that these porcelain cats found 1,600 miles from where she enjoyed hers aren't hers. Porcelain cats that land in the $0.99 bin at Goodwill don't move very far, even in an era of globalized secondhand.

I take them out of the bin and set them on the table. I'm sure Cathy, the store manager, will let me buy them before they go on the shelves.

And then I put them back.

Better that someone else, someone like my mom, has a chance to enjoy them. And if nobody buys them, if those porcelain cats end up in a desert landfill, I take solace in knowing that somebody, somewhere, had a chance to enjoy them before they ended up in a tote at Goodwill. When I started this book, I wanted to find out what happened to my mother's stuff after I donated it. More or less, I think I have. I just wish I'd snapped a picture of those porcelain cats with my phone before they slinked away to their own version of obsolescence. In retrospect, however, I knew the answer long before Tucson, Tokyo, or anywhere else I traveled while reporting. At heart, every consumer sort of knows. Sooner or later, we all know: it's just stuff, and stuff isn't forever.

For an author with a partner or spouse, a book becomes a family project. My wife, Christine, was the first person to hear about my trips to cleanouts, to clothing markets, to the donation door, to the Yokohama warehouse where Bookoff performs triage on tons of used books per day. The experience impacted both of us. I was never much of a shopper in the first place, and I became less of one.

Christine listened to my stories and often took them more personally. One evening early in this project, I noticed she was examining the books in the personal library that she's been carefully collecting since childhood. She does this often, flipping through favorite passages. But on this occasion there was a slightly frantic nature to her page turning. She wasn't reading; she was looking for and finding damage. We live in a suburb of Kuala Lumpur, and the tropical heat and humidity take a toll on books: mold, foxing, pages sticking together, pages turning yellow and brown. So in the days and weeks and months that followed, Christine did something unexpected. She decided to give away her books. Rather than have them rot on the shelves, only to be opened once in a while, she wanted someone else to have the chance to enjoy them.

First she tried donating them to charity shops. But the charities were already inundated with books and didn't want them. So she sought out local book exchanges and book lovers, and the books started moving off her shelves. As they did, Christine realized something lucrative: people wanted her books badly enough to buy them. So she sold them. And when she sold them, she found, they disappeared more quickly than when she tried to give them away.

Soon buyers started inquiring about titles Christine didn't have, so she started acquiring secondhand books and selling those, too. In other words, she happened upon her own secondhand business. These days, she hunts flea markets, remainder shops, online sites, and any other place that carries titles appealing to Malaysia's thriving community of readers.

Money is one reward. The other is a more bookish life filled with even more bookish friends. As it happens, Malaysia has a wildly committed community of readers (the KL Book Appreciation Club has—as of this writing—8,422 members), many of whom constitute Christine's social circle. At all hours, she's immersed in book-related messages on her phone.

One evening, as I was nearing the end of this manuscript, a college student messaged Christine to ask about *Goodbye, Things: The New Japanese Minimalism*, by Fumio Sasaki. It's an international bestseller by a self-described "regular guy" who decided that his life was too full of stuff. Sasaki's fix was to become a minimalist. He pared his life to its material essentials: a bed, a table, a few changes of clothes, his laptop, and a few other items. For those occasions in which he finds himself needing to acquire an actual item, he requires that the object meet these minimalist criteria:

(1) the item has a minimalist type of shape, and is easy to clean;
(2) its color isn't too loud; (3) I'll be able to use it for a long time;

(4) it has a simple structure; (5) it's lightweight and compact; and (6) it has multiple uses.

As pictured in his book, Sasaki's home looks like a tech-loving monk's cell (for the record: I have visited monk's cells, both in Japan and the United States). My guess is that most of the millions of people who buy his book admire him more than emulate him.

"I need to declutter," wrote Christine's college-age book-loving friend. "But I don't know how."*

Christine likes to sell books. She's good at it. But not that evening. "I don't find all these books particularly helpful," she messaged back. "The method I use for myself is, imagine myself dead and all my stuff chucked." The student responded with a heart, and Christine continued: "Sad right? So better let go now, especially if I can see the recipient and know the stuff will be loved or used."

I call Christine's method Preemptive Morbid Decluttering (PMDC), and I think there's probably a short, morbid-advice bestseller to be written about it. The idea isn't entirely original to Christine, of course. I've met numerous cleanout professionals in the United States and Japan who have their own variations on it (some are mentioned in these pages). Years spent cleaning up the messes of others instill in them a powerful desire to avoid placing that same material curse on their relatives (and the cleanout professionals those relatives might hire). If readers come to this book in search of advice—as in real-world, what-can-I-actually-do advice—Preemptive Morbid Decluttering is the best I've got.

---

* To be clear: I am not in the habit of reading my wife's text messages. The only reason that I know about this exchange is because Christine mentioned it as it was happening. Later, I asked to see it—and then asked permission to use it.

By the way, Christine's copy of *Goodbye, Things* remains in her possession, stored in a plastic bin, where it's protected from the humidity and insects. "Because we're hoarders," she told me when I asked about it. "But mainly I hung on to it for you."

Christine's online friend bought a new copy.

ACKNOWLEDGMENTS

In ways visible only to my beloved wife, Christine Tan, and me, this book chronicles a conversation that started four years ago. My grandmother would have called her "a find," and she'd be right. I am grateful for Christine's advice, patience, and support during the years we lived and grew with this project.

Thank you to my agent, Wendy Sherman, for her enthusiasm and confidence. She makes everything possible.

Thanks to Anton Mueller at Bloomsbury USA. He embraced the concept behind this book and trusted me to follow it to unexpected places and conclusions. Additional thanks to Sara Mercurio for bringing my work to a much wider audience than I ever imagined possible.

Gratitude to David Shipley and Jonathan Landman at Bloomberg Opinion for their support of this project from its earliest stages. Thanks, too, to Nisid Hajari and Timothy Lavin. Many of my ideas about secondhand were developed in columns that they edited, and I am a better writer for having worked with them.

Joel Weber at *Bloomberg Businessweek* embraced my reporting on Japan's home cleanout industry, and Jillian Goodman edited it brilliantly.

My interest in the globalized secondhand market was sparked during a 2015 reporting trip to Kenya and Ghana for *Scrap*. Thank you to Kent

Kiser and Rachel Pollack for sending me and the many years of friendship and guidance.

Companies and organizations that allow a reporter to roam their operations take a massive leap of faith. In the course of reporting this book no organization took a bigger leap than Goodwill Industries of Southern Arizona. I am particularly grateful to Judith Bucasas for putting it all together. Additional thanks to the many Goodwill employees who shared their time and knowledge: Lisa Allen, Mary Bremerman, Anissa Brown, Tara Carmody, Kevin Cunningham, Brittney Drake, Jason Flores, Chris Foster, Kathie Greco, Laurie Gulick, Liz Gulick, Michelle Janse, Frank Kaphan, Faye McCorry, Abel Medina, Lance Meeks, Mike Mellors, Kylene Parker, Lupita Ramos, Julie Sanchez, Erich Schmidt, Melinda Sparling, and Mackenzie Williams. A special thanks to Cathy Zach for hosting me in her store and making an introduction that enriched this book.

Finally, I'm grateful for the patience and trust of the international secondhand traders at the Goodwill outlets on Irvington Road in Tucson and Grand Avenue in Nogales.

To my friend "Shoe Guy"—thank you for taking me along for the ride and sharing your wisdom.

Sharon Fischman of Empty the Nest inspired more of this book than just the sections in which she and her company are featured. Sharon Kadet was a patient and generous teacher in the art, business, and metaphysics of the cleanout. Additional ETN inspiration and information came from Kristy Dueffert, Ally Enz, Tracy Luke, and Amy Rimington. Finally, thanks to Neal Simonson and Lesley Novich of Coldwell Banker Burnett for the hospitality and wisdom.

I am especially grateful to Denise Dixon and anonymous others in Minnesota and Japan who allowed me to attend that most personal of events, the cleanout of family property.

Diane Bjorkman of Gentle Transitions introduced me to the scale and professionalism of the American move management industry and the sorters so crucial to it. I am grateful for the wisdom and stories shared by the following Gentle Transitions employees: Melissa Doerr, Jill Freeman, Barb Holmquist, and Tammy Wilcox.

In Japan, Toubi Cho translated language and culture for me, and Rina Hamada, the editor of the *Reuse Business Journal*, shared her extensive knowledge and contacts in Japan's secondhand industry. Thanks to both. Additional thanks to Pontus Nylén for his help in Kamakura.

Jeongja Han of the Tail Project brought me inside Japanese homes and the important work the Japanese cleanout industry performs. She also introduced me to Tetsuaki Muraoka of Muraoka. Hideto Kone of the Association of Cleanout Professionals offered crucial industry history, insights, and introductions.

One evening my friend Irfan Muhammad told me about Malaysia's history with secondhand from Japan, and pointed me in the direction of Bookoff. I am very grateful to him. Thanks to the efforts of Takaharu Kominato, Bookoff opened its doors to me. Additional thanks to the following Bookoff employees: Mayumi Hashimoto, Toru Inoue, and Kenichi Tanwa; Hisato Mori and Harumi Yamakoshi of the New York City branch of Bookoff; and Koji Onozawa of Jalan Jalan Japan.

Finally, thanks to to Bookoff founder Takashi Sakamoto, now of Oreno Corporation, for sharing perspectives on his career.

My reporting at Midtown Antiques was coordinated and enriched by Dick Richter. Thanks to him, Julie Kranz, and the following Midtown dealers: Judi Gerber, Linda Hemberger, Joe Heyring, Trevor Kartarik, and Dale Kenney.

The Amcorp Mall weekend flea market in Petaling Jaya, Malaysia, has been a source of secondhand market knowledge and stuff. I owe particular thanks to Azalina Zakaria.

BooksActually is a great bookstore and you should visit. Appreciation goes to its owner Kenny Leck, who shared his knowledge of Singapore's antiques and culture. Additional Singapore thanks to Jamie Teo.

Nick Huzar of OfferUp provided me with insights into the evolving world of P2P e-commerce.

Shigeru Kobayashi of Hamaya revealed the scale of globalized Japanese secondhand. Thanks to him, and to Yuki Ohkuma, for arranging and translating my visit.

Among the most enjoyable visits I made while reporting this book was to daidai. Mio Ojima is the manager and—in my opinion—the artist-in-residence and curator. I am grateful for her time, wisdom, and art.

Mohammad Faisal Moledina of Used Clothing Exports introduced me to Mississauga's secondhand textile industry. Thanks to him and his father, Abdul Majid Moledina. Additional thanks to Maple Textiles, and Ashif Dhalwani and Salim Karmali of Five Star Rags.

In Cotonou I relied upon the translations, guidance, and negotiations of Michael Ogbonna. I gratefully acknowledge the traders, trading houses, and sorting houses that we visited and which asked that their businesses remain anonymous.

Nobody I met in the course of my reporting was more enthusiastic about secondhand than Todd Wilson of Star Wipers. Thank you for your hospitality and example. Additional thanks to Amity Bounds and her colleagues.

Thanks to Nohar Nath of Kishco Group for his insights into India's shoddy industry and for inviting me to accompany him to Panipat. I also thank Ramesh and Puneet Goyal of Ramesh Knitting Mills, and Sumit Jindal of Jindal Spinning Mills.

My education in child safety seat regulation was helped along by several individuals who asked to remain unnamed. They know who they are. Additional thanks to the U.S. National Highway Traffic Safety

Administration, Maria Krafft at the Swedish Transport Administration, and Professor Anders Kullgren at Folksam.

Poshmark hosted me at the 2017 Poshfest and during a visit to their headquarters. Thanks to Sera Michael for arranging everything, and Manish Chandra and John McDonald for their insights into the evolving world of secondhand P2P. I benefited from the wisdom of several poshers, including Kristin Bachman, Estrella Gallegos, Jade Myers, Kate Ray, and Priscilla Romero.

I am grateful to Phil Graves of Patagonia for agreeing to speak with me about the company's Worn Wear program.

My journey to Alliance Laundry Systems was inspired by my aunt Jane Zeman and her new Speed Queen washer. Thanks to Jane and the following members of the Alliance Laundry Systems family: Tom Friederick, Jay McDonald, Susan Miller, Randy Radtke, and Mike Schoeb.

Wahab Odoi Mohammed introduced me to Ghana and the intrepid West African entrepreneurs who supply their home region with second-hand stuff. I am grateful for his patience, insights, and friendship.

Additional thanks to the representatives of Ghana's tech sector who contributed to my education in West African repair and reuse, starting with Steve Edison at Bugi Computers in Accra and Kamil Chendiba at Chendiba Enterprises in Tamale. I received additional instruction from Kamaldeen Abdulasalam, Ibrahim Alhassan, Clement Atinyo, Zachariah Karim, Abdul Jaleel Musah, Olu Orga, Awudu Pan, Ishmael Rahman, and Elvis Yawson. In Agbogbloshie, I was hosted by Awal Muhammad, Razak Muhammad, and Yaro Muhammad. Finally, thanks to Suleiman Jawula, who shone light on the accident car export trade in the South Bronx.

For a decade Robin Ingenthron has shared his observations on secondhand with me. He also invited me to accompany him for portions of three business trips to Ghana, and (with his wife, Professor Armelle

Crouzières) hosted me in Middlebury while I poked around Good Point Recycling. I am grateful for his friendship, trust, and guidance. In addition, I thank the following Good Point employees: Elias Chinchilla, Dan Emerson, Andy Huntley, Jhimmy Sabillon, and Jim Tighe.

Kyle and Jen Wiens hosted me in their home and at iFixit. Thanks to both of them, Luke Soules, and the following iFixit employees: Kay-Kay Clapp, Samantha Lionheart, Brittany McCrigler, and Kelsea Weber.

Scott O'Connell at Dell was one of the first people to hear that I was working on this book, and he quickly extended an invitation to visit the Dell refurbishment facility run by FedEx Supply Chain. Thanks to him and Andrea Falkin, and John Coleman and Sean Templin of FedEx Supply Chain.

Additional thanks to Tom Becker, Colin Hall, and Joseph Suchodolski at Allen Edmonds Shoes; Jennifer Killinger at the American Chemistry Council; Yusuke Mitsumoto of Bank; Hans Eric Melin of Circular Economy Storage; Jeff Coyne and Jack Hawkins at Earthworm Recycling; Takeshi Futagami, Kaori Goda, Kazunari Kuwata, Yasuyuki Mizobe, and Tatsuya Tsukimura at EcoRing; Zubair Ahmed and Saddam Ali of Golden Power; Hiromasa Kobayashi of Happy Price Group; John Atallah, Ellen Jackowski, and Jade McNorton at Hewlett-Packard; Alec Oxenford at LetGo; Adele Meyer at NARTS: The Association of Resale Professionals; Jackie King at the Secondary Materials and Recycled Textiles Association; Jimmy Vosika at Shopjimmy.com and MN Home Outlet; and Tom Allison, Arun Karottu, and my dear friend Shelly Li at Smart Metals Recycling.

As I researched and wrote this book, the following academics inspired me with their scholarship on the past, present, and future of the second-hand world: Grace Akese, Jenna Burrell, Chen Liwen, Josh Goldstein, Josh Lepawsky, Dagna Rams, Yvan Schulz, Eiko Maruko Siniawer, Susan Strasser, and Carl Zimring.

With gratitude, I recognize the family members who were so critical to completing this project: John Tan and Michelle Ku, Bruce and Joanne Gruen, Amy Minter and Michael Bachrach, Michael Minter, Rita Sandstrom, and Edward and Jane Zeman.

Finally, my son, Samuel. When he was three and a half, I asked him what this book was about. His response: "Blah, blah. Let's play cars." That's a good idea.

NOTES

PREFACE: THE DONATION DOOR

1. Arnold, Jeanne F., Anthony P. Graesch, Enzo Ragazzini, and Elinor Ochs. *Life at Home in the Twenty-First Century: 32 Families Open Their Doors.* Los Angeles: Cotsen Institute of Archaeology Press, 2012.

2. Kaza, Slipa, Lisa Yao, Perinaz Bhada-Tata, and Frank Van Woerden. *What a Waste 2.0: A Global Snapshot of Solid Waste Management to 2050.* Urban Development Series. Washington, D.C.: World Bank, 2018.

CHAPTER 1: EMPTY THE NEST

1. Epstein, Reid J. "Liberals Eat Here. Conservatives Eat There." *Wall Street Journal*, May 2, 2014. https://blogs.wsj.com/washwire/2014/05/02/liberals -eat-here-conservatives-eat-there/.

2. Oxfam. "3.6 Billion Clothes Left Unworn in the Nation's Wardrobes, Survey Finds." https://oxfamapps.org/media/press_release/2016-06-over -three-billion-clothes-left-unworn-in-the-nations-wardrobes-survey -finds/.

3. The history of Anglo-American consumption in this section relies on Strasser, Susan. *Waste and Want: A Social History of Trash.* New York: Henry Holt, 1999.

CHAPTER 2: DECLUTTERING

1. This passage and the following section rely on Siniawer, Eiko Maruko. *Waste: Consuming Postwar Japan.* Ithaca, NY: Cornell University Press, 2018.

2. Ibid., 32.

3. Ibid., 35.

4. Ibid., 203.

CHAPTER 3: THE FLOOD

1. This history is laid out in Susan Strasser's landmark *Waste and Want: A Social History of Trash.* New York: Henry Holt, 1999. I relied on it while writing this chapter.

2. Ellen MacArthur Foundation. *A New Textiles Economy: Redesigning Fashion's Future*, 19. 2017. http://www.ellenmacarthurfoundation.org/publications.

3. thredUP. *Resale Report*, 2018. https://cf-assets-tup.thredup.com/resale_report/2018/2018-resaleReport.pdf.

CHAPTER 4: THE GOOD STUFF

1. Houston Public Media Staff. "Are Millennials Behind Price Drop in Houston Antiques?" *Houston Public Media*, June 6, 2017. https://www.houstonpublicmedia.org/articles/news/2017/06/06/203563/tuesday-air-are-millennials-behind-price-drop-in-houston-antiques/.

CHAPTER 5: DANSHARI

1. For the following translation and discussion of *danshari*, I rely on Siniawer, Eiko Maruko. *Waste: Consuming Postwar Japan*, 266–78. Ithaca, NY: Cornell University Press, 2018.

CHAPTER 7: FRAYED BELOW THE STITCH

1. Farrell, Sean. "We've Hit Peak Home Furnishings, Says Ikea Boss." *Guardian*, January 18, 2016. https://www.theguardian.com/business/2016/jan/18/weve -hit-peak-home-furnishings-says-ikea-boss-consumerism.

2. Frazer, G. "Used Clothing Donations and Apparel Production in Africa." *Economic Journal* 118, no. 532 (October 2008): 1764–84.

3. For more on this important topic, see Jerven, Morton. *Poor Numbers: How We Are Misled by African Development Statistics, and What to Do About It*. Ithaca, NY: Cornell University Press, 2013.

4. The best analysis of the many complicated factors that contributed to the decline of African textiles and clothing is Brooks, A., and D. Simon. "Unraveling the Relationships Between Used-Clothing Imports and the Decline of African Clothing Industries." *Development and Change* 43, no. 6 (September 2012): 1265–90. https://doi.org/10.1111/j.1467-7660.2012.01797.x.

5. Opoku, Darko. "Small-Scale Ghanaian Miners and the Textiles and Garment Industry in the Age of Chinese Economic Onslaught." In *Challenges to African Entrepreneurship in the 21st Century* (United Kingdom: Palgrave MacMillan, 2018), 147–78.

6. Yebo, Yeepoka. "Chinese Counterfeits Leave Ghanaian Textiles Hanging by a Thread." *Christian Science Monitor*, May 31, 2015. https://www.csmonitor .com/World/Africa/2015/0531/Chinese-counterfeits-leave-Ghanaian -textiles-hanging-by-a-thread. Marfo, Nana. "The Death of Ghana's Apparel Industry." *Worldwide Responsible Accredited Production*, August 31, 2018. http://www.wrapcompliance.org/blog/the-death-of-ghanas-apparel -industry.

7. Foster, Rosina. "National Friday Wear Program Creating Jobs for the Chinese." 3News.com, January 25, 2017. https://3news.com/national-friday -wear-program-creating-jobs-for-the-chinese/.

8. Burgis, Tom. "Nigeria Unraveled." *Financial Times*, February 13, 2015. https://www.ft.com/content/b1d519c2-b240-11e4-b380-00144feab7de.

9. Mallett, Whitney. "Inside the Massive Rag Yards That Wring Money Out of Your Discarded Clothes." *New Republic*, August 18, 2015. https://newre public.com/article/122564/inside-massive-rag-yards-wring-money-out -your-old-clothes.

CHAPTER 9: ENOUGH TO SELL

1. For more on this topic, see Catlin, Jesse R., and Yitong Wang. "Recycling Gone Bad: When the Option to Recycle Increases Resource Consumption." *Journal of Consumer Psychology* 23, no. 1 (January 2013): 122–27. https://doi.org/10.1016/j.jcps.2012.04.001. Zink, Trevor, and Roland Geyer. "Circular Economy Rebound." *Journal of Industrial Ecology* 21, no. 3 (2017): 593–602. https://doi.org/10.1111/jiec.12545.

2. Bank of America. "Homebuyer Insights Report," 2018. https://info.bank ofamerica.com/homebuyers-report/.

3. Accel and Qualtrics. "The Myth of the 'Don't-Own' Economy." *Millennial Study*, 2017. https://www.qualtrics.com/millennials/.

4. Ranzini, Giulia, Gemma Newlands, Guido Anselmi, Alberta Andreotti, Thomas Eichhorn, Michael Etter, Christian Hoffmann, Sebastian Jürss, and Christoph Lutz. "Millennials and the Sharing Economy: European Perspectives," (October 30, 2017). http://dx.doi.org/10.2139/ssrn.306 1704.

CHAPTER 10: AND IT LASTS FOREVER

1. Consumer Reports. "Are Secondhand Car Seats Safe?" January 28, 2017. https://www.consumerreports.org/car-seats/are-secondhand-car-seats -safe/.

2. Krafft, Maria. "Köp Gärna Begagnad Bilbarnstol." *Trfiksäkerhetsbloggen*, September 25, 2009. http://trafiksakerhet.folksamblogg.se/2009/09/25/kop -garna-begagnad-bilbarnstol/.

3. The history of lightbulb lifespan engineering is laid out in very readable form by MacKinnon, J. B. "The L.E.D. Quandary: Why There's No Such Thing as 'Built to Last.'" *New Yorker*, July 14, 2016. https://www.newyorker .com/business/currency/the-l-e-d-quandary-why-theres-no-such-thing-as -built-to-last.

4. Slade, Giles. *Made to Break: Technology and Obsolescence in America*, 45. Cambridge, MA: Harvard University Press, 2006.

5. For more on the scale of the problem, and how it was ultimately resolved, see chapter 10 of *Junkyard Planet*.

6. Dupre, Mikael, Mathieu Jahnich, Valeria Ramirez, Gaelle Boulbry, and Emilie Ferreira. *The Influence of Lifespan Labelling on Consumers*. Brussels: European Economic and Social Committee, 2016.

7. The textile-related data in this paragraph is derived from Ellen MacArthur Foundation. *A New Textiles Economy: Redesigning Fashion's Future*, 2017. http://www.ellenmacarthurfoundation.org/publications.

8. Prakash, S., G. Dehoust, M. Gsell, T. Schleicher, and R. Stamminger. "On the Impact of the Service Life of Products on Their Environmental Impact (Creation of an Information Basis and Development of Strategies Against Obsolescence)." German Federal Environment Agency, 2016.

9. Waste and Resources Action Programme. "Switched On to Value: Why Extending Appliance and Consumer Product Lifetimes and Trading Used Products Can Benefit Consumers, Retailers, and the Environment," 2014. Retrieved from www.wrap.org.uk.

10. This quote and account are from the web-based narrative of Ol' Lonely's evolution, published on the website Character, the marketing agency hired

to consult on the character's transformation: http://www.characterweb.com/maytag.html.

11. Janeway, Kimberly. "How to Make Your Washer and Dryer Last." *Consumer Reports*, 2018. https://www.consumerreports.org/laundry-cleaning/how-to-make-your-washer-and-dryer-last.

12. Dupre et al. *The Influence of Lifespan Labelling on Consumers*; and Artinger, Sabrina, Susanne Baltes, Christian Jarchow, Malte Petersen, and Andrea Schneider. *Lifespan Label for Electrical Products*. Berlin: Press and Information Office of the Federal Government, 2017.

CHAPTER 11: A RICH PERSON'S BROKEN THING

1. These figures are based on interviews with several Northern Region electronics repairmen and traders, including Ibrahim Alhassan, Karim Zachariah (in Tamale), and Kamal Chendiba (also in Tamale). For a national and regional perspective, I am heavily indebted to Awudu Pan of Kumasi. Pan is a leader in that city's sprawling television repair industry and a key organizer of its nascent trade association.

2. Strasser, Susan. *Waste and Want: A Social History of Trash*, 22. New York: Henry Holt, 1999.

3. Brignall, Miles. "'Error 53' Fury Mounts as Apple Software Update Threatens to Kill Your iPhone 6." *Guardian*, February 5, 2016. https://www.theguardian.com/money/2016/feb/05/error-53-apple-iphone-software-update-handset-worthless-third-party-repair.

4. Koebler, Jason. "Apple Sued an Independent iPhone Repair Shop Owner and Lost." *Motherboard*, April 13, 2018. https://motherboard.vice.com/en_us/article/a3yadk/apple-sued-an-independent-iphone-repair-shop-owner-and-lost.

5. Shaer, Matthew. "The Pentalobe Screws Saga: How Apple Locked Up Your iPhone 4." *Christian Science Monitor*, January 21, 2011. https://www.csmonitor.com/Technology/Horizons/2011/0121/The-Pentalobe-screws-saga-How-Apple-locked-up-your-iPhone-4.

6. Cook, Tim. "A Letter from Tim Cook to Apple Investors," January 2, 2019. https://www.apple.com/newsroom/2019/01/letter-from-tim-cook-to-apple-investors/.

7. Chapter 6 of *Junkyard Planet* includes a profile of Net Peripheral, a now-defunct Malaysian television refurbishment company that was once one of Robin's key customers.

8. The 1975 Magnuson-Moss Warranty Act prohibits manufacturers from placing repair restrictions on a device for which it offers a warranty. In other words, a Samsung Galaxy Note consumer can't lose a warranty if a corner repair shop replaces a cracked screen. In 2018, the U.S. Federal Trade Commission went so far as to warn several companies, including Microsoft, Hyundai, and Sony, that their "warranty void" stickers are illegal.

CHAPTER 12: MORE SUITCASES

1. Amoyaw-Osei, Yaw, Obed Opuku Agyekum, John A. Pwamang, Esther Mueller, Raphael Fasko, and Mathias Schluep. "Ghana e-Waste Country Assessment." Secretariat of the Basel Convention, March 2011. http://www.basel.int/portals/4/basel%20convention/docs/ewaste/e-wasteassessmentghana.pdf.

2. Adjei, Asare. "Life in Sodom and Gomorrah: The World's Largest Digital Dump." *Guardian*, April 29, 2014. https://www.theguardian.com/global-development-professionals-network/2014/apr/29/agbogbloshie-accra-ghana-largest-ewaste-dump.

3. CBC Radio. "The World's Largest e-Waste Dump Is Also Home to a Vibrant Community." CBC Radio, November 3, 2018. https://www.cbc.ca/radio /spark/412-1.4887497/the-world-s-largest-e-waste-dump-is-also-home-to -a-vibrant-community-1.4887509.

4. McElvaney, Kevin. "Ghana's e-Waste Magnet." Al Jazeera, February 12, 2014. https://www.aljazeera.com/indepth/inpictures/2014/01/pictures-ghana-e -waste-mecca-2014130104740975223.html.

5. *Frontline.* "Ghana: Digital Dumping Ground." PBS, June 23, 2009. http:// www.pbs.org/frontlineworld/stories/ghana804/.

6. Akese, Grace A., and Peter C. Little. "Electronic Waste and the Environmental Justice Challenge in Agbogbloshie." *Environmental Justice* 11, no. 2 (2018): 77–83.

7. Mathias Schluep, Andreas Manhart, Oladele Osibanjo, David Rochat, Nancy Isarin, and Esther Mueller. "Where Are WEEE in Africa? Findings from the Basel Convention E-Waste Africa Programme." Secretariat of the Basel Convention, December 2011.

8. Ellen MacArthur Foundation. *A New Textiles Economy: Redesigning Fashion's Future,* 2017. http://www.ellenmacarthurfoundation.org/publications.

9. This account of the Joe Benson prosecution relies heavily on documents collected and shared with me by Robin Ingenthron and, equally important, the detailed account and analysis of the case offered in Lepawsky, Josh. *Reassembling Rubbish: Worlding Electronic Waste,* 49–67. Cambridge: Massachusetts Institute of Technology Press, 2018.

10. Puckett, Jim, Chris Brandt, and Hayley Palmer. *Holes in the Circular Economy: WEEE Leakage from Europe,* 32. Basel Action Network, 2019. http://wiki.ban .org/images/f/f4/Holes_in_the_Circular_Economy-_WEEE_Leakage_from _Europe.pdf.

11. Several organizations and individuals are working hard to bring modern waste management to the developing world. Among the best is WasteAid, a U.K.-based nongovernmental organization that's campaigning to increase waste management funding to 3 percent of international aid spending. It also helps communities obtain waste management systems.

12. Burrell, Jenna. "What Environmentalists Get Wrong About e-Waste in Africa." *Berkeley Blog*, September 1, 2016. https://blogs.berkeley.edu/2016/09/01/what-environmentalists-get-wrong-about-e-waste-in-west-africa/.

INDEX

A NOTE ON THE AUTHOR

ADAM MINTER is the author of *Junkyard Planet: Travels in the Billion-Dollar Trash Trade* and a columnist for *Bloomberg Opinion*. He lives in Petaling Jaya, Malaysia.